T0319370

# THE POVERTY OF CLIO

# THE POVERTY OF CLIO

## RESURRECTING ECONOMIC HISTORY

*Francesco Boldizzoni*

PRINCETON UNIVERSITY PRESS  PRINCETON AND OXFORD

Published by Princeton University Press,
41 William Street, Princeton, New Jersey 08540

In the United Kingdom: Princeton University Press, 6 Oxford Street,
Woodstock, Oxfordshire OX20 1TW

press.princeton.edu

Library of Congress Cataloging-in-Publication Data
Boldizzoni, Francesco, 1979–
The poverty of Clio : resurrecting economic history
     p. cm.
ISBN: 978-0-691-14400-9 (hardcover : alk. paper)
Truth on the cross : science and ideology—Economics with a human face?—
The fanciful world of Clio—microeconomic history—macroeconomic perspectives—
Building on the past : the creative power of history.

                                                        2011002663

British Library Cataloging-in-Publication Data is available

This book has been composed in Sabon

Printed on acid-free paper. ∞

Printed in the United States of America

10 9 8 7 6 5 4 3 2 1

**To My Father** _____

# Contents

# Preface

THE STORY OF THIS BOOK BEGAN IN CAMBRIDGE on a warm day in April 2007 in the soberly furnished rooms of Emmanuel College. I was enjoying an agreeable ritual that takes place several times each year and having lunch with Peter Burke. Our conversation touched on certain twentieth-century historians and their hopes for a history that was economic and cultural at the same time. Peter is an incomparable example of historical intelligence and his effortless creativity, his aptitude for penetrating the significance of human activity through its languages and signs, and his flair for writing history with whatever sort of material are qualities that would impress even the most experienced scholar. The discussion of the evolution of economic history soon got me thinking of new ideas. The more I reconsidered the goals that had been reached and the innovative methods tested in the past century, the more evident did the decline that the discipline has undergone in recent years appear to be. More than anything else the claims to originality in this field seemed to be the result of ignorance of the past.

My initial plans were to write a study of historiography showing that a change of direction was needed. When my idea later reached the Princeton University Press, the external readers highlighted two important elements, and these were to have a decisive effect on the book's destiny. One of the scholars realized intuitively that I was challenging the "new economic history" and encouraged me to clarify the terms of the dissension, while the other suggested I should speak to the social sciences. I owe my thanks to both of them because they understood my intentions even better than I did myself. It is especially thanks to them if I have managed to say what I wanted.

However, I do not wish my criticism to sound hostile toward the colleagues who are defending the approach from which I distance myself so firmly. A few years ago they were good enough to prepare a delightful textbook for evangelizing humanistic historians (Rawski et al. 1996). I hope they will welcome my own book as a historian's attempt at evangelizing economists. Historians generally have two attitudes toward what they do not understand; they either reject it or admire it. Fortunately, I do not run either of these risks. Before becoming a historian, I was trained as an economist, and hence I am quite familiar with the tricks of the trade. Knowing its strengths and weaknesses enables me to take a somewhat detached view of economics.

More generally, my hope is that the issues raised in these pages may be of some interest for all scholars in the humanities and social sciences. The wish to address a readership that is as wide as possible has led me to avoid overspecialized language and excessive detail and to focus instead on method and principles. Readers might well find that developments in the respective disciplines have been treated schematically and important debates simplified, but here too I have tried to focus on their essence, namely the relevance of their results for economic history.

During the research and writing phase I accumulated countless debts. While at Dartmouth College in the Fall Term 2009 as Fannie and Alan Leslie Visiting Fellow in the Humanities, I was able to work full time on chapters 3 and 6. My grateful thanks go to the Leslie Center and especially to Adrian Randolph, its eclectic director, for the magnificent hospitality and the generous support given to me. Of course, it goes without saying that the peace and quiet of New England and access to some of the finest libraries in the United States were no less congenial.

The preparation of lectures for the Ecole des Hautes Etudes en Sciences Sociales in Paris has provided me with the opportunity to reflect on recent trends and future prospects for economic history, and this invitation, which takes me to a place that is very dear to me, is a very great honor. In addition, the opportunity of convening the Cambridge Seminar in the History of Economic Analysis at Clare Hall over the past three years has brought with it incomparable occasions for discussion.

I have benefited enormously from advice given by several colleagues, mentors and friends, who include Franco Amatori, Maurice Aymard, Peter Burke, Marco Cattini, Gervase Clarence-Smith, Martin Daunton, Norman Davies, Nicola Di Cosmo, Antonio Di Vittorio, Mark Elvin, Peter Garnsey, Jack Goody, Mark Granovetter, Jean-Yves Grenier, Steve Gudeman, Pat Hudson, Marcin Kula, Colin Lewis, Susan McKinnon, Paul Millett, Craig Muldrew, Patrick O'Brien, John Padgett, Roberto Scazzieri, Walter Scheidel, Leigh Shaw-Taylor, Alessandro Stanziani, and Dan Tompkins. Some of them have provided me with useful information or unpublished material, and many took upon themselves the burden of carefully reading large sections of the manuscript, if not the whole work. Naturally, I do not wish to implicate anyone in my theses.

At Princeton University Press, it has been a real pleasure working with Richard Baggaley and Seth Ditchik, my editors, and with Kimberley Williams. I am equally indebted to Peter Dougherty, who showed faith in the project right from the start. Last but not least, many thanks to Katharine Hunt, who has turned my convoluted prose into English. Financial support from Bocconi University is gratefully acknowledged. Quotations from the Finley Papers appear courtesy of the Master and Fellows of Darwin College and the Syndics of Cambridge University Library. Figure 4.2 is reproduced by kind permission of its author.

# Chapter 1 _____

## TRUTH ON THE CROSS
### Science and Ideology

IN GREEK MYTHOLOGY, Clio is the muse of both history and epic poetry. The verb *kleio* means to celebrate or extol, while *historia* means inquiry or investigation. In Herodotus, the combination of fabulous elements and concrete facts still reflects this ambiguity. Thucydides broke more decidedly with the traditional view by delivering a style of investigation that we today would call "positivistic," even though he did not really consider himself as a historian but as a sort of political scientist.

Time in antiquity passed at a somewhat slow pace, so that half a millennium later the Syrian-born Lucian could refer to Thucydides as if he had been a contemporary. His pamphlet *How to Write History* is probably the first work on historical method to come out of the Greek cultural world. Lucian was reacting to the rather mediocre literature that had arisen in celebration of the victories of the Romans against the Parthians (A.D. 161–66). As the army of Lucius Verus gradually advanced in the Middle East, it found new adulators ready to manipulate the truth as it suited them. They produced accounts that were so improbable as to seem grotesque, and they even distorted the Greek language, cramming it with pointless Latinisms. Hence, it was necessary to reestablish the rules of Thucydides:

> Here is then what the historian should be like: fearless, incorruptible, free, genuinely truth-loving, one who calls a fig a fig and a boat a boat, as that comic playwright used to say; someone who does not pass judgment motivated by hatred or withhold it out of compassion, deference, or shame. An impartial judge, well disposed to all, but never to the point of conceding to anyone more than his due, who when he writes has no fatherland, no city and no sovereign; one who does not calculate what will please this one or that, but reports what has happened. (*How to Write History* 41, my translation)

Lucian uses forceful adjectives and alludes to renunciation, the voluntary renunciation that is required of the historian as the price of objectivity. When he operates, the historian has to be like a foreigner (*xenos*) without a city (*apolis*) and without a sovereign (*abasileutos*). For modern scholars to adhere to these precepts means coming to terms with membership of a community and avoiding the often unconscious influence that it exerts on their way of thinking. It means shunning power (not only political power) and giving up the advantages that it offers to whoever submits to it. But Lucian also warns against following fashions and conforming to trends; otherwise historiography becomes an exercise in serial imitation.

## The Roots of Economic History

Before considering how Clio comes into this book, we need to introduce the main character: economic history. As in all stories worthy of the name, one cannot guess the direction in which someone is heading without knowing where they started from. The tale of Little Red Riding Hood opens in the mother's kitchen and finishes in the wolf's stomach. The perils of the wood would be difficult to imagine without the prior experience of the reassuring peace of the village.

In the first place, economic history has not always existed. During the Renaissance, nobody would have found it of very great interest to deal with the economies of the past. When in the 1510s Machiavelli wrote his *Discourses on Livy*, his concerns were the structure of republics, warfare, and leadership. Machiavelli would enter his study dressed in "regal and courtly" attire, as he told Vettori, to converse with the ancients, the great statesmen now departed, and they could respond to him precisely because they knew how to write. He would ask them about "the reason for their actions" (1513, p. 142) and not about what they produced or how their fellow citizens made a living.

Two centuries later, Edward Gibbon (1776–89) did not find it beneath him to deal with manners and customs as long as it could be useful for understanding the political collapse of an empire. Nowadays it would be considered as coming within the domain of social and cultural history. Yet the economic past started to become a matter for investigation precisely at that time. Gibbon's contemporaries sensed that the economy was changing irremediably and that new values were coming to the fore. Even when they are not historical works, historical references abound in the writings of Smith, Malthus, or Marx. One of the first cases in which the elevated term "history" is applied to a subject that is anything but elevated is the *History of the Cotton Manufacture* written by Edward Baines (1835), a forerunner of David Landes's triumphalistic account *Unbound Prometheus* (1969)!

However, only when economics became a deductive science, and one prone to universalize particular, culture-specific patterns of behavior, did economic history acquire its own identity. This transition was completed in the final quarter of the nineteenth century and was not entirely unexpected.

As early as the 1840s, the German economist Friedrich List, who was heir to the cameralist tradition, had targeted the theories of the British classical economists. Because he also questioned their policy views, his attack had obvious practical implications. List criticized the "prevailing theory" for the way it hastily generalized conclusions drawn from observing the first industrial nation and mistaking them for laws of nature. "Not considering historical facts, except so far as they respond to its particular tendencies," he maintained, "it knows not or disfigures the lessons of history which are opposed to its system" (1841, p. 65). Hence, Smith overlooked the importance of the nation as an economic actor, while Ricardo interpreted rent as the price of the natural fertility of land and based his whole political economy on this principle:

> An excursion into Canada would have afforded him proofs, in every valley and on every hill, that his theory was built upon sand. But having only England in view, he falls into the error of supposing that the English fields and meadows, the apparent natural fertility of which produces such large returns in the shape of rent, have been always the same. (List 1841, p. 335)

Richard Jones (1831), the Englishman who opposed Ricardo, had been motivated to investigate comparative economic systems by considerations of a similar tone.

But these were relatively minor sins. Despite the shortsightedness of their insular perspective and their inclination to overgeneralize, the classics in any case started from an analysis of social aspects: this involved in Smith's case the separation of the public from the domestic sphere and in Ricardo's a theory of the conflict between classes and groups. In the late nineteenth century, on the other hand, the unit of analysis adopted by marginalism was disembedded individuals who lived by maximizing their own gratification and monetary income. In the most extreme version of this approach, known today as neoclassical economics, one presumes the agents are aware of the rules of differential calculus and how to apply them to all the possible combinations of goods and production choices that exist. Marginalism spread to Britain, Austria, Switzerland, and the United States, while France and Italy were only mildly affected. Germany remained practically immune until World War II.

The great dispute on method, the *Methodenstreit*, broke out in the 1880s. On one side was Gustav Schmoller (1883), the leader of the German school, in whose view one could not formulate any economic theory that was not based on the historical analysis of society. On the other side was the Austrian Carl Menger (1884), who maintained that it was possible to know the principles of economic behavior of individuals a priori. Similarly in Britain, William Cunningham (1892) argued against Alfred Marshall, but the outcome of the controversy was less fortunate, one reason being that Marshall had embraced marginalism only very tentatively (Hodgson 2001, p. 107). Arnold Toynbee (1884) also devoted himself to the study of the "industrial revolution" (he actually popularized this expression) motivated by the wish to reject theoretical commonplaces such as the universal benefits of free trade.

Once it had entered through the back door into the pantheon of history, which Edward A. Freeman, a contemporary of Cunningham's and Regius Professor at Oxford, used to define as "past politics" (Bentley 2005, p. 192), the study of the economic past made great advances after the 1920s. In this difficult conjuncture, the Great Crash, the instability of the interwar period, and increasingly complicated industrial relations made a deep impression on public opinion and reminded contemporaries of the need to look back into the past.

But as the "civic" significance of economic history made headway, it became more and more divorced from economics. Berlin ceased to be the intellectual heart of the Western world, and the model of historical-institutional economics that the Germans had exported to some extent everywhere soon lost ground. In the postwar period, John Maynard Keynes, the second antagonist of neoclassical theory was no longer. He had conceived economic knowledge as an art that was supposed to guide "practical men." His intuition, with its far-reaching import, that disequilibrium was the rule in capitalist economies and equilibrium the exception, was ably neutralized in the classrooms of MIT, following a famous article by Hicks (1937).

Having abandoned the ambition of formulating grand theories based on empirical evidence, economic historians dedicated themselves entirely to the interpretation of the latter. "History for its own sake" might be the most suitable motto to describe this new phase. The change of direction certainly brought with it some positive aspects, because economic history was worthy of a professional body of devotees, but it also left open a latent conflict with the discipline it had separated itself from, namely economics.

## The Crisis of Economic History

Today economic history is going through a deep identity crisis brought about by the development of a movement founded in the United States at the end of the 1950s and known as "new economic history" or "cliometrics."

History is normally expected to improve our understanding of the past. It is probably agreed that what distinguishes good historical research is its capacity to throw light on the workings of societies that differ to varying degrees from our own. On the other hand, the (unconfessed) aim of cliometrics is not to increase our knowledge of the past. It is to create narratives of the past compatible with neoliberal economics, and often it is a highly ideological exercise to endorse specific worldviews, theories, and policy recommendations.

Until relatively recently, European economic historians tended to ignore this phenomenon, and starting a dispute with cliometricians was considered a waste of time, because, it was said, "they do not form part of the historical profession." As long as these scholars were operating in the United States and dealing mainly with American history, they were no great menace. But nowadays this line is no longer tenable. Two decades ago one might have smiled at McCloskey's claim that the new economic history had "won the West," imposing a "Pax Cliometrica" (1987, p. 77), but in the 2010s the risk appears to be more real. In twenty years there has been a burgeoning of armies of American-trained PhDs on European soil, and even if they are still a minority, it is a very aggressive minority. Moreover the cliometricians use increasingly sophisticated tools of persuasion, and their works are sometimes taken to be reliable by historians who are specialized in other fields and who are not familiar enough with economics to be able to form an independent judgment. Cliometricians occupy a large share of the publishing market in the English-speaking world and enjoy great visibility. This "literary genre" now covers the history of all five continents, and its timeline stretches from antiquity to the present day.

But in the meantime dissatisfaction has been building up not only among historians but also among dissident economists. Writing from a neo-Schumpeterian perspective, Freeman and Louçã, for example, have called for "remarrying economics and history as an alternative strategy to that of cliometrics" (2001, p. 39). Their appeal for a "reasoned history" recalls that of Fritz Redlich, who was one of the first critics of the new economic history: "In my opinion," he wrote, "the future belongs to both analytical qualitative and quantitative economic and social history" (1968, p. 96). At the time, "analytical" history meant problem-oriented history, an approach that was as much against narrative history as against cliometrics.

The problem is to define what the "alternative strategy" is today. There still seems to be general confusion about the nature of the "new institutionalism," which Freeman and Louçã themselves see as a break with neoclassical economics. It is in fact an attempt at product differentiation with deference to the mainstream and is dictated solely by the requirements of academic politics. Its invention became indispensable the moment Douglass North realized that the application of neoclassical models to history was something "that quickly runs into diminishing returns and leaves the economist with the conviction that we are marginal if not dispensable to the profession" (1978, p. 78). He has recently acknowledged that in the 1970s "economists came to see economic history as a luxury rather than as adding a new dimension to economics. . . . The result was that the demand for economic historians decreased. . . . The new institutional economics inspired by Ronald Coase's work was a consequence" (2008, p. 211).

What was needed was a formula that differed from neoclassical theory just enough not to become an identical copy or to contradict its basic principles; it also had to sound familiar to the dominant orthodoxy. The new institutionalists collected the accusations of unrealism that had tormented neoclassical theory since its beginnings and exploited them to their own advantage. They patiently subjected it to a patching-up operation and then presented themselves to mainstream economists as the ones who could save them from the attacks of historians, sociologists, anthropologists, and the like; and this way their chairs were kept safe.

Chapter 2 gives a detailed analysis of the new institutional paradigm and its strange alliance with rational choice theory. The most recent developments of American-style economic history are discussed in chapter 3. The second part of the book presents an alternative way of practicing economic history that developed mainly in Europe in the postwar period. Chapter 4 is dedicated to microeconomic history, while chapter 5 covers macroeconomic issues. The potentialities of these approaches are highlighted in the light of recent theoretical results in fields such as economic sociology and anthropology. Chapter 6 is a manifesto for the reconstruction of economic history and calls for a new pact between history and the social sciences in order to counter the way economists have abused the past.

The main point being made here is that we need a different paradigm of historical research that is not subject to economic theory but contributes toward renewing it. If theory is to be based on facts, it makes sense that history should correct theory and not vice versa. It is not a question of inventing this paradigm out of nothing but of learning from the lessons of certain innovative economic historians of the twentieth century. They suggest a third way between a narrative type of history and one reduced to applied social science.

It is important to avoid a possible misunderstanding from the outset. Given the target of my criticism, some may be tempted to think that this book wishes to offer up a "progressive" reading to set against a "neo-liberal" reading. The stereotype of the Rive Gauche intellectual looking down on economic activity and conceiving the market as grubby and immoral is so deeply rooted that some have even felt the need to write books to defend "bourgeois virtues" (McCloskey 2006). I am convinced that ideology of any type taints the work of the historian, and in this book a special effort has been made to avoid it. The unnatural effort at alienation that Lucian demanded would certainly be hard for anyone, but constantly striving toward such an objective is what distinguishes honest historical research (Cipolla 1991, p. 66). Thus, if the neoliberal drifts are the subject of this book, this is only because they reflect recent developments in the discipline; the same thing could have been said about certain forms of Marxism, if that did not now belong to another phase.[1]

Even in the past history was largely conditioned by ideology, and it would be pointless to deny it. In the twentieth century, Marxism and liberalism produced influential paradigms and informed the work of hundreds of scholars, but this influence was generally kept within the limits of decency and only rarely did it go so far as to pervert the work of the historian. Two authors such as Eric Hobsbawm and Walt Rostow certainly started from differing ideological positions, but advantages could be gained from reading both once their premises had been allowed for. Nowadays, however, a well-organized group of scholars seems to believe it holds the monopoly of knowledge; what is more, they demand the respect for their theses, presented as objective truths, that is due to the hard sciences.

## On the Shoulders of Giants?

When historians are convinced that earlier interpretations of the past are correct and not some fashionable trend of the moment, too often they tend to dilute their arguments by adopting a halfway line between "old ideas" and fashionable trends. In rehabilitating a former generation of historians, the present book takes a necessarily inconvenient stand and does not seek facile compromises.

At this point, it would be useful to clarify my view of the evolution of historiography. I do not think that in the historical sciences there is necessarily any progress, as there is not in economics where rival theories have always coexisted (see Boehm et al. 2002). What the historians of a generation write may or may not be better or more informed than what their immediate predecessors wrote. In other words, history is not completely

[1] In 2004 a conference organized by the British Academy was significantly called "Marxist Historiography: Alive, Dead, or Moribund?"

cumulative knowledge. Each generation constructs and reconstructs the past guided by the sensibility of the moment.

A work such as the medievalist Otto Brunner's *Land und Herrschaft* was considered orthodox in the Germany of 1939, when it was published, not because it represented the official position of the Nazi regime, but because it responded to the common feeling at the time. Brunner argued that lordship was not the product of constitutional history drawn up at the table; institutions were not of a legal nature and did not originate in a contract but evolved from patriarchal rule over the household (see also Brunner 1958) and from the relationship that bound a charismatic leader to his band of warriors. Orthodoxy in the world after 1989 is represented by the neo-Hobbesian account of North, Wallis, and Weingast (2009), which maintains an entirely antithetical truth. Brunner clearly had in mind the role of the *Volk*, which he believed could have a direct and nonmediated relationship with forms of authority; likewise, it is clear that North and his coauthors wish to elevate economics over politics, the individual over society, and impersonal interactions over social bonds.

Even when it is a highly academic activity, the writing of history is still connected to the process whereby society maintains, transforms, and passes on public memory. The anthropologist Mary Douglas puts the question this way:

> Every ten years or so classroom text books go out of date. . . . The revisionary effort is not aimed at producing the perfect optic flat. The mirror, if that is what history is, distorts as much after revision as it did before. The aim of revision is to get the distortions to match the mood of the present times. . . . When we look closely at the construction of past time, we find the process has very little to do with the past at all and everything to do with the present. (1986, p. 69)

Should this awareness result in embracing relativism and asserting that everything we write is irremediably linked to the moment and place in which we live and to our particular point of view? No, of course it should not. Today, a century and a half after first investigating the archives, we know a great deal more about the past than at the time of Leopold von Ranke, but the point is that there is no reason to prefer one historical explanation only because it is recent or more in line with the consensus of the moment. I have always found this attitude extremely naive, which among other things fosters conformism. Not only can we measure ourselves with the scholars of the past, but we have a duty to do so. The historians of the postwar period, in particular, were working on the same sources that we are using and were often even more scrupulous and systematic. It is paradoxical that, while the rational choice narratives are based on the argument that human nature is always the same, our academic predecessors are seen as being in some way psychologically inferior or less rational.

But there is another reason why the historians of the past should be taken seriously. A good knowledge of historiography—and the same could probably be said of the history of economics or the history of sociology—greatly diminishes the current practitioners' claims to being innovative. When economists say that "history matters," they invariably think of "path dependence," the concept introduced by Paul David (1985) and often cited as if it was a Copernican revolution. This idea not only is not new but had already been shown to be unhistorical at least seventy years ago. In his *The Historian's Craft*, published posthumously in 1949, Marc Bloch warned against the "idol of origins," which leads to "confusing ancestry with explanation" (p. 27). Just as the seed from which it develops contains the destiny of a plant only to a minimum degree, so the history of social facts results from forces that are not found in the "initial conditions" to any great degree and whose effects are not propagated automatically.

## Understanding the Context

The new economic history is an unmistakably American phenomenon that cannot be understood without taking account of a combination of cultural factors, the intellectual climate, and institutional circumstances in the United States between the 1950s and 1960s.[2] With regard to cultural factors, it is worth hearing what Joseph Schumpeter, a direct witness, had to say. With the excuse of opening up a parenthesis on Ricardo, in a footnote in his *History of Economic Analysis* he comes out with a harsh verdict on his students at Harvard:

> I do not think that Ricardo ever did much historical reading. But this is not what I mean. The trouble with him is akin to the trouble I have, in this respect, with my American students, who have plenty of historical material pushed down their throats. But it is to no purpose. They lack the historical *sense* that no amount of factual study can give. This is why it is so much easier to make theorists of them than economists. (1954, p. 472n)

[2] Its reception in Europe was decidedly cool (Van der Wee and Klep 1977). In Britain, thanks to Charles Feinstein, cliometrics managed to penetrate Oxford, even though Roderick Floud (2001) had previously practiced it as a graduate student under the influence of Lance Davis. Today, along with the London School of Economics and perhaps Warwick, Oxford is still the only British university where such an approach has a significant presence. By contrast, about 50 percent of the articles currently published in the *Economic History Review* are in the cliometric style.

There is undoubtedly some truth in this argument, but Schumpeter may have jumped to his conclusions too quickly. It is by no means easy to have a "historical sense" if one has grown up in a young town with perpendicular streets named "Main Street," "North Street," or "South Street." In the Old World, borders between states and regions reflect linguistic and cultural identities that have resulted from a millennial relationship between man and his natural barriers, while in the New World they have been drawn up with a stroke of the pen, though this can hardly be considered a peculiarity of the United States. Besides, how can it be explained that some of the most brilliant historians of the twentieth century, and of the present century, are American? How can their unique capacity for combining their close study of the present with a depth of vision be explained?

The problem is probably related to the mindset of the students who enrolled in an economics program. The standard of American secondary education is still quite low in comparison with that of a European lyceum or a British grammar school. At high school, students receive very practical training but are denied the study of philosophy, which underlies critical knowledge, and they are used to thinking of history as coinciding with the constitutional and political events of their own country. Hence, their first serious contact with the humanities takes place at university; but this applies only to those who decide to specialize in these disciplines. Yet, even philosophy is a dangerous exercise if it is divorced from history, and it can easily lead to baseless argument. One wonders if the author of the following passage has any idea of what the "economy" she is speaking about really is: "We have, in sum, a Parmenidian economic world. The flux of everyday life is illusory. Homo oeconomicus has never evolved, at least since the emergence of capitalism and possibly long before that. . . . One wonders why it took economic historians so long to catch on" (Schabas 1995, p. 198).

In any case, though Paul Samuelson did stand out from among Schumpeter's students, Alfred Conrad and John Meyer, the founding fathers of what would be called cliometrics, were also among them. What was meant by the term "cliometrics"?[3] Even though it would like to suggest the application of certain statistical methods to history, the distinctive contribution of this approach "has not been so much the use of 'econometrics' but the use of *economics*—the application of standard economic reasoning in the posing and answering of historical questions" (G. Wright 1971, p. 416). Others went as far as to define economic history as "a form of applied neo-classical economics" (Temin 1973, p. 8).

[3] The term was coined by Stanley Reiter, a mathematical economist at Purdue, in 1960.

The intellectual elements out of which the new paradigm was able to develop, starting at Purdue University—a center of excellence for aeronautical engineering, with an abundance of "computers but no library books" (Hughes 1991, p. 233)—were linked to a milieu open to new ideas. This type of environment gives American academic life its characteristic and unequalled dynamism, but it also has less positive aspects, which according to the late Bob Coats include "the concomitant tendency to exaggerate claims to originality; a disrespect for past achievements . . .; the overinvestment of resources in academic trivia and gimmickry; the academic pressure to 'publish or perish'; and—especially in this case—the veritable passion for quantification and measurable standards of performance" (1990, p. 14).

Compared to Britain, economic history had never enjoyed real disciplinary autonomy but had grown up under the wing of history as well as of economics departments (Cochran 1969, p. 1563). In the postwar period, the latter underwent important changes, when axiomatization and the development of econometrics gave the decisive boost to transforming economics into a mathematical science (Weintraub 2002). Consequently, on the one hand "'making like economists' meant looking down on the practitioners of 'softer' subjects . . . in an era when a simplistic concept of the scientific ideal prevailed" (Coats 1990, p. 15), while on the other it was a survival strategy for those having to live with a much more powerful neighbor (Coats 1980, p. 190).

The new economic historian had to go to the great supermarket of economic theory and select a model to apply to the concrete circumstances of the past as need be. Anyway, it is significant that the chosen theory has always been the one practiced in mainstream departments; there has never been a post-Keynesian cliometrics, or an Austrian cliometrics! Considering the axiomatic nature of neoclassical economics, this implied believing in the existence of universal laws of human behavior that were recognizable a priori. However, it would be wrong to attribute the first cliometricians with undue methodological awareness. In many cases, there were superficial reasons for choosing to become applied economists. A more perceptive author, Lance Davis, condemned the poor critical sense of his colleagues and defined the theory as the "siren lure" (1968, p. 78), but the warning seems to have fallen on deaf ears.

The faith in theory is part of a more general mental attitude. Recently I happened to attend the seminar of a PhD candidate from an Ivy League school. In his paper, the size of the population of early modern towns was used as a proxy for wealth to test "economic growth." One of those present pointed out that Naples was the most populated city of the preindustrial West, yet it certainly did not have the aspect of a rich or dynamic place. At this point, the PhD candidate produced an astute argument (from the point of view of an economist), saying that what was important was not the population stock but the rate of its growth. From the historian's perspective, this is a rather clumsy attempt at putting matters right; by the same token, one could object that, being notoriously passionate, Neapolitans reproduced just as quickly.

What distinguishes the gaze of the economist from that of the historian? It is mainly the fact that it is based on deduction rather than on induction. In the foregoing example, the explanation given was a logical one, but it was not plausible, and it fell short as soon as the reasoning was transferred from the vacuum of the imaginary model to a concrete situation. In 1973 Carlo Cipolla, who had a unique penchant for wit, wrote a celebrated parody of this way of reasoning. He invented a longing that Peter the Hermit had for pepper; this longing was to cause the First Crusade and set off an unlikely sequence of changes in population, trade, and the production of goods and services in the twelfth century. The "aphrodisiacal constant of pepper" was inserted into the multiplier model to form the equation of the "economic development of the Middle Ages." In this way Cipolla was able to show that totally implausible, but perfectly logical, narratives could be fabricated.

The second distinctive trait of the new economic history that can still be recognized, even though it has become routine and is no longer at the cutting edge of the profession, is the particular use of statistics that qualified it as "econometric history." It developed out of the need for model validation. This method also differs in one fundamental aspect from sophisticated techniques of descriptive statistics and time series analysis. While the latter leave the responsibility of interpreting quantitative data entirely up to the historian, a multivariate regression gives rise to a set of correlations between a dependent and several independent variables, each potentially able to explain the phenomenon with a certain probability and magnitude. Multivariate analysis thus becomes an *explanatory tool*. However, it is extremely dangerous to attribute the significance of a causal link to this type of connection. Two or more variables can be correlated for the most diverse reasons, but, more importantly, there is no guarantee that the ones that really matter have been included in the model.

An interesting example is contained in an influential theoretical work of Acemoglu and Robinson. Four regressions, carried out by combining different indices, suggest a negative association between democracy and inequality. Apparently, "countries that are more unequal . . . tend to be less democratic." However, Acemoglu and Robinson recognize in all honesty that it is impossible to establish causal relations between the two phenomena. "Moreover," they continue, "these correlations are not always robust to the inclusion of other variables in a regression model" and, after citing the results of studies that are incompatible with each other, conclude: "The existing empirical literature is, therefore, rather contradictory" (2006, pp. 59–62).

The fact that even economists are beginning to consider econometrics as inconclusive, or at the very least to realize its limits, should induce cliometricians to start seriously asking themselves questions.

## Reality and Fiction

The hope of transforming economic history into a deductive discipline initially found expression in the enthusiasm for "counterfactual history." Robert Fogel's book *Railroads and American Economic Growth* (1964) led the way for this enterprise. Historians had traditionally considered the railroads an important factor in the economic development of the United States in the nineteenth century. Fogel thought of these conjectures as being little more than idle chatter and wished to subject them to rigorous testing. He built a model that would allow him to have an idea of what the American economy would have been like in 1890 without the railroads. The economy was represented as being in general equilibrium, something which even on paper is problematic. Albert Fishlow (1965), who embarked on a similar but less audacious exercise, chose a different year (1859) and came to opposite conclusions.

Fogel did not stop at "removing" the railroads but thought up the details of an alternative system of transport. He designed a network of canals and roads that were suited to transporting the same amount of goods and following identical trajectories. In particular, he started from the assumption that the railroads did not create traffic and that the volume of goods was not related to the cost of the service. Under these hypotheses, he calculated that the macroeconomic impact of the railroads had been modest.

The limits of this imaginary construction lie precisely in the fact that it is imaginary. It cannot be excluded that a different and more costly system of transport would have followed different trajectories and conveyed fewer quantities of goods; moreover, the prices of raw materials, starting with coal, are certainly not an independent variable. But the problem lies at the root: was it the towns and trade that attracted the railroad, or was it the railroad that brought about the rise of the towns and stimulated trade and industry? Right from the start, Fogel implicitly adopted the former standpoint and thus predetermined the outcome of his investigation. Paradoxically, he depicted an economy without railroads benefiting from the effect of the railroads!

The cliometricians argued that resorting to counterfactuals in history writing was inevitable and that they had only made a quite widespread way of reasoning explicit. According to Lance Davis, "the unique contribution of the historian lies in his ability to understand sequences of events (*i.e.*, to interpret causal relationships). Any step in this direction, however, leads necessarily to the use (implicit or explicit) of a counterfactual argument" (1968, pp. 75–76).

Here there is a fundamental misunderstanding. History is not a futile search for immediate causes. The historian is not interested in knowing *if*, but *why*. If Franz Ferdinand of Austria had not been assassinated at Sarajevo, World War I would not have broken out on July 28, 1914, and perhaps not even that summer. But does it make sense to wonder how things would have turned out? No, it does not, unless one believes that events are the driving force behind history. Would it not be of far greater interest to explore the relationship between the war, late nineteenth-century nationalism, and the second industrial revolution?

Wondering what the world would be like if the Axis had won World War II and other puzzles of this type that enthuse military historians so much is very tempting (Ferguson 1997; Tetlock et al. 2006). Could the Axis have won the war? If Hitler had been satisfied with the successes achieved up until 1941, and the Allies had accepted the existence of a continental empire, the scenario does not seem to be implausible. It would undoubtedly have involved dramatic changes for the lives of millions of people, but from the point of view of the history of geopolitical structures, would it not have been a *déjà vu*? After all, in the previous century, a similar empire had materialized with Napoleon. It lasted ten years and, even then, the invasion of Russia was fatal. In chapter 5, we return to the relationship between event and structure in the historical explanation.

Yet the counterfactual reasoning that Davis speaks about is to do with the causes of certain phenomena and not with their repercussions. It is in fact a form of post hoc fallacy, that is to say: "A precedes B," therefore "A causes B." Furthermore, the interactions between A and B cannot be isolated from elements C, D, E. . . . If A does not happen, then D is also likely to change, and so on, in a way that is certainly not automatic. This is what underlies the harsh (and somewhat crude) judgment of E. P. Thompson, in a book otherwise dedicated to criticizing Althusserian Marxism, when he mentions "the counterfactual fictions; the econometric and cleometric groovers—all of these theories [that] hobble along programmed routes from one static category to the next. And all of them are *Geschichtenscheissenschlopff*, unhistorical shit" (1978, p. 108).

## The Defining Moment

The year 1974 was a turning point in these matters. What for fifteen years had been a movement of Young Turks became institutionalized. Counterfactual history, all in all, had been a passing fashion. *Time on the Cross*, Fogel's next book, which was coauthored with Stanley Engerman, was a compendium of all the essential ingredients of the new approach: the quantitative techniques just described were there; the ample recourse to deductive reasoning was there; there was sensationalism, with strong claims aimed at shocking the audience; and a profound lack of respect for historical scholarship was also displayed. The publishing operation was carefully studied, and the book was entrusted to a major trade publisher and organized in two volumes. The first volume was aimed at a general readership; it was without footnotes and contained the narrative. In the second volume were the calculations and a summary indication of the primary sources.

The thesis put forward by Fogel and Engerman was very simple. The historians who had up until then dealt with slavery in the antebellum American South had completely misunderstood the phenomenon, because they had not adopted the conceptual framework of neoclassical economics and did not have the econometric tools. Fogel and Engerman argued that slavery was a highly efficient system based on a mutual agreement between benevolent, profit-maximizing masters and responsible, income-maximizing slaves. The former did not act according to "patriarchal commitments" but followed their capitalist instincts. The latter had absorbed the ethic of hard work and Victorian values from their masters; they were more productive than midwestern agricultural laborers and enjoyed a higher standard of living than "Yankee" industrial workers.

The claim about the efficiency of slave agriculture in the Old South had already been made and had been much debated since the time of Conrad and Meyer (1958). The radical innovation of *Time on the Cross* was the system of motives attributed to the actors, who reacted to incentives exactly in keeping with a microeconomics textbook.

The values of the Protestant slave owners were certainly different from those of the slave owners in the ancient world, and their family lives had little in common with the customs of the Portuguese in Brazil (see Freyre 1933). Like the New England settlers, they had a sense of their economic interests, and behind the importation of slaves there was a calculation of this type. But this does not mean that the slaves were *homines oeconomici*, or that they had given up their traditional culture to adopt WASP values (M. Smith 1998). Historical research is not required to discover this: the cultural peculiarities of the various ethnic groups that make up American society are still evident (see chapter 6), just as more than two centuries of coexistence have not eliminated differences between the Québécois and the English-speaking Canadians.

Fogel and Engerman set themselves up as fighting a battle in the name of science, but in *Time on the Cross* the ideological element lurking behind the math played a role that was without precedent. Slavery was like a heavy stain on the history of a country that had made a banner out of civil and political rights. Showing that it had been profitable for the South, and that the slaves were well treated and by no means hostile, responded to a need to blot out the original sin of the nation and assuage its sense of guilt in a period marked by great social struggles.

Even the most superficial reader is struck by the work's systematic decontextualization of the data from any qualitative reference. But there are more serious problems. Herbert Gutman's book-length review *Slavery and the Numbers Game* (1975) divulged the biased samples, factual errors, and numerous exaggerations in the quantitative analysis. Equally ferocious criticism came from cliometricians (Walton 1975; David et al. 1976). A year after its publication, *Time on the Cross* did not seem to have an academic future despite the strong impact it had had on the media. Thomas Haskell wrote an obituary in the *New York Review of Books*, which ended with the charge that "now [Fogel and Engerman] must prove . . . that their book merits further scholarly attention" (1975, p. 39). But the tone of the controversy gradually died down, and Fogel's fidelity to the economists was rewarded with the Nobel Prize, which he shared in 1993 with North. It comes as no surprise that in a recent publication dedicated to the self-celebration of cliometric achievements there is hardly any mention of these early controversies (Lyons et al. 2008).

The way for the new economic history had been pointed. If nothing else, *Time on the Cross* had shown something: namely, that it is very simple to condition the result of a regression through the choice of independent variables with the aim of confirming or refuting a theoretical hypothesis. This is what led the cliometricians away from primary sources and toward a selective and opportunistic use of data. As Bernard Alford has noted, "some practitioners of the new approach—unencumbered by the need for archival research—frequently overreached themselves as they sought to graft selective historical evidence onto the latest fashion in economic theory and sell it as economic history" (2004, pp. 640–41).

Among outside observers, the idea had long prevailed that this unfortunate trend could not last. In his essay on the method of economic history about twenty years ago, Cipolla wrote: "If the 'new economic historians' want to come to grips with historical reality in all its complexity they will have to abandon their *esprit géométrique* for the subtler if less elegant *esprit de finesse*. This may actually happen sooner than expected" (1991, p. 70).

The *esprit de finesse* is essential for understanding the past, but unfortunately it does not enable us to foresee the future. If Cipolla's prediction had proved to be right, the rest of this book would never have been written.

# Chapter 2

## ECONOMICS WITH A HUMAN FACE?

A MAJOR MISUNDERSTANDING about cliometrics comes from the subsequent spread of Douglass North's new institutional approach. Unlike Fogel, North claims to have challenged traditional economic theory, which he found inadequate. Many think that this is the case, and North has used history to "humanize" economic theory. In fact, what he did was to extend the neoclassical explanatory model to the realm of social relations.

North noticed the absence of institutions from standard economics and decided that they should have a part in it. But while he restored them to economic theory, he explained their genesis in terms of the same theory he wished to improve. This is a circular procedure, as epistemologists would call it. Its roots lay in North's assumption about the universal nature of certain social arrangements (North et al. 2009) and in his methodological individualism. To put it in his words: "The strength of microeconomic theory is that it is constructed on the basis of assumptions about individual human behavior. . . . Institutions are a creation of human beings . . . hence our theory must begin with the individual" (North 1990, p. 5).

If the effects produced by the microfoundations program on the realism of economic theory have turned out to be deleterious (Hodgson 2000), the new institutionalism carries even more serious risks, because it is presented first of all as a theory of society (and of history). In other words, the new institutional economics does not remain on the abstract plane of model building and axiomatization, but seeks to gain legitimacy from historical and biological material, and is offered in its turn as an explanation for human history. Along with the explanation, the prescriptive message that was already contained in the premises filters through as if it was a self-evident reality. The persuasive force of the deduction from a few simple principles is reinforced by an appeal to the natural sciences that is no longer merely metaphorical, as in the neoclassical approach, but is fundamental. North's (2005) recent attempt to build a fully evolutionary theory is supposed to make the principles of economics potentially applicable even to the workings of the human mind.

In this chapter, I show how this approach, besides being patently unhistorical (Daunton 2010), rests on flimsy foundations. In order to do so,

I draw on a variety of evidence from the social and historical sciences. I also compare North's synthesis with the example of social science history offered by Moses Finley, the eminent ancient economic historian. Finley made a powerful argument against the application of modern economic theory to the past. Furthermore, he developed an alternative interpretation for the origin of institutions, rigorously demonstrating the logical precedence of society over the economy.

But before I do that, we need to step back and return to the criticism that Karl Polanyi made against neoclassical economics in the mid-twentieth century. In fact, both North's and Finley's works can be read as a response to Polanyi.

## Back to Polanyi's Problem

In his essay "The Economy as Instituted Process" (1957b), Polanyi argued that a great deal of conventional economic analysis was based on a misunderstanding arising out of a semantic trap. This misunderstanding concerned the twofold meaning of the term "economic." The "formal meaning" of the word was to do with the most advantageous way of achieving one's own ends in conditions of scarcity and was to be distinguished from the "substantive meaning" that corresponded to the actual operation of present and past economic systems. The prevalence of market exchange as an allocation system since the mid-eighteenth century had led to these two meanings coinciding in practice. But this overlapping of meaning was quite incidental and contingent.[1]

Asserting that the substantive meaning is the only truly universal parameter for carrying out comparisons in time and space is the equivalent of denying that economic activity is autonomous from other spheres of society. Just like politics, it is subordinated to the general ends of society as a whole and takes on a specific aspect in relation to them. Polanyi was not the only one to take these premises as his starting point. A similar vision is found in the social anthropology of A. R. Radcliffe-Brown (1952), who built up a theory of the dependence of various social functions on the "social structure." But precisely because of the latter's central position, Radcliffe-Brown ended by viewing economic activity as a subject

---

[1] For Polanyi (1957b, p. 244) the advent of price-making markets seems to be the direct consequence of an ongoing or accentuated situation of scarcity ("acts of exchange . . . involve the participants in choices induced by an insufficiency of means"). The scarcity of resources is thus an element determined institutionally, that is to say, dependent on the regime of exploitation to which they are subjected and on the juridical constraints that characterize it. The substantivist critique of economics, however, does not imply this particular historical reconstruction or this concept of scarcity.

for study that on the whole held little interest, and he preferred to concentrate on the prime mover. Polanyi, on the other hand, made it the center of his interest. As starting points for his analysis, he distinguished three "forms of integration": reciprocity, redistribution, and (market) exchange.

In outlining this scheme, he was influenced by two notable ethnologists who were also from central Europe. The first was the Berlin professor Richard Thurnwald (1916; 1932), while the second was Bronislaw Malinowski, one of the founders of the British school. During the 1910s both carried out extensive fieldwork in the archipelagoes of the Western Pacific and gave detailed descriptions of the way the first two forms of integration operated. Malinowski's work, *Argonauts of the Western Pacific* (1922), introduced what was to be a textbook example of reciprocity, the *kula*. This was a complex system of ceremonial exchange carried out by the Trobriand Islanders and characterized by a circular flow of gifts going in opposite directions. Armshells were passed from one hand to another in one direction, and necklaces in the other. As Polanyi writes: "We describe it as trade though no profit is involved, either in money or in kind; no goods are hoarded or even possessed permanently; the goods received are enjoyed by giving them away" (1944, p. 52).

Reciprocity, as practiced in this extreme form by the indigenous peoples of Melanesia, is thus represented as a system of multiple obligations involving transfers of wealth that have the aim of reinforcing membership of a group and also of acquiring prestige. This needs to be distinguished from redistribution, whereby the transfer of wealth instead starts from a center, usually corresponding to the political or religious center of the society, on which the services of the producers converge. These forms of integration can be adapted to varying degrees of social complexity, from communities of hunter-gatherers to the early empires of the Near East: they were allocation systems that prevailed in Europe in antiquity, as well as in the Middle Ages and beyond. This does not mean that they were exclusive and could not exist alongside other systems. Despite his inclination for "primitivism," Polanyi did not deny the emergence of markets during the long evolution of Euro-Asiatic civilization, especially after the Neolithic revolution, and he was aware of the role played by money in these civilizations. But he maintained that reciprocity and redistribution, in appropriate combinations, defined the majority of transactions performed outside the household and conferred a distinctive character on these economies.

The real change took place in Europe sometime on the eve of the modern period. The economy became gradually disembedded from social relations, and wealth ceased to circulate by means of the first two forms of integration in order to be allocated through market exchange. This differs radically from the other two allocation systems because of its anonymous nature: the contract frees the parties from personal bonds, and each single transaction stands by itself. The shift to the new system started in the sixteenth century with the English enclosures and culminated in the nineteenth century. It is the subject of Polanyi's best-known work, *The Great Transformation* (1944).

The expansion of the self-regulating market was to cause a similar, though not identical, phenomenon of commodification to the one that Marx had described, which triggered off a reaction of the self-protection of society. A "double movement" thus took place: there was, on the one hand, the formidable drive toward globalization and, on the other, a protectionist counterdrive to rescue land and labor from being "fictitious commodities," to which state the assimilation to the mercantile system had reduced them. Twentieth-century fascism was the most dramatic, yet inevitable, outcome of this need for self-protection.

This is where Polanyi the social scientist ends and Polanyi the ideologist begins. His antipathy for the self-regulating market—though he had no liking for socialist planning either—led him to believe that underlying its emergence there was a perversion, with the economy being unnaturally extracted from the bedrock of society where it was organically incorporated. It is possible to reject this thesis—and we will see that there are good reasons for so doing—but there remains the problem with which economic historians have to contend: that modern economics arose to describe the modern market economy, and is therefore unsuited for analyzing previous periods. The economic activity of the past needs to be understood with reference to its substantive meaning.

## The Universalization of Contingency

In an article entitled "Markets and Other Allocation Systems in History: The Challenge of Karl Polanyi," North acknowledged that Polanyi had raised an objection that could put neoclassical economics, and hence the type of economic history inspired by it, into a predicament. Both disciplines had placed the market at the center of their attention; until the nineteenth century, however, the market had been a relatively marginal phenomenon in human history and in the twentieth century had again lost in importance (1977a, p. 706).

Primitive, archaic, and preindustrial economies had been dominated by the other two "transactional modes" of reciprocity and redistribution, and even in the nineteenth century, the heyday of the market economy, they had not completely disappeared. After all, resources had continued to be allocated, but not by market prices, in households, voluntary organizations, and governments.

At this point, North wondered: "Is there an economic explanation for these "transactional modes" or must we retreat to the ad-hoc explanation that has characterized historians and scholars from the social sciences?" (1977a, pp. 708–9).

Here it might be objected that the question is badly put and reveals an initial prejudice: that only economics is capable of providing exhaustive, and not ad hoc, explanations for human behavior. But in fact the social sciences are able to construct organic theories that frequently have great explanatory power, in the same way that it is not unusual to come across ad hoc "economic explanations." And what if North's was one of these?

North defines "families, firms, guilds, manors, trade unions, cooperatives" as "substitutes for price-making markets." The term "substitutes" is not neutral and indeed here does not mean "alternatives." *Substitutes* expresses the idea that the natural allocation system is the market, and the others are surrogates for it, intervening when conditions are imperfect and unfavorable. In other words, according to North, it is not the emergence of the market system that requires explanation, but why other institutions "allocate resources *in place* of markets" (p. 709; emphasis added).

This is an extraordinary starting point. First the market is said to be the exception, and then it is taken as a yardstick. But there is no justification for this choice. One can suppose that the latter prejudice arises out of his conviction that the most efficient system, in terms of greater profit and utility for all, is the market, and, since human beings are maximizing actors, they cannot but tend toward this type of efficiency when there are no obstacles.

The obstacles are transaction costs, which are defined as "the costs of defining and enforcing property rights," given that property rights are a necessary condition for the existence of the market. Where transaction costs exceed the benefits that the market would offer, society adopts other allocation systems, such as reciprocity and redistribution, and the existence of public services would be an example of the operation of this decision-making process, because resorting to the market to meet certain needs involves irreducible costs. But with technological progress transaction costs generally tend to decrease; and as progress continues, nonmarket transactions gradually give way to market transactions in a growing number of sectors. North wishes to show that in this way neoclassical theory can also explain nonmarket phenomena, countering Polanyi's objections.

The idea of the market with property rights as society's natural (and ideal) condition has been at the heart of new institutional economics right from the start.[2] Two Marxist authors have recently reappraised Oliver Williamson's *Markets and Hierarchies*, calling attention to his assumption "for expositional convenience" that "in the beginning there were markets" (1975, p. 20). After a close analysis of the unhistorical implications that necessarily follow from similar premises, they reach a surprising conclusion: "Williamson himself is an institution of capitalism" (Ankarloo and Palermo 2004, p. 427). One does not need to be a Marxist, and see "bourgeois plots" lurking everywhere, to see how much truth there is in this colorful expression. One merely needs to be aware that certain cultural biases do exist. Each human group, living immersed as it does within a specific system of values and with specific institutions, sees its own institutional arrangements as being natural. It requires an effort of alienation and rationalization to understand that it is an illusion. Without this effort, or if it is insufficient, it becomes difficult, in the economic system one happens to live in, to distinguish the cultural elements from the "constants of nature," if there are such things in this field. If hardly excusable for an economist, this is especially serious for anyone claiming to practice the historian's craft.

Historical knowledge shows that whether societies are based on market or nonmarket allocation systems does not generally depend on opportunistic calculation, nor is it is a matter of choice. This argument also needs to be kept in mind when it comes to explaining the presence of public services in a market economy. In certain countries, public services could never become private because their culture abhors it. In the United States, if keeping the health care system private or not can become the subject of a cost-benefit analysis, this is because it does not upset people's sensitivity. But even this is framed within certain limits, if it is true that Barack Obama achieved victory in the 2008 presidential elections by stating that health care "should be a right for every American," and that the insurance companies had to appeal to equally sentimental or ideal principles (typically "freedom of choice") in campaigning against the health reform. On the other hand, in Europe, the problem of privatizing the health system does not even arise, being a sort of social taboo. In a country such as Italy, the idea that health care is a right is felt so strongly that even clandestine immigrants are granted the right to treatment, without doctors being able to report them.[3] An outcry within the entire medical profession was created in 2009 when a draft law was presented to make

---

[2] Mirowski (1988, p. 71) refers to this fallacy as the "*as if*" inconsistency—no need to say that here "as if" has nothing to do with counterfactuals.

[3] Decreto Legislativo 286/1998, Art. 35, no. 5.

it easier to report illegal immigrants by taking advantage of their presence in a hospital, and the government was forced to withdraw it.

But what happens when there are no property rights at all? From the standpoint of the new institutional economics, where this occurs, it is due to the excessive cost of setting them up. This deduction is equally unfounded. In the first place, there needs to be a *wish* to do something before any costs are assessed. Can it possibly be assumed that private property is a universal aspiration of mankind in all periods?

According to North, the most conspicuous "substitute" is the government in the sense of economic actor: "Throughout economic history," he writes, "activities (such as, the provision of old-age security) have shifted from households to markets to government" (1977a, p. 709). But assuming this is the sequence—which cannot be generalized, and the intermediate phase in particular cannot be—the explanation certainly does not lie in transaction costs. It is necessary to look in other directions. Population trends (prolonged average life expectancy in particular), the evolution of family structure in relation to these trends and to social change, the evolution of the idea of state and citizenship (with their relative rights and duties) in political thought—all these elements contributed to increasing the influence of the public sector.

Then there are the more unwavering attitudes to do with the culture of each society as it has settled down over the long term. They explain the "horizontal" differences from one country to another. Why is the welfare state stronger in Scandinavia or in France than in the United States? Is it perhaps a question of costs? Among the values that modern democracies identify in themselves, apart from the equality of citizens before the law, the French Republic emphasizes *fraternité*, while in the United States particular stress is laid on "freedom." This means that the French will be ready to accept higher taxation to have a greater degree of social security. In actively laying down these principles ever since the Enlightenment, I think it more plausible that the ruling elites in both nations have taken into account the culture of their people rather than made an economic calculation.

But even if we consider the origin of the most profit oriented of organizations, the modern firm, is it realistic to assume that the explanation given by Coase (1937), that it exists to minimize transaction costs, is historically true? Mechanizing and carrying out all the productive phases under one roof (actually to exploit a new source of energy—steam—with its economies of scale, and not so much to minimize the use of the market) are only the final act of a long historical process, which began with the enclosures and continued with the putting-out system (Landes 1986). In order to be completed, this process required the existence of specific social relations (capitalists and waged workers) and a society that accepted its aims, that is, economic acquisition. In particular, it required (*pace* Coase) the parallel formation of a market (for labor, raw materials, and finished products). On the other hand, even in the early modern period, centralized manufacturing plants existed. One imposing example is the Venetian Arsenal (see R. Davis 1991)—other examples can be found in glassmaking, papermaking, metallurgy, construction, and so on. These were all sectors in which separate production would have been physically impossible, or where precious raw materials or secret techniques needed to be protected. But they have nothing to do with the modern firm. This is the outcome of Western social and cultural history, of Western power structures and technology.

## Institutions as Constraints

The existence of allocation systems other than the market is thus explained by the new institutional economics in neoclassical terms as the product of cost minimization (which, as the microeconomists teach, is equivalent to profit maximization). This position, which we have already discussed, is fully expounded in *Structure and Change in Economic History* (North 1981). But North's aim is more ambitious. He is not only interested in explaining in this way how economic institutions arise but wants to construct a general theory of social institutions. At that point, it would be possible to assess the impact of different social institutions on economic performance, whose program had already been proclaimed in 1990 in *Institutions, Institutional Change and Economic Performance.*

Institutions are presented as "the humanly devised constraints that shape human interaction," in the sense that they "define and limit the set of choices of individuals" (North 1990, pp. 3–4). Choices need to be limited; otherwise people would be lost in uncertainty. Any activity that arises out of human interaction requires a knowledge of how to do it, and institutions are an indispensable guide. Activities such as greeting friends, driving a car, buying oranges, borrowing money, forming a business, and burying the dead (to cite the examples given by North), would be extremely costly in terms of time, resources and energy if we had to reinvent a way for carrying them out each time. This post hoc argument would undoubtedly have exerted an irresistible fascination on the Dr. Pangloss described by Voltaire; besides, it has the gift of great elegance and simplicity. But is it a realistic explanation? Let us analyze it in detail.

Institutions take on a dual form, of informal and formal constraints (North 1990, chs. 5–6). Conventions, codes of conduct, norms of behavior, and also "beliefs" and "belief systems" belong to the first group (North 2005, ch. 5). In complex societies, these informal "rules of the game" need to be complemented by formal constraints, which include a wide range of instruments—constitutions, laws, and so on up to contracts. These enhance the efficacy of the former.

The maximizing actor is still the starting point, but he is subject to the objective constraint of uncertainty. To begin with, we do not know the features of other people, not to mention their thoughts or intentions. If it were not for this state of things, people would have no need of society and could quietly live their lives like atoms performing day-by-day transactions in order to obtain what they need, from food to sex.

According to Northian anthropology, the latter state, that is a state of nature rid of uncertainty, is also the ideal condition of society. It envisages free individuals that carry out their activities on a market with well-defined and enforced property rights and zero transaction costs. How close a given institution manages to come to this condition by lowering the definition and enforcement costs of property rights reflects its efficiency. Hence, there are better institutions and "inferior institutions" (North 1990, p. 7). The difference vis-à-vis Alchian (1950) is that competition is not able to select the better institutions in a Darwinian fashion and assure survival only for them. This is because institutions do not operate by themselves but need organizations. They are "the players," that is to say, "groups of individuals bound together by some common objectives," such as firms, labor unions, political parties, the Congress, religious bodies, and clubs (North 2005, pp. 59–60).

Organizations "are created to take advantage" of the set of opportunities defined by institutions (North 1990, p. 7). But they are often equipped with incomplete information "and process the information that they do receive through mental constructs that can result in persistently inefficient paths" (p. 8). In their turn, "as the organizations evolve, they alter the institutions" (p. 7), and this gives rise to institutional change. But whether organizations are successful in promoting positive change depends largely on the nature of the institutions to start with. If the institutions are generally good, then a virtuous circle will be set off; otherwise, it will be a vicious circle. If the institutions are wrong, the organizations will become more and more efficient at perpetuating them. This explains, for example, the economic performance of the United States versus that of the Third World (pp. 8–9). Quite simply, some "got it right" and others "got it wrong" (North 2005, p. 116).

In the next chapter, we will see how this vision, which is shared by political economics, has strongly influenced cliometrics. On the next pages, it will be shown that it is an ideological and unfounded one. In particular it will be demonstrated:

1. how the assumption that the market with property rights is the ideal state of mankind is an ideologically biased apriorism;
2. how institutions, organizations, or allocation systems do not originate in an economic calculation (cost minimization) but instead exist in societies that view the economy and economic considerations as of marginal importance;
3. how the market itself is a social institution, and institutions cannot therefore arise as substitutes for the market; and
4. how the methodological individualism on which this theory of society is based is misleading.

## Was the Soviet System against Nature?

North presupposes that mankind (or at least its most enlightened sections) tends toward the institution of efficient, impersonal property rights, because the state of nature is dominated by violence. Where there is a communal regime, people spend time defending their belongings, taking it away from productive activities. In the intermediate evolutionary stage, in which most of the world still finds itself, the political system assumes great importance: it controls the violence by creating "economic rents." However, only open-access societies (currently twenty-five countries and 15 percent of the world population) "regulate economic and political competition in a way that uses the entry and competition to order social relations" (North et al. 2009, p. xii). But the state does not fade away, because its function is still that of providing "third-party enforcement" (p. 7).

In these premises, it is not difficult to see emerge the Hobbesian image of the *bellum omnium contra omnes*, the war of every one against every one, which forms the basis for the idea of the social contract (Hobbes 1642; 1651). It is a theory of society that is the opposite of Aristotle's, according to which the human being is *politikon zoon*, a naturally political animal (*Politics* 1253a1–18). For Aristotle, social coexistence does not need to be sanctioned by any contract. In other words, it does not need to be negotiated, as it is the very essence of the human condition: "the individual, when isolated, is not self-sufficing . . . he who is unable to live in society, or who has no need because he is sufficient for himself, must be either a beast or a god" (1253a26–29). Clearly, our knowledge of the animal world has greatly evolved since then, and no biologist would be ready to define a clear boundary between the human faculty of speech (*logos*), which was so important for Aristotle, and the "mere voice" (*phone*) of the other species with their forms of sociability. But Aristotle's fundamental intuition, as we will see when we consider the Durkheimian tradition, is still the basis of modern sociology.

According to the law and economics school, the institution of property rights is so remote as to belong to a mythical phase of the history of humankind. As the Yale lawyer Robert Ellickson tells us, with a touch of solemnity:

> Then, about 10,000 years ago, prehistoric civilization achieved a great breakthrough. In the Fertile Crescent of the Near East, human groups, which had shortly before begun operating out of permanent settlements, mastered the skills of cultivating crops and domesticating animals. The breakthrough required innovations not only in husbandry, but also in property rights. A prehistoric community had to develop a set of land rules that provided incentives for its members to engage in the small events involved in raising crops and animals. The Promethean invention was likely the classic usufruct. (1993, p. 1365)

It is astonishing how such statements can be made—and made, what is more, without any backing from historical or archaeological scholarship. Is perhaps an act of faith demanded of readers? The distinguished Assyriologist Johannes Renger writes: "As for ancient Mesopotamia, we are able to observe land tenure systems in varying degrees of accurateness from the end of the fourth millennium B.C. until Late Achaemenid times towards the end of the first millennium B.C." (1995, p. 269).

Thus, for around half the period mentioned by Ellickson, no information is even available. Yet the preconception that economic activity, any economic activity—even subsistence cultivation—needs "incentives" to be performed, overrides any objective and reasoned approach to the question. Actually, incentives of an economic nature work well in a system that is already a market system. In many cases, even in the most complex economies, the motivation to take part in the division of labor is not the expected material reward but social recognition.

In *Understanding the Process of Economic Change*, a central chapter (ch. 11) is dedicated to the Soviet Union, which is presented as an attempt to intentionally deviate from a natural condition, as a sort of colossal cognitive error on the part of the rulers. The "belief system" worked out by Marx and Engels was imported into Russia by Lenin in order to "break away from a capitalist mode of production." This attempt to break with the past in order to introduce an unnatural regime was translated into an uninterrupted history of "altered perceived reality" and of "outcomes deviate[d] from intentions." Both the beliefs and the players' responses reflected "the very imperfect and primitive understanding" they had of the economy and of the incentives that were necessary to make it work (North 2005, pp. 3–4, 146ff.).

Many Western economists who deal with transition economies seem to be candidly convinced that everything changed with 1917 (Gregory

1994; Spulber 2003). One of them, wishing to rehabilitate the tsarist economy against the Soviet economy in order to draw lessons from it to apply to post-Soviet Russia, asks "How well did the tsarist economy perform under conditions of market-resource allocation?" (Gregory 1994, p. 12). There is no sense in this question because the prerevolutionary economy did not operate in conditions of this sort. Whatever one thinks of Gerschenkron's (1962) general thesis, historical research has unequivocally shown that the state never ceased to be the driving force behind Russian industrialization and, what is more important, that Russia remained essentially an agricultural country (R. W. Davies 1990). In 1913 five-sixths of the total population still lived in the countryside. "Most peasant households were organised into rural communes: their land was divided into strips, and in many communes was periodically redistributed" (p. 12).

The Russian agrarian structure, which became consolidated over the centuries, was organized around the *mir* (sometimes referred to as *obshchina*), the commune. Each *mir* included a certain number of peasants, without any individual property at all, who were bound by mutual obligations and duties toward the landed aristocracy. It governed itself by means of the *skhod*, or the village assembly, which periodically allocated and reallocated the strips of land available for the various households according to the size as recorded in the census. As proof of the total, even psychological, identification of the peasants with the *mir*, it has been pointed out how the Russian word *mir* also means "universe" and, in a variant spelling, "world" (Hoch 1986, p. 2). The reforms of the mid-nineteenth century, and in particular the emancipation of the serfs in 1861, did not substantially change the situation (see Braudel 1987, p. 545). The collective constraints that affected the members of the *mir* did not disappear, and the aristocracy continued to exert its control over the latifundia. The revolution that led to communism was carried out against the latter, and not in the name of peasant property rights. The *soviet* replaced the *skhod*; the *kolkhoz*, the *mir*; and the *sovkhoz*, the manorial estate.

Studies on the evolution of state bureaucracy and on labor relations in the nineteenth and twentieth centuries have highlighted the strong continuity between the dirigistic style of the tsarist administration and that of the USSR, between the organization of labor before and after emancipation, as well as before and after the revolution of 1917 (Stanziani 1998; 2008b). A significant example of the resistance of these deep-seated attitudes, which Fernand Braudel called "structures," is the Stolypin Land Reform, which was carried out by the tsarist state immediately after the revolution of 1905 (Pallot 1999). In response to the discontent arising out of the recurring agrarian crises, the imperial bureaucracy of Saint

Petersburg, living under the influence of the myth of liberal Europe, suggested uprooting the peasants from the *mir* and transforming them into independent farmers on the Western model. Pyotr Stolypin and the other reformers believed that by providing the peasant "with a separate plot of land taken from the state domains . . ., making sure that there was adequate water and that it satisfied all the other requirements for proper cultivation, then . . . there would arise an independent, prosperous husbandman, a stable citizen of the land" (quoted in Pallot 1999, p. 1). This attempt produced disappointing results, because the peasants refused to enclose land from the commune. When some of them tried to enclose, the others hindered their plans by putting up various forms of resistance. Hence, it can be asserted with reasonable certainty that, with or without the revolution of 1917, Russia was by no means on the path to agrarian individualism.

The case of Russia is also particularly appropriate for highlighting the contradictions in North's theory of the state. If the state exists to set up and defend property rights, then in tsarist Russia, where such rights were not recognized, we should find relatively weak forms of central power. Yet around the mid-seventeenth century, government bureaucracy was already exerting widespread control over the country, and the absolutism of the Romanovs after Peter the Great (1672–1725) sanctioned the principle that state, nation, and territory were one and the same thing.

North's conception of the state is reminiscent of the doctrine of the "night-watchman state" developed by social contract theorists such as Nozick (1974), in comparison to whom even Adam Smith (1776) would seem interventionist. But it reflects only a particular political culture and cannot be universalized. Moreover, it is an idealization and not so much a model, and has never been fully realized in the United States or anywhere else, which in fact happens for many products of philosophical speculation. In spite of the doctrine that Hobbes had expressed in the *Leviathan*, when a few decades after the Battle of Trafalgar (1805) the British erected a column to commemorate Admiral Nelson, it is clear they saw themselves as a nation and not a group of people held together by mere interests.

Furthermore, the concept of full ownership is a recent one, even in most parts of the modern West. In the past, one limitation was due the extent of collective property, whose importance in early modern Europe has been widely documented (Grossi 1981). This was a land right pertaining to a group rather than to an individual. The origins of these forms of property lay in Indo-European collectivist institutions: the Russian *mir*, the Teutonic *Mark* (a form of collective dominion over undivided property), the Celtic community, the Scottish township. Depending on the penetration of Roman law and on many other environmental variables, in due course of time these institutions became modified, but they never completely disappeared. In various regions of the European mainland, they were still relatively important in the nineteenth century (Demélas and Vivier 2003). Another limitation to private property in the meaning it usually has today came about as a result of the paramount rights that had developed during the feudal period and operated until at least the beginning of the nineteenth century.[4] With the dissolution of feudalism, such rights did not vanish but were still controlled by individuals who had previously exerted them as a privilege. The Code Napoléon (1804), a product of the French Enlightenment and on which the civil law of most of continental Europe and Latin America is currently based, generally did away with these medieval vestiges, just as it abolished primogeniture and established equality between heirs. However, they were so deeply rooted that they still survived in a bland form. Observing these forms is rather like observing the fossils trapped in geological strata for the paleontologist. To give just one example, emphyteusis, which is a much greater limitation than servitude or usufruct, still exists in some of these countries at least theoretically. It is a hereditary right on someone else's immovable property. The holders of this right and their heirs gain the exclusive use of the land, on condition that they look after it and pay a small rent. Against payment of a large enough sum, they can become its owners, and under certain conditions the right can even be ceded.

## Lessons from the Ancient Economy

We have seen therefore that the existence of a strong state does not imply the existence of property rights. But where both state *and* clearly defined property rights do exist, does that necessarily mean there is a market economy?

Let us start from a general assumption that law and order produce the market. If the absence of markets is due to the high transaction costs originating from a lack of effective political superstructures, then it would be enough to remedy this lack in order to make them magically appear. Archaeological research on Bronze Age polities such as Hawaiian chiefdoms and the Inka Empire disprove any such link. Despite the

---

[4] In early medieval Europe, the three particular cases envisaged by Roman law—the *dominium*, the absolute right to landed property; the *possessio*, the right to effectively dispose of that property; and the *ius in re aliena*, limited rights in another's property—had become mixed in various ways, in theory and in practice. This state of things does not reflect a crisis in legal thought, but rather the fact that in this period control over the land, and the labor to which it gave access, became functional to political power (see Davies and Fouracre 1995).

imposition of a lasting territorial peace in both cases and the construction of a functional infrastructure of connections (in the case of the Inka
Empire, around 30,000 kilometers of roads), there is no evidence of a
growth in exchanges (Earle 2002).

Put in these terms, however, the question is still too vague. The really interesting case is the one where property rights do effectively exist.
And in order to be able to provide evidence for them with any certainty,
we have to necessarily leave prehistory and enter history. In this section,
I introduce the model of classical antiquity developed by Moses Finley
in his *The Ancient Economy*, first published in 1973. It will provide an
opportunity to observe how a historical explanation is constructed and
to appreciate the difference with regard to ahistorical forms of reasoning. We will see that an authentically historical approach is ultimately
decisive for understanding the workings and evolution of economic and
social institutions.

The Greeks and Romans had property rights extending not only over
things but also over human beings. The Romans built up a highly sophisticated system of rights based on the concept of *dominium*. The Greeks
had a less elaborate concept of ownership (in line with the lesser degree
of technicality of their legal tradition), but they clearly distinguished
between ownership and possession and had an efficient system for the
general enforcement of rights, in addition to public notice requirements
for property transfers. The property rights established under Roman
law, with the notion of individual rights being reinforced by Scholastic
thought, were taken up in the Code Napoléon. Thus, Roman law is the
foundation of modern civil law on which most of western Europe is
still based.[5]

The economy of the ancients was not a primitive one (Finley 1985).
Well before the fourth century B.C., there is evidence of widespread exchanges of consumer goods and long-distance trade. Markets did therefore exist, just as they did in early modern Europe. But there was no
*market economy*, nor could one have developed for reasons that we
will see. In the final analysis, the market economy is the typical allocation system of capitalism, and the ancient economy was not a capitalist
system.

In the ancient world there were no guilds, but not because there was a
culture of free trade; rather because commerce (especially that on a small
scale) was held in such low consideration that the interests involved were
not considered worth defending. The aim of long-distance trade was not

[5] On Athenian property law and procedural matters, see Harrison (1968, part II). On rights
and enforcement in Athens, see Hansen (1998, pp. 93–94, 96); on Roman property law, see
Garnsey (2007, pp. 186ff.).

exports but consumption and supplies for the city. Neither was there any market for land, labor, or capital. On the subject of land, Finley pointed out that "the normal purchase of land in antiquity . . . was windfall purchase" (1985, p. 119; also 1976, p. 1). Which did not mean that "windfalls were rare" but that there was no incentive for systematic speculation with a view to maximizing one's gain. The Greco-Roman social organization was such that hired labor was casual and marginal, which is clearly different from what happens with capitalism. Loans on interest were for financing consumption rather than investment. Citizens generally kept away from such activities, which were the reserve of foreigners, slaves, and former slaves, the freedmen.

The only type of productive activity that the ancients really approved of was agriculture, carried out in the *oikos* (the *familia* of the Romans). This was a very complex and articulated organization, involving "all the people of the household together with its land and its goods" (Finley 1977, p. 58). Production was intended for achieving self-sufficiency. This does not imply that the *oikoi* lived at a level of subsistence; the autarkic ideal was not incompatible with affluence. But making profit was not their aim. The trader or banker, those who made a living outside this closed system, was pitied for his state of "dependence." Not that the landowners looked down on making money on occasion, which they did mainly indirectly through the intervention of low-ranking intermediaries. But these actions were aimed at maintaining their lifestyle (including the upkeep of their clients) and hence their status.

In the mentality of the Greeks and Romans, economic activity was inseparable from other aspects of social life to such a degree that they had no concept of economy or of economic system. Xenophon's *Oikonomikos* (c. 360 B.C.), a treatise on the management of the *oikos*, gives reflections on how the head of the household (the Roman *paterfamilias*) should exert his authority and control over the people, as well as the property, that make up his household. These elements (people and material goods) appear to be indistinguishable from one another. People might be free men or slaves, bound by blood ties or not. The conception of the family on the intimate lines that we are used to was alien to the ancients in much the same way as was the conception of a separate existence between goods and people.

Therefore *oikonomia* (the art of household management) is not the "economics" of Alfred Marshall, nor is it a business administration. The vocabulary of economics, made up of abstract terms such as labor, production, capital, investment, income, circulation, demand, entrepreneur, and utility, is untranslatable in Greek or Latin, and there are no equivalent words. (By contrast, the word "entrepreneur," in the sense of universal decision maker in the economic and political activity of all times and places, recurs seven times in the eight-page introductory chapter of Douglass North's *Understanding the Process of Economic Change*.)[6]

Xenophon is concerned not with productivity but with the quality of the goods being produced. In the *Oikonomikos*, as Finley points out, "there is not one sentence that expresses an economic principle or offers any economic analysis, nothing on efficiency of production, 'rational' choice, the marketing of crops" (1985, p. 19). On the contrary, it aims at teaching *how to avoid* exchanges. The ideal of self-sufficiency was also shared by the Roman citizens. They extolled contemplative idleness (*otium*) over business, which was regarded as a necessary evil (the Latin word *negotium* literally means "time taken from *otium*"). Cicero translated Xenophon into Latin, and was full of praise for him for those reasons (*De officiis* 2.87; *De senectute* 59).

As the political philosopher James Booth puts it when referring to classical Athens, "Aversion to the market (as well as to other productive functions, e.g., necessary physical labor and the sale of one's labor) had as its foundation not a theory of the costs of enforcement and measurement associated with the market mechanism but rather a view of the instrumentality of the economy for the sake of the good life, a view that, to repeat, required the greatest possible exclusion of it from the lives of free persons" (1993, p. 89).

At this point one might well ask if there was not a gulf between the full citizens and the other Greek and Roman people. A neoclassical economist would surely say: "Agreed, the aristocrats remained in their villas idling away their time, the thinkers in the academies working on their great theoretical systems, and the slaves, the freedmen and the foreigners were left with the dirty work, but all the same these lower-status people did trade. They left no writings, as is only logical, but their values were not those of the elite, and there is nobody to tell us that this silent majority did not have a modern economic spirit." First, it needs to be seen whether it was indeed a majority. But an objection of this sort would not grasp the main point, because it would assume there was a freedom in ancient society that did not exist. Ancient society was one in which inequality (not economic, but of kind) was accepted as natural, one in which there were no social classes, only social orders. It was not a society

[6] On a similar note, Landes et al. (2010). The concept of *entrepreneur* or *Unternehmer* is closely linked with the development of continental capitalism, in particular French and German. It has no equivalents in other economic cultures, even Western cultures, and does not appear in the vocabulary of the British classical economists. Its widespread use in the United States is due to Schumpeter (1934) in particular, although it had already been used by Francis Walker, who justified himself for borrowing "a word from the French" (1892, p. 74).

that contemplated slavery, but it was a "slave society" (Finley 1980, ch. 2; Cartledge 2002b).

Even when they could go into business for themselves, the slaves did not feel they were united by economic interests, and, apart from the times they rebelled in order to gain their freedom, they were not united by an esprit de corps.[7] The freedmen, whatever their formal condition, also occupied their place in a static world that offered very few opportunities for social mobility. The comedies of Menander, Plautus, and Terence give an idea of the derision to which parvenus were subjected in the Greco-Roman world and of the mistrust of rapidly accumulated fortunes: for them, "this type of wealth and the mentality that is associated with it contrasts with the wealth that derives from the ancestors with its very different solidity. . . . [It] has been gathered not against the will of the gods, but indeed with their help, and this is an endorsement of its legality, is evidence for its good origins and guarantees its duration" (Gabba 1988, pp. 76–77).

The Greeks and Romans did not gather statistical data on their economies, and nor did they reason by figures to show trends. On the other hand, they kept meticulous accounts of the number of hoplites, cavalrymen, and ships, and the reserves of cash available for the immediate requirements of war. Should we perhaps attribute this "statistical innocence" to the absence of adequate conceptual tools? Clearly not: "A society that produced the work of Apollonius of Perge on conic sections had more than enough mathematics for what the seventeenth-century English and Dutch called 'political arithmetic' and we call 'statistics'" (Finley 1985, p. 25).

Again, it is an interest, or lack of interest, in specific questions that creates the need or not for analysis.[8] The example of Aristotle is indicative (Finley 1970). Aristotle was prompted by the analytical aim of classifying the branches of knowledge. He wrote *Logic*, *Physics*, *Metaphysics*, *Ethics*, *Politics*, *Rhetoric*, and *Poetics*: but he wrote no *Economics*. He applied his versatile mind to biology and meteorology, but he never concerned himself with providing an explanation for price formation.

Aristotle dealt with the household and forms of exchange in book I of the *Politics* and in book V of the *Nicomachean Ethics*, but not with the mechanics of market exchange. The only passage in the *Ethics* that might

---

[7] For the Romans, the "servile wars" did not merit even being considered civil wars (Plutarch, *Crassus* 11.8; Florus, *Epitome* 2.8). In 71 B.C. the followers of Spartacus were treated in accordance with their status and were given a mass crucifixion (Appian, *Civil Wars* 1.120).

[8] Arguing that "economic behaviour did not depend on having a theory about it" (Erdkamp 2005, p. 8) is a superficial objection and betrays a failure to appreciate the links between economic and intellectual history.

effectively explain how exchange values between one good and the other are determined sounds totally incomprehensible to the modern reader. He says that exchange values are determined by "reciprocal proportion." The quantity of product A equivalent to a given quantity of product B is inversely proportional to the ratio of the producer of A to the producer of B. In other words, equivalence, or justice (which for Aristotle are the same thing), is determined by the relative status of the respective parties and by the prestige they enjoy within society.

Finley comments:

> As an explanation of exchange values in a market economy nothing could be more absurd. The first principle of a market economy is the indifference in the calculations of the persons of the buyer and the seller. Yet for Aristotle, it is the persons who constitute the first principle, so to speak, of the calculation. And modern commentators have had a time with this, for, having committed themselves to the notion that Aristotle was talking about commercial trade and a supply-and-demand market, they have had no choice but to treat Aristotle as an idiot or to insist that the text does not say what it so patently does say.[9]

Aristotle was not unaware of the existence of speculation. He knew that markets existed on the fringes of the world of the household where price was determined by supply and demand. This was "a commonplace in Greek life in the fourth century B.C." (Finley 1970, p. 47). But he did not concern himself with it, believing, along with his fellow citizens, that it was a perversion of natural ethics, and that it could not therefore be an object of knowledge. Aristotle's analysis is concerned with the world of the household on which Greek society was based. Applied to that context, and to that context alone—and thus to relations between the *oikoi*—does it make sense. In order to understand this point, we need to refer to the *Politics*. Here Aristotle introduces *chrematistike*, the "art of acquiring property," saying that wealth is a means that is instrumental in maintaining the household and the *polis*. Moreover, he condemns loan against interest, as well as commercial trade (*kapelike*), defining them as practices that go against nature. The reason is simple. Whereas wealth by its nature is limited—and this is an idea that pervades the whole of

---

[9] Moses Finley, "Aristotle on Exchange," ms., March 1954, pp. 10–11, box 16/G3, Finley Papers, Cambridge University Library. Finley prepared this paper for the seminar "Economic Aspects of Institutional Growth," convened by Karl Polanyi and Conrad Arensberg at Columbia University. His study on Aristotle was to have been included in Polanyi et al. (1957). However, the disagreement over the excessively primitivist interpretation that Polanyi made of ancient economies led him to withdraw it (see Polanyi 1957a; Finley 1975, p. 117). On the complicated relationship between Polanyi and Finley, see Tompkins (2008, pp. 126–27, 134).

classical antiquity—the market cannot be seen as anything other than a zero-sum game.

Aristotle was no reactionary, and he knew he was no longer in an archaic Greece where exchanges "simply served to satisfy the natural requirements of self-sufficiency," making up for shortages and surpluses of individual households (*Politics* 1257a24–30, as quoted in Finley 1970, p. 17). But nonetheless he thought that exchange relationships within the framework of the *koinonia* (community) were the natural state of society, not a utopian ideal.

Marcel Mauss was certainly right to state that "it was precisely the Romans and Greeks who, possibly following the northern and western Semites, invented the distinction between rights over things and rights arising from obligations, separated sale from gift and exchange, disassociated moral obligations from contracts, and, above all, conceived the difference that exists between ritual, rights and interests" (1923–24, p. 139). However, in the ancient economy a certain degree of "reciprocity" still operated. It was smaller than Polanyi (1957a) supposed, when automatically transferring to the study of classical antiquity the categories that anthropology had worked out for "primitive" and archaic societies. But it was still a significant degree, comparable to that existing in medieval and early modern Europe.

Hence, Finley's reply to the question about which of the social sciences should be the most suitable mentor for ancient history: "I deliberately select anthropology, not sociology, as the mentor. . . . Ideally, we should create a third discipline, the comparative study of literate, post-primitive (if I may), pre-industrial, historical societies" (Finley 1975, pp. 118–19).

Among these societies, the case of classical antiquity is particularly significant, because property rights existed that were far more widespread than they were in medieval western Europe. Yet the "other allocation systems" that North spoke of had by no means disappeared.

## North and Finley on Archaic Exchange

In regard to the instances of reciprocity described by Polanyi, North is particularly attracted by the more archaic forms, known to anthropologists as the "gift economy." His aim is to show that they do not depend on noneconomic factors but can be perfectly explained with a neoclassical schema that takes transaction costs and property rights into account. We have examined the weak points in this reasoning. However, it might be useful to point out how the very criticisms that North makes against Polanyi are misdirected and based on a distorted interpretation of his works. Neither Polanyi nor his sources ever stated that "giving is good in itself and not carried out for any ulterior motive" (North 1977a, p. 712). On the contrary, they argue that gift-exchange in archaic societies does have an ulterior motive, but this is political and social, namely the assertion of power and prestige through establishing relations of mutual commitment. Whoever shows he is able to give more, to the point where the other, or others, are not able to reciprocate, binds them into an asymmetrical relationship with himself.

Interpreting the gift system as an exchange of equivalents, to the point of stating that "reciprocity societies can be considered as a least-cost trading solution where no system of enforcing the terms of exchange between trading units exists," means to completely misinterpret what Mauss (1923–24) defined as the "spirit of the gift." Just as misleading is to state that exchange ratios remained constant over time "so that there would be assurances that trade would not be interrupted" (North 1977a, p. 714).

Moses Finley made a rigorous analysis of the system of reciprocity in archaic Greece in his work *The World of Odysseus*, first published in 1954. He demonstrated the considerable importance, and the frequent recurrence, of the gift-exchange in the Homeric poems, and how it intervenes in a variety of circumstances. It serves to strengthen friendships, seal alliances, or acts as a reward for a favor that has been granted. Gift-exchange needs to be distinguished from "trade," where the exchange of goods is the end in itself and is present in the *Odyssey* as well. However, "trade" is carried out only for reasons of consumption or to meet specific needs: "Hence, in modern parlance, imports alone motivated trade, never exports. There was never a need to export as such, only the necessity of having the proper goods for the counter-gift when an import was unavoidable" (Finley 1977, p. 67).

In this early phase of Greek civilization, money was still absent. The measure of value (typically cattle) did not coincide with the medium of exchange, which took on a variety of forms. In the Homeric world, the function of fixing equivalents between goods in an exchange, which in the modern world is entrusted to the market, depended on custom and convention. Not supply and demand but "the actual practice of exchange over a long period of time had fixed the ratios, and they were commonly known and respected" (p. 68).

This could not be otherwise, for "behind the market lies the profit motive, and if there was one thing that was taboo in Homeric exchanges it was gain in the exchange" (p. 67). Gain at the expense of others was certainly contemplated, but it belonged to a different sphere, not the economic sphere. It belonged "to warfare and raiding, where it was achieved by acts (or threats) of prowess, not by manipulation and bargaining."

But the Homeric poems help to understand the genesis of another two aspects of Greek culture—namely, the attitude toward traders and that toward hired labor.

On the island of the Phaeacians, Odysseus is confronted by a local aristocrat who challenges him to prove that he is not "a master of sailors who traffic, one who remembers the cargo and is in charge of merchandise and coveted gains" (trans. Finley 1977, p. 69). In the ears of Odysseus, this rings like an intolerable insult. Although there is no lack of references to the Phoenicians and their trafficking, it is significant that neither the *Iliad* nor the *Odyssey* contains a single word that is synonymous with "merchant" (p. 70).

The second element that is worth reflecting upon is the figure of the *thes* (*thetes* were unattached landless laborers who worked for hire). In his comment on the meeting between Odysseus and Achilles in Hades, and Achilles' famous phrase: "I would rather be bound down, working as a *thes* for another, by the side of a landless man, whose livelihood was not great, than be ruler over all the dead who have perished," Finley points out: "A *thes*, not a slave, was the lowest creature on earth that Achilles could think of. The terrible thing about a *thes* was his lack of attachment, his not belonging" (p. 57).

Since these early times, the Greeks had derived their social identity from belonging to the *oikos*, to its system of norms, solidarity, and obligations. Thus, it was better to be a slave (*dmos*, from *domos* = house) in the *oikos* than a free man with no land or bonds. True freedom was identified with the possibility of having labor of one's own and maintaining control over one's livelihood this way. If slaves were seen as victims of destiny (it was not uncommon for foreign nobles to be made prisoners of war), the *thetes*, who had deliberately chosen to sell their own labor, were not pardoned the ignoble renunciation (p. 71).

## Embeddedness Generalized: The Social Construction of the Market

North's argument is based on the dichotomy between market and institutions, whereby the latter arise as substitutes for the former. But the market itself is an institution, or social construct. Thus, there is no sense in seeing institutions as alternatives to the market, or vice versa. Paradoxically, the arguments of the new institutional economics come to depend on Polanyi's hypothesis that market exchange is disembedded. The merit of having understood this goes to the economic sociologist Mark Granovetter, who, in 1985, reconsidered the problem of embeddedness in his article "Economic Action and Social Structure."

The neoclassical representation of economic behavior, with its atomized agents ever ready to make contracts, was criticized as being undersocialized. But the idea that the actors were so conditioned by social norms as to see their active capacity for transforming them annulled was also considered implausible, as it was oversocialized. The new institutional economics, exemplified by Williamson's theory of the firm, embodied both defects, because it was a "mixture of under- and oversocialized assumptions" (Granovetter 1985, p. 494).

Granovetter pointed out that nonmarket economies were probably less embedded than was supposed by the oversocialized interpretations and that, vice versa, market economies were more embedded than the undersocialized interpretations were ready to recognize. The result was that the level of embeddedness did not vary significantly with modernization. This redefinition, which some have wished to interpret as a compromise (Beckert 2009), in fact offered a concept that was more powerful than the original one and had a much wider range of application.

The fact that we live in an economic epoch is indisputable. Martha Nussbaum (2010) invites reflection on one particularly noteworthy circumstance, namely the changed idea of knowledge. In our society, even knowledge tends to be seen as having a value not in itself but as a function of the practical results—especially economic results—that can be achieved with it. Hence, the admiration for fields such as business administration, which once would not have even been a subject for teaching at university, and the low status in which the humanities are commonly held.

But does this authorize us to believe that the modern economy has absorbed society? Have social relations been subordinated to the "cash nexus"? No, in fact the extraordinary role that economic calculation has assumed in contemporary life has been made possible by its compatibility with shared beliefs. If the market is such an important phenomenon today, it is still society that has made it so. In *The Social Structures of the Economy*, Pierre Bourdieu (2000, p. 1) cites a famous witticism of the philosopher Henri Bergson: "It takes centuries of culture to produce a utilitarian such as John Stuart Mill." Now, regardless of whether Mill was the most suitable target for Bergson's irony or not, the sense of the phrase is clear, which is that utilitarianism is a cultural construct. To assume that the economy has a corrupting power that can erode the foundations of social coexistence (even if only for a limited time span, as in Polanyi's view) is the equivalent of conceding that it has an autonomous nature and existence. But is that not what those who embrace economic reductionism want? The emphasis on economic activity that is found more or less everywhere in modern times is not the fruit of a pathological inversion—disembeddedness—but is due rather to the fact that the culture of society prefers the values of economic acquisition.

In chapter 6 we will return to the problem of explaining the rise of these values in the modern Western imagination. Here I simply recall that it has been a central preoccupation of sociological analysis since the times of Max Weber and Werner Sombart. In any case, it is interesting to observe that the convergence between society and economy is never total, and this is a confirmation that the former logically precedes the latter:

> Despite intimate connections between social networks and the modern economy, the two have not merged or become identical. Indeed, norms often develop that limit the merger of sectors. For example, when economic actors buy and sell political influence, threatening to merge political and economic institutions, this is condemned as "corruption." Such condemnation invokes the norm that political officials are responsible to their constituents rather than to the highest bidder and that the goals and procedures of the polity are and should be different and separate from those of the economy. (Granovetter 2005b, p. 36)

The most innovative contributions of the new economic sociology have emerged precisely from this observation. In the past thirty years, it has extensively explored the social relations underlying markets. Both horizontal relationships (involving trust and cooperation) and vertical relationships (those of power and compliance) have continued to lie behind economic action in modern times (Granovetter 2002, p. 36). The decisions of economic actors are not taken in isolation, as in the hypothesis of atomized individuals, and the market is a much less anonymous and competitive system of exchange than it might seem to be. Factors that have little to do with business at times influence the choice of trading partners, and as much as one tries to keep them out of this sphere, nonpecuniary motives come into play even in the most impersonal of transactions. Some markets, such as the labor market, tend to be more regulated than others, where conventional commodities are bought and sold. There is no need for a long account of the role of the labor unions and laws that in many countries prevent dismissals; one only needs to think of the familiar example of the "academic job market," which moreover does not exist in most of Europe, Asia, and Latin America. These aspects will be taken up again in chapters 4 and 6.

## Structure and Agency: The Individualistic Fallacy

Flaws in the new institutional accounts are often a direct consequence of methodological individualism, whereby society can be reduced to the sum of the individuals who form it, and institutions are the product of their actions. Whoever takes this point of view as his starting point often assumes that there is no need to justify it, as its validity seems to be self-evident. As Jon Elster, a champion of such an approach puts it: "This view . . . is in my view trivially true" (1989, p. 13).

The program of methodological individualism has a long history of association with politics. Hayek and Popper avoided holism because they saw in it a possible source for legitimizing totalitarianism (one needs to bear in mind the historical climate in which they were writing). Elster was against the way his fellow Marxists utilized functionalism as a post hoc explanation. He firmly anchored methodological individualism to rational choice theory, even if he has somewhat toned down his positions more recently (see Elster 2007).

Methodological individualism is typical of only two academic contexts: the Austrian and the Anglo-American. The contrast with continental Europe had already been evident in the very early days of social science, with Spencer and J. S. Mill on one side, and Comte and Durkheim on the other, and this continued into the twentieth century. "The contrast is so striking as to suggest that we should interpret the debate itself in structural terms, as a clash of cultures" (Burke 2005, pp. 127–28). But this does not imply that we should give up trying to overcome the contrasting positions. We will see how over the past forty years attempts to do this have been made from different sides, and we will see that positions such as North's contradict the conclusions of most contemporary social theory. But first we will need to go back to Emile Durkheim, whose contribution formed the starting point for subsequent research.

Durkheim considered society as being an outright organism and introduced the category of the "collective consciousness" to explain how it was held together by a cohesive force that transcends individual motivations: "We must . . . seek the explanation of social life in the nature of society itself. It is quite evident that, because it infinitely surpasses the individual in time as well as in space, it is in a position to impose upon him ways of acting and thinking which it has consecrated with its prestige. This pressure, which is the distinctive property of social facts, is the pressure which the totality exerts on the individual" (1895, p. 102).

Socialization is the natural state of individual existence. This is proved by the fact that when the former fails, for whatever reason, human beings sink into a state of malaise, and even continuing to live becomes a problem. In his famous study on suicide, Durkheim (1897) interpreted "egoistic suicide" as the extreme reaction to a state of severe undersocialization. But he recognized that oversocialization, or identification with the norms of a community pushed to such a point that individual identity is annulled, is an equally pathological state that can end in "altruistic suicide." The predictive capacity of this conceptual scheme is evident over a century later: one only needs to consider the crisis in the model of social coexistence in present-day large metropolitan areas on the one hand and the Islamic suicide terrorist attacks on the other.

It is clear that it is always individuals who think and act—and British scholarship with its proverbial pragmatism reminds us of this. But this does not mean that society can be described in terms of the sum of its parts; without a "grand theory," the behavior of individuals cannot be understood. To be satisfying, a theory has to be able to explain the micro-macro link in particular (Alexander and Giesen 1987). This seems to be the main point.

Mary Douglas has tackled this problem in a book significantly entitled *How Institutions Think* (1986). She argues that the possibility of individuals to think derives from the existence of a common institutionalized knowledge (note that "understand" and "think" are two distinct mental acts). Right from the very earliest experiences of life, and hence from the relationship with our mothers, from society we learn to make classifications. We classify objects on the basis of a similarity between them that appears to us intrinsic, but in reality it is in the eye of the beholder, because systems of classification vary from one society to another. We have all experienced how difficult it is to convey certain concepts in another language. This is due not to a lack of linguistic ability but to the very close link between linguistic and cultural structures. As we will see in chapter 6, cultures can be understood, because they are endowed with an internal logic, but they cannot be translated. People from different cultural backgrounds tend not only to face problems differently but also to pose them differently. The framework developed by Mary Douglas makes it possible to explain this variability.

The most influential twentieth-century contribution to making the link between action and structure is probably that of Pierre Bourdieu in his *Outline of a Theory of Practice* (1972).[10] The concept of *habitus*, at the center of his theory, reconciles the subjective and objective dimensions. The *habitus* is "structured structures predisposed to function as structuring structures" (1972, p. 72), or even "the system of structured, structuring dispositions" (1980, p. 52). They generate and structure practices and representations that appear ordered without being the product of blind obedience to the rules but neither are they the product of individual intentionality, that is, "collectively orchestrated without being the product of the orchestrating action of a conductor" (1972, p. 72). The *habitus* is essentially internalized experience: "The *habitus* is a spontaneity without consciousness or will, opposed as much to the mechanical necessity of

[10] But Norbert Elias (1939) is an obvious rival with his figurational sociology.

things without history in mechanistic theories as it is to the reflexive freedom of subjects 'without inertia' in rationalist theories" (1980, p. 56).

But the experience in question is not purely individual, because it reflects the participation of the agent in a collective history. The objective social structure is absorbed by the subject in the form of *doxa*, the particular values of the community to which he or she belongs, but which are perceived by the subject as natural, almost as if they were universal truths. "Every established order," Bourdieu pointed out, "tends to produce . . . the naturalization of its own arbitrariness" (1972, p. 164), emphasizing the role of power in this process. While I quite agree with Jeffrey Alexander (1995, ch. 4) that the solution adopted by Bourdieu has its limits and ambiguities, I believe, however, that the overall picture is nonetheless valid. This seems to me confirmed by the fact that European sociology in the 1970s and 1980s was particularly fruitful with regard to attempts in this direction.

Drawing on a vast literature, Anthony Giddens (1979; 1984) has brought about a notable effort at synthesis that has led him to work out his scheme of "structure" and "agency." This scheme, though perhaps it is more correct to define it as a paradigm, has the advantage of being more flexible and less bound to the individual vision of an author. He opposes the "theory of structuration" to the strong structuralism of Peter Blau and methodological individualism. Structure and agency are interdependent, in the sense that neither of the two could exist separately from the other. Thus, the "constitution of society" is not the result of a contract between individuals.

Giddens defines action as "a continuous flow of conduct" or "situated practices" (1979, pp. 55–56). Action has a recursive character; it "occurs as a durée. . . . 'Action' is not a combination of 'acts'" (1984, p. 3). It is clear how close the concept of "routine" (p. xxiii) is to the *habitus* of Bourdieu. The *durée* however transcends the individual life cycle; it has to do with the "long-term existence of institutions"; it is the dimension of "institutional time," of "social reproduction" (p. 35). It will be evident, in the second part of this book, how this formulation has been influenced by the French historical school. But what are institutions? They are "the most deeply layered practices constitutive of social systems" (1979, p. 65). Their existence is linked to social reproduction rather than to any strategic aim, such as the reduction of uncertainty (1984, p. 17). It is important to note that the concept of social reproduction does not imply the adoption of a functionalist perspective, but it is seen as a fact of human life, something that takes place automatically. Generations succeed one another, but for a certain period they overlap. In this period, each conveys to the other a map that serves not so much to face reality as to *inter-*

*pret* it.[11] As we will later see, this map is culture. Cultural transmission is thus largely an unconscious process, that is to say, not intentional.

Among the contributions of recent years, one of the most interesting seems to me that of Margaret Archer. According to Archer (2003), neither are individuals the passive objects of social conditioning, nor do they make their decisions autonomously as if they were isolated from the context in which they live. Human reflexivity is expressed through "internal conversation," a continuous process of mediation between structure and agency. This approach does not exclude the cognitive contribution of neuroscience, but it clarifies that genetic determinism as much as social determinism offers an unrealistic vision of the behavior of our (and other) animal species. In chapter 6 we return to the implications of this result when we need to put together the elements of a theory of culture and realize that the problem of culture is closely linked to that of self-awareness and reflexivity.

## The Selfish Gene, or the Evolutionary Turn of Northian Narratives

The biological analogies are not distinctive of the new institutional economics (Rutherford 1994, pp. 110ff.). Alchian's idea, which has already been mentioned, whereby competition selects the best firms by producing efficient results, undoubtedly sets a precedent. The theory of Nelson and Winter (1982) is another perhaps more sophisticated example of this type. However, there is a substantial difference between utilizing biology metaphorically and utilizing biology as an explanatory tool, a path followed all the way by a few social scientists after Herbert Spencer.[12] North completed this step in the 1990s, developing an increasingly systematic attempt to weld his ideas on institutional change onto the biological

---

[11] I maintain that one of the problems in North's theory (2005) is not to have grasped this basic logical difference. The interpretation of reality lies behind any strategy of the actors. Taking it for granted that everyone interprets it the same way, instead he sees institutions as cognitive constructs aimed at action that differ only in their degree of efficiency.

[12] Rosenberg (1994, p. 403). According to Mokyr, there is also a third way: a more wide-ranging evolutionary theory that includes nonbiological phenomena. Its rules are to be taken by analogy from biology, somewhat similar to how those of standard economics have been taken from classical physics (2000, p. 58; 2005, p. 203). But is it really something more than a metaphor? And, above all, is it useful? Its applications are unconvincing. Why, for example, should profitability be the equivalent of fitness? And why should the QWERTY keyboard suggest "the role of accident and chance in forming our environment"? (1991, pp. 129, 134). Rather, it appears to me that both the origin and the survival of this device can be explained in deterministic terms, respectively, with convenience and force of habit, two very commonsense concepts.

theory of evolution. He pointed out how "reputation, trust, and other aspects of human behavior . . . on the surface appear to be altruistic and not consistent with individual wealth-maximization." Then the concept of maximization needed to be extended by including adaptation fitness, because these behavioral aspects "turn out to be superior survival traits under certain circumstances" (1990, p. 21).

The controversial book of the British biologist Richard Dawkins, *The Selfish Gene*, proved to be an endorsement. According to Dawkins, any behavioral tendency is dictated by our genes' need to reproduce themselves: "we are survival machines," he wrote, "robot vehicles blindly programmed to preserve the selfish molecules known as genes" (1976, p. x). The underlying assumption is that natural selection does not operate at the level of organisms and species, involving phenotypes, but instead maximizes the replication of the genes. The Oxford theologian Keith Ward, a noted supporter of Darwin, has stressed that Dawkins's ultimate aim was to prove the nonexistence of God, a rather unusual aim for a scientific work, or at least for a popularizing work of science.[13]

Why choose a work of this sort to form a marriage between economics and biology? The reason is quite clear. North is not so much concerned with arguing for wealth maximization, as for human nature. He is ready to forgo the former but not the latter. He wants to show that individuals are not altruistic; even if they appear to be, this is only a mask behind which a stronger form of self-interest is hiding. The same concern to defend self-interest had led him to misunderstand, rather unsubtly, Polanyi's interpretation of the *kula,* as we have seen. Because in this chapter I am not dealing with moral philosophy, it is not my intention to enter into how well founded or not the beliefs of Dawkins and North are. But it is important to highlight these ideological premises that impinge on different trends in cliometrics.

The other progenitor of the Northian evolutionary approach is the sociobiology founded by Edward Wilson (1975). This is how Marshall Sahlins described this "new synthesis" in his *The Use and Abuse of Biology*:

> In place of a social constitution of meanings, it offers a biological determination of human interactions with a source primarily in the general evolutionary propensity of individual genotypes to maximize their reproductive success. It is a new variety of sociological utilitarianism, but transposed now to a biological calculus of the utilities realized in social relations. (1976b, p. x)

Sociobiology was an immediate success among economists. One only needs to see how soon Gary Becker (1976a) utilized it to base his theory

---

[13] Ward (1996). Detailed criticism of *The Selfish Gene* is given on pp. 136ff.

of self-interested altruism on kin selection (see Trivers 1971). Unfortunately, sociobiology became "so interested in the fact that in helping others one helps himself," it forgot "that in so doing one also benefits genetic competitors as much as oneself" (Sahlins 1976b, p. 87). In spite of this inner contradiction, some still claim that reciprocal altruism extended to society once it proved successful among genetically related individuals.

Today the foremost discipline for this type of argument is the self-proclaimed "new science" of evolutionary psychology, which has its guru in Steven Pinker (1997; 2002) and its best-known popularizer in the journalist Robert Wright (1994). Because it chooses the human mind as the unit of analysis, it is even more suited to combining with the methodological individualism of the new institutional economics.

According to North, the most important contribution of evolutionary psychology is "explicating the . . . inference structure of the mind that appears to account for the predisposition of the mind to entertain and construct 'non-rational' beliefs such as supernatural explanations and religions that underlie so much of the decision framework of individuals, groups, and organizations in societies" (2005, pp. 29–30). Indeed, North places "myths, superstitions, and religions" on the same plane. They are instrumental in creating "ideological conformity" (p. 42). His guide in this ground is Pascal Boyer (2001) according to whom "religious concepts are parasitic upon moral intuitions"; it goes without saying that such intuitions, because humans are a species of cooperators, are inscribed in their genes (North 2005, p. 41).

Biological anthropology and developmental psychology contradict this vision of the human mind. According to the neurobiologist Kathleen Gibson (2005), who has made a long study of brain maturation and the cognitive development of human and nonhuman primates, the mind is not characterized by function-specific mechanisms with the function of solving particular adaptive problems. Instead, it works by means of very general mechanisms that make the brain a flexible tool suited to solving a wide range of problems and to responding to the new challenges that are constantly being set by the changing environment. Human evolution has not taken place in a static environment, and our species and those of the other primates would certainly not have gotten very far with a model of mind like the one described by the evolutionary psychologists. This extraordinary brain plasticity, which allows for open programs of behavior, explains the importance of the activity of mental construction that leads to culture. Culture is made possible by our genetic base, but it develops largely independently from it. There is no one-to-one correspondence between the genes and behavioral traits. This is confirmed by the fact that most genes are pleiotropic, which means they have different phenotypic effects. Recent research in linguistics, which proves the absence of linguistic universals (including the distinction between nouns and verbs), provides a picture that is perfectly compatible with this, confirming that there are no innate mental structures. But not even the human sensory and perceptual experience seems to have very much that is universal about it, being modeled more as a consequence of interaction with the environment (Foley 2005; Danziger 2005). Anyway, the tendency to atomize organisms into "traits," and to explain these traits (including suboptimalities) as structures designed by natural selection for their functions, was already shown to be Panglossian in a much-cited article by Gould and Lewontin (1979).

In her biting criticism of what she calls "neo-liberal genetics," the cultural anthropologist Susan McKinnon (2005) has shown how evolutionary psychology is based on such weak evidence that it almost smacks of science fiction. The function of this discipline, she says, is actually to produce "moral tales" about the "naturalness of neo-liberal economic values of self-interest, competition, rational choice, and the power of the market to create social relations; about the survival of the fittest and the determinant force of genes" (p. 144). Evolution is represented as if it was the product of a design aimed at the maximization of genetic self-interest. In so doing, the genes are unduly attributed the agency that human beings have been deprived of, reduced as they are to acting as containers for genes. It is clear that this has nothing to do with Darwin: it is an atheistic teleology as baseless as the intelligent design of certain religious fundamentalists (pp. 14–16).

Yet, for North the sense of appealing to evolutionism and the neurosciences is generally more subtle. He concedes that not all behavior can be interpreted as an unconditional reflex of genetic inheritance, and he does not even borrow Dawkins's theory of the "memes" (the equivalents of the genes that supposedly explain the intergenerational transfer of cultural attributes). But North ascribes everything that does not fall into the dominion of genetics to individual rationality, though bounded: accordingly, "institutions must be explained in terms of the *intentionality* of humans" (North 2005, p. 42, emphasis added). At the same time we are "interchangeable cogs in a larger machine" (p. 24). The result is a two-headed and discontinuous theory. The plane of the unconscious, of collective phenomena, of routine, has no place, and neither could it have any. North wishes to set up a naturalistic basis for institutional failure, namely to demonstrate that some cultures are worse than others, quite apart from the cognitive errors that affect organizations.

The key to understanding institutional failure lies in the combination of nonrational and rational beliefs that guide human behavior (p. 42). The former create "ideological conformity," which is "a major force in reducing the costs of maintaining order," but unfortunately they also prevent institutional change, which is indispensable in a world of uncertainty (or "non-ergodic world"), because "no one can know the right path to survival." Rationality, competition, and institutional diversity are closely linked; path dependence does the rest. On a historical plane, there follows an exaltation of the Protestant Reformation as a product of the freedom of thought and an unconditional condemnation of "Muslim conformity" responsible for the "ever widening gap between the Muslim and Western world" and for "religious fanaticism" (pp. 43–44). However, with the triumph of the "impersonal exchange which underlies modern economic growth," the importance of institutional diversity suddenly seems to come to nothing. What has happened to evolution? Could it have inexplicably stopped?

McKinnon points out that "culturally specific ideas, once naturalized into deep genetic and evolutionary history, have the effect of privileging and validating certain cultural ideas and social arrangements over others" (2005, p. 12). This is applied to evolutionary psychology but describes the strategy of *Understanding the Process of Economic Change* equally well.

## The Road to Tautology

It has been pointed out that with the new institutionalism, economics has entered the second phase of aggression toward the other social sciences that started in the 1970s and is defined by its own creators as "economic imperialism."[14] It is an offensive aimed at demonstrating that economics can also explain noneconomic phenomena better than the social sciences that focus on doing just that.

As Edward Lazear has argued in a text that transudes aggression even in its style,

> Economists generally believe in the market test. Economic imperialism can be judged to be successful only if it passes this test, which means that the analyses of the imperialists must influence others. The effort to extend the field measures its success by inducing others to adopt the economic approach to explore issues that are not part of classical economics. One possibility is that scholars outside of economics use economic analyses to understand social issues. Political scientists, lawyers, and sociologists come to use the methods of economics to answer the questions that are of interest

[14] Stigler (1984). Earlier uses of the term, in the critical sense, appear in Thurow (1977; 1983) and Harcourt (1982). There is now an abundant literature on economic imperialism: see Fine and Milonakis (2009); Milberg (2009). On the ideological premises of the Chicago school, see Freedman (2005).

in their fields. Another possibility is that economists expand the boundaries of economics and simply replace outsiders as analysts of "noneconomic" issues, forcing noneconomists out of business, as it were, or at least providing them with competition on an issue in which they formerly possessed a monopoly. . . . both routes have been followed with success. (2000, p. 104)

Although in its strong form it is a relatively recent turning point in economic thought, its roots lie in the famous formal concept of economics as formulated in 1932 by Lionel Robbins. According to the exponents of this current, scarce means and alternative ends are to be found in practically all spheres of human action, and this makes neoclassical economics a sort of passe-partout.

In its initial phase, exemplified in the work of Becker and the Chicago school, economic imperialism "was based upon reducing the noneconomic to the economic, treating the former as if it were equivalent to a perfect market even in its absence" (Fine and Milonakis 2003, p. 547). On the other hand, in its more recent version, it emphasizes the role of market imperfections, especially informational imperfections: "These are claimed, in typical reductionist fashion, to explain economic *and* social outcomes, the latter as the potentially collective but individually rational response to market imperfections." Conformity to social institutions and norms is reduced to economic rationality in conditions of uncertainty: "In short, the new version of economics imperialism extends its explanatory power by inserting the rational individual into a world of statistical uncertainty and, equally, extends its appeal by adopting and adapting the language and concepts of colonized subject matters" (p. 547).

We will see in the next chapter how the latter point is a central aspect of the strategy adopted, a sort of aesthetic disguise whose aim is to facilitate the penetration of the paradigm. Here, however, I would like to highlight elements of continuity between the two phases. I would also like to caution historians and social scientists against the attraction held out by the economists' bridge building. Rather than bridges, they are often baits.

The most obvious point of contact between Becker and North is the hypothesis of "implicit markets." As Becker says, the rational choice approach assumes that "the behavior of different individuals is coordinated by explicit and implicit markets" (1991, p. ix). It is precisely this concept that enables rational choice theorists to see markets and transactions where there are none, as, for example, within the family. The assumption of the new institutional economics that there are also transaction costs in nonmarket economies and organizations has a similar implication.

However, resorting to invisible transactions and shadow costs and prices does not take one very far. It is as if a physicist explained the opening of a door in the dead of night with the presence of a ghost. Because the ghost is invisible, nobody will be able to refute this theory. But the physicist would immediately be expelled from the profession. Karl Popper would say that the ghost theory is not falsifiable. Yet how nonfalsifiable theories manage to gain an audience in economics is a fascinating problem that deserves to be studied in its own right. Here I limit myself to pointing out that it is the very conception of economics as a formal science that does not admit falsification. After all, even mathematicians can imagine inexistent entities with an internal consistency. But none of them would dream of asserting that they might be useful for historical explanation. Economists do just that. And I cannot see how Lazear can possibly assert the following: "The power of economics lies in its rigor. Economics is scientific; it follows the scientific method of stating a formal refutable theory, testing the theory, and revising the theory based on the evidence. Economics succeeds where other social sciences fail because economists are willing to abstract" (2000, p. 102).

The superiority of economics is supposed to lie in the fact that, unlike the other social sciences, it can formulate predictions in new situations because it uses the hypothesis of maximization; "the maximum of a function is a well-understood concept; other rules are not, especially when they vary from situation to situation" (p. 100). But this is nonsense: it is as if an astronomer argued that the Earth is triangular and based a defense of this bizarre idea on the fact that a triangular model of the Earth makes it possible to apply the Pythagorean theorem.

The distinguished anthropologist Clifford Geertz (1978) was ready to compromise with economists by drawing on the economics of information. He considered a large urban market in Morocco in an area that had been linked to trade in the Mediterranean for centuries, namely the bazaar of Sefrou. He then interpreted bargaining as a mechanism in which both parties seek to maximize their respective objectives (the one to sell as dear as possible, and the other to buy at the lowest possible price), with clientelization as a method for reducing uncertainty.

While the latter assumption is reasonable but trivial—it is the Sunnah itself that ordains that trade should be free from uncertainty, the *gharar* (Saleh 1986)—his interpretation of bargaining does not grasp one essential aspect, which anyone entering the market of a country whose culture is Islamic cannot help noticing. The vendor feels offended if the buyer accepts the first offer and does not negotiate in order to lower the price. This attitude is viewed as a refusal to enter into relations, or set up a relationship of personal trust.

The last time I visited the Spice Bazaar (Mısır Çarşısı) of Istanbul, in 2007, I remember sitting and bargaining for half an hour in front of a seller of nuts. Could there possibly be anything rational (in the sense of economic theory) or maximizing in this? Should I deduce that the apple tea that I was offered in that situation was a technique for creating a loyal customer? The vendor knew he would not see me again or, more optimistically, that if he did it would not be for some years, assuming I was able to locate his shop in the gallery of nut sellers. In short, reduction of uncertainty and maximizing behavior appear to be rather a contradiction in terms.

Even with the best of intentions, attempts at dialogue with economics like Geertz's end up by laying themselves open to instrumentalization. Richard Posner, one of the self-styled Chicago imperialists, did not hesitate to gain legitimacy from such a dialogue in order to proceed to a personal reformulation of the principles of economic anthropology. It is the response of rational choice theory to the "challenge of Karl Polanyi" that North was writing about.

According to Posner, the debate between formalists and substantivists was based on a "misconception of the nature of economics" (1980b, p. 608). Both shared "an excessively narrow view of what is economic" (1980a, p. 2). Posner argued that "primitive" peoples are unrefined and have a scarcity of resources because they have a limited (unscientific) knowledge of nature and rudimentary communication technologies. But the hypotheses of scarcity and rudimentary knowledge had both already been fully refuted by the field research of ethnologists in the 1960s and 1970s (see chapter 4).

These types of limitations of "primitive" societies are carried over into just as many other deficiencies. The crudeness leads to a lack of government; the scarcity of technical knowledge leads to a limited variety of consumer goods (another circumstance that the fieldwork of specialists had disproved). Both elements combined give rise to the lack of contract enforcement, linguistic differences, and a lack of money, which in their turn are conveyed into high transportation and transaction costs. The result is the isolation of communities, with few intertribal trade relations. Again, the crudeness, whether technological or institutional, is the reason for the impossibility of stocking goods, in the first place food (which creates perennial uncertainty with regard to future food supply), and for the lack of private gain for innovations (no private property or privacy).

Posner builds up his theory on the basis of these dubious premises. The scarcity of goods and the lack of supplies explain the mechanisms of reciprocity, such as the gift-exchange: it is a form of insurance, produced by a strategic calculation. However, because there is no government, and thus no contract enforcement, reciprocity between strangers might not be respected. Here lies the explanation for the importance that family and kinship take on in these societies.[15]

But is there any sense in assuming there is a logical precedence of exchange over kinship, the latter developing to make up for a defect in the exchange, namely the possibility of free riding and moral hazard? (Posner 1980a, p. 16). Might not reciprocity-among-strangers, such as Posner assumes there is in the state of nature, be a contradiction in terms? Is the gift perhaps a "contract" that needs to be enforced, as he writes? Posner confuses reciprocity (a mechanism for the circulation of wealth *arising out of* personal bonds, which reflects relations of power and prestige) with bartering (which is a market without money, an abstraction imagined by the Enlightenment thinkers that has never existed).

Thus, Posner replaces formal institutions with informal ones such as "kinship insurance," in a subtle game of interlocking puzzles. It is rather like when schoolboys, tackling an arithmetical problem and finding a result that does not coincide with the solutions in the textbook, try to "work out the sums" by altering the original conditions as a function of the desired result. It is a totally artificial procedure. The contradiction lies precisely here: conclusions about the inadequacy of "primitive" institutions are drawn by comparison with twentieth-century America, which is used as a universal yardstick. In this sense, the procedure is very similar to that of the new institutional economics.

But Posner transcends North. If North's objective is to explain institutions in economistic terms, Posner is engaged in Gary Becker's mission to extend the "nature of economics" to the point of making it comprise everything and its opposite. Here is how status is explained: it makes up for the lack of insurance-type contractual relations. The sense of honor is explained as taking the place of law enforcement by sanctioning the wrongs suffered with reprisal. In addition, the assignment of social roles according to age and sex is the most rational way to economize information: such parameters are supposedly "proxies" for skills. This reasoning inevitably leads to a short circuit: once carried to its extreme, it leads Posner to assert that even superstition is rational.[16]

[15] A similar model to Posner's has been more recently developed by Janet Landa: "In a society that lacks institutions for protecting life, property, and contracts, an institution like the Kula Ring may be interpreted as a clublike arrangement for economizing on costs of transacting across tribal boundaries" (1994, p. 165). See Gudeman's critique (2008, pp. 117ff.).

[16] Posner says that the belief in and practice of magic, sorcery, and witchcraft promote the economic well-being of society and constitute a rational response to the demand for insurance (1980a, p. 23).

# Chapter 3

## THE FANCIFUL WORLD OF CLIO

NORTH'S APPROACH HAS been influential. One might say that it has survived in Darwinian fashion, because nowadays hardly anybody still practices Fogel's type of economic history.[1] The result is that cliometrics has evolved into a literary genre having little to do with numbers in the sense of econometric testing, though a lot to do with the deductive stance of the new institutional economics and of rational choice theory. At times these two approaches, which are not completely compatible, coexist even in the same author, giving rise to a sort of analytic schizophrenia. While the Northian approach admits the existence of other allocation systems besides the market (with this existence being explained in terms of neoclassical economics or ad hoc hypotheses, when the whole fabric comes apart from the point of view of the logic), the rational choice approach does not. Instead, it attempts to prove that the market is omnipresent and extends to every sphere of social action and has done so ever since the earliest times.

The current practitioners of cliometrics are eclectic in many senses. They draw on evolutionary economics, they use (and misuse) cultural explanations, and they eagerly cite biologists and cognitive scientists. They consider themselves all-around social scientists. This strategy of dissimulation often leaves scholars in other fields disorientated, especially those who are not familiar with the "imperial" turn of economics in recent decades and the new branches of law and economics, political economics, economics of the family, economics of religion, and the like. And at times it even baffles the economic historians themselves. In his historiographical account, the Dutch cliometrician J. W. Drukker praised the new economic history for its increased range of interests, maintaining that it had finally freed itself from the confines of neoclassical economics to reincorporate the cultural and institutional factors that it had initially ejected (Drukker 2003, p. 16). He received a gentle scolding from Joel Mokyr (2003), who pointed out to him that recent developments were perfectly in line with neoclassical economics. Sadly, Mokyr is right.

---

[1] Among recent exceptions, see Goldin and Katz (2008), Rosenbloom (2008), and the economic history papers in Diamond and Robinson (2010).

In this chapter we analyze the most significant trends of this "newer" economic history. From the standpoint of methodology, as has been pointed out (Fine and Milonakis 2003, p. 552), it shows the confusion between history and path dependence or presence of "multiple equilibria" in a predetermined deductive schema. It is not actually difficult to recognize that underlying these trends is an ideological slant, whether conscious or unconscious, aimed at exalting values such as individualism and materialism, which are typical of certain segments of contemporary Western society, and at projecting them unduly onto the past. Which leads to paradoxical narratives and to patently obvious anachronisms.

## The West Is Best

In the 1990s, the end of the Cold War caused a great deal of excitement among American intellectuals. Conservative thinkers proclaimed that the values of Western-style democracy and the free market would prevail once and for all: it was the "end of history" that Francis Fukuyama (1992) had prophesied. Samuel Huntington (1996), a little more to the left, upheld the less optimistic version of the clash of civilizations. Edward Said (2001), a great deal further to the left, condemned this stereotyped vision of Islam as a monolithic entity necessarily in conflict with the Western world in his famous paraphrase "the clash of ignorance."

Huntington's ideas, on one hand, had the merit of reviving the cultural explanation in social sciences but, on the other, were translated into an assumption that some cultures were more favorable, or less favorable, to human progress, and hence into policy recommendations for promoting cultural change (Harrison and Huntington 2000). These issues were very soon adopted by the new discipline of political economics, a blend of economics and political science.[2] The final outcome was not very different from Fukuyama's idea. Democracy and the universal development of markets were still the ultimate goal. Their advent, however, would not be automatic but would be an objective to pursue through what came to be defined by its critics as the "evangelical mission of westernization" (Shweder 2000).

In the years of the George W. Bush administration, neoconservative narratives multiplied, even in economic history. Whereas the ideological dimension was explicit in public discourse, in academic products it was thinly disguised to present the desired outcome as the consequence of a

---

[2] Persson and Tabellini (2000); Acemoglu and Robinson (2006); Guiso et al. (2006); Tabellini (2008); it is interesting to note the crescendo in the cultural focus. Robert Nelson (2001, ch. 9) provides an amusing account of new institutional attempts to promote "efficient religions."

series of necessary conditions. Once again, the tools of persuasion were in the hard sciences or in mathematics.

Let us take Avner Greif's (2006) influential book on institutions and trade in the medieval Mediterranean, which draws on a series of published articles that started to appear in 1989. In the preface, Greif claims to have produced a sophisticated example of social science history. There is no doubt that it is a very sophisticated work, though serious doubts can be raised as to whether it is actually history.

The book contrasts Genoese traders to Maghribi traders in the eleventh and twelfth centuries. The Maghribis were a Jewish community that migrated from Iraq to Tunisia and adopted the values of the Muslim society. According to Greif, the Genoese had individualistic cultural beliefs, whereas the Maghribis had collectivist habits. The former adopted competitive strategies and allocated resources, including labor, through impersonal channels, whereas the latter's behavior was cooperative and tended to share information and resort to kinship and social ties.

But it soon becomes clear that what Greif is actually talking about is the present, and what gives these essays a unitary argumentative force is the revival of the cultural conflict after September 11, 2001. At a certain point we are explicitly told that the Genoese represent "the developed West" of our day, whereas the Maghribis "the Muslim world" or, more generally, "contemporary underdeveloped countries" (Greif 2006, p. 301; see also p. 273). After having found that both the systems have pros and cons, the conclusive syllogism states that "formal enforcement institutions that support anonymous exchange facilitate economic development. Individualistic cultural beliefs foster the development of such institutions, enabling society to capture these efficiency gains. An individualistic society also entails less social pressure to conform to social norms of behavior, thus fostering initiative and innovation" (p. 301).

Thus, the message is that individualism has brought economic achievement to the West, while collectivism condemns the Muslim world to a subordinate position, and the failure of the Muslims in "building effective, welfare-enhancing states" further reflects this original sin (pp. 247–55).

One's immediate reaction is to remind Greif that there are countries under the umbrella of Islam such as Mauritania with a per capita GDP of two thousand dollars, as well others with a GDP ten or twenty times larger than that. And one would not define the United Arab Emirates as an underdeveloped economy.

Reasoning in terms of "cultural beliefs" instead of adopting an organic concept of culture leads to vague assertions, such as the one we find a few pages further on that cannot be documented: "Genoa was well known among the Italian city-states for its individualism" (p. 301). Now, it is reasonable to hold that the Genoese were relatively more individualistic than the Muslims, but one cannot see why they should have been more so than the Tuscans or the Lombards. Sombart and Weber spent much of their lives, and several thousand pages, showing how the mercantile individualism of that period was rather weak compared with the individualism typical of modern capitalism. I believe the idea of presenting the Genoese as the archetypal *homines oeconomici* would have left them somewhat bewildered. Besides, history offers excellent examples of societies that are certainly not individualistic but that have nonetheless experienced economic development. The case of the economic development of postwar Japan is illuminating. The events in Germany at the end of the nineteenth century, and in the China of today, are just as illuminating, if not even more so.

These are weaknesses that Greif's work shares with the traditional "Whig" history à la David Landes (1998). The difference lies in the persuasive techniques they use. In the case of Greif, game theory allegedly demonstrates the superiority, from a mathematical point of view, of certain social arrangements over others. It should be pointed out that this type of mathematics is purely deductive, a long way from any form of statistical quantification. It leads to the assertion of truths whose principles are valid by virtue of the intrinsic properties of the model and hence in all the actual cases that the model is supposed to represent. For instance, the deduction that individualistic social arrangements are better suited to resolve what he calls the problem of "cheating" (to which the explanation for the origin of the social contract is almost exclusively attributed) depends on the initial assumption that an agent will not cheat if, and only if, he is offered a wage equal to, or above, a certain level $W^*$ (Greif 2006, pp. 275–76)—hence, in those cases where the honesty motivation is an economic incentive.

This is clearly an arbitrary assumption, and thus far Greif is still in the realm of logical possibility (R. Boyer 2009, p. 679). When the moment comes to establish a link between the model and actual reality, or to show how a specific case might reflect the hypothetical logic of the model, textual evidence then becomes essential. The idea that a single example or a few examples isolated through painstaking research could confirm a certain theory of the past is more suggestive of the attitude of the collector than the historian. But we can overlook methodological questions and come to the substance. As proof of the competitive individualism that, in his view, makes the Genoese of the Middle Ages resemble the Americans of today, Greif puts forward the notion that an "economic motivation" lay behind the establishment of the commune itself (2006, p. 222). This supposedly emerges from the "historical records," regarding which he states: "I used them extensively" (p. 221). This approach was praised by many of his fellow cliometricians who were quick to point out in endorsements and reviews that historians could not ignore this contribution because of its masterly use of the sources.

In support of his argument on the economic motivation of the commune, Greif provides a quotation from the *Codice diplomatico della Repubblica di Genova* (the collection of public records of the state): "A consul had to swear 'not to diminish the honor of [the] city, nor [its] profit[s]'" (Greif 2006, p. 222). According to him, this expression is to be found in document 20 of volume 1. My curiosity aroused, I decided to search out the passage that he had quoted. I discovered, somewhat to my dismay, that not only does it not exist but document 20 of volume 1 has nothing to do with the consuls swearing the oath but is a deed of donation to the Cathedral of San Lorenzo in 1107.

There and then I thought there might have been a mistake in transcribing the number of the volume, and so I looked in the other two volumes of the collection, but I could find no trace of the passage he had quoted. Document 20 of volume 2 is an act for the emancipation of the serfs who belonged to traitors of the commune, while in volume 3 it is a letter from the Byzantine emperor Isaac Angelus regarding the granting of privileges to the Genoese. On checking Greif's bibliography and the list of abbreviations, I soon realized that the *Codice* itself had been listed incorrectly. The years of publication refer to the complete collection (in three volumes), while the period referred to in the title (from 1164 to 1190) corresponds only to volume 2, a mistake that anybody actually consulting these texts would be unlikely to make.[3]

The consuls' swearing of the oath (1143) is to be found in document 128 of volume 1, where one reads: "Nos non minuemus honorem nostre civitatis, neque proficuum nec honorem nostre matris Ecclesie nobis scientibus" (*Codice*, vol. 1, p. 154). This translates into: "We will not intentionally lessen the honor of our city, nor the revenues and the honor of our mother church." The "profits" (which in any case would be more correctly translated as "revenues") that Greif mentions are those relating to the church, not to the city![4] *This* makes sense, and indeed the whole document emanates a sense of great subjection to the authority of the clergy and is concerned with safeguarding its temporal interests.

Yet this is not the only peculiarity to be found in Greif's book. A little further on he continues: "That economic considerations motivated establishing and joining the commune is reflected in the fact that the ultimate

---

[3] Volume 1, published in 1936, covers the period 958 to 1163; Volume 2, published in 1938, covers from 1164 to 1190; Volume 3, published in 1942, covers from 1191 to 1202 (in the frontispiece of the latter there is a printing error).

[4] Cf. the comment of S. A. Epstein (1996, p. 34).

punishment for refusing to participate in its activities was exclusion from its overseas trade" (2006, p. 223).

According to Greif, this concept can be deduced from document 285 of volume 1. Because there were no quotations or indication as to page, I went through the document searching for a passage to back up this statement. The only point where mention is made of the exclusion from maritime trade is on p. 352. Regrettably, however, neither the phrase nor the document as a whole have anything to do with the point Greif is making. Instead, it deals with the statutes ("brief") of the Compagna. This was an oligarchic association of Genoese citizens that gradually took over the government of the city after a transitional phase during which the church acted as guarantor for institutional stability (Imperiale 1936, p. xxxviii). At this point everything becomes clear.

In connection with this document, Van Doosselaere has pointed out: "The administering of an oath was the typical feudal way to assert reciprocal social obligations. By swearing to defend the commercial interests of the city, the Genoese adapted that traditional institution. The 1157 document does not refer to a protectionist policy, but is the military commitment of a feudal social organization to defend its space" (2009, p. 29).

This leads to a fundamental aspect, which this excellent study of the social dynamics in medieval Genoa has not failed to highlight: "It is important to note that the Commune association was of 'all arms-bearing men' . . .—clearly not a commercial or occupational but a military criterion—who swore allegiance to the Compagna and its emerging institutions. It is a modern interpretation to believe in the commercial foundation of the Commune" (p. 35).

But there is another valid reason to quash the idea that the Genoese commune was a sort of sanctuary set up to glorify capitalist gain. For the Genoese of the time, sailing the seas was a practical necessity because there was no cultivable hinterland from which to draw a subsistence and in particular where cereals, the basis of the Mediterranean diet, could be grown (Cattini 2005; Sauner-Leroy 2001, p. 492). For the majority of Genoese, this activity was a way of supplementing their income. Hence, if many of them were involved in Mediterranean trade in one way or another, only for a minority was trade the main occupation (Van Doosselaere 2009, p. 79).

The statutes of 1157 did not envisage economic disincentives for anyone who did not want to form part of the commune. Instead, after many preambles of a religious nature—first an oath was sworn to honor "God and the mother church of Genoa, and the other churches of the city of Genoa and the archbishopric" with one's deeds (*Codice*, vol. 1, p. 351)— and a ban on aiding rival cities in the event of war, they prohibited the members of the Compagna from transporting money on behalf of those who had refused the invitation (or rather the order) of the consuls to join. Anything to the contrary, namely that they would have benefited them with their own means, would have been absurd. The association was clearly an elitist one and closed to outsiders: that is, "those in the compagna were only a subset of the larger pool of adult Genoese men, and only those of a certain local importance found themselves invited to join." (S. A. Epstein 1996, p. 35). Moreover, what is being disciplined is the insubordination of these merchants to the political authority of the consuls. Interestingly, "the consuls . . . had jurisdiction over trade, though commerce is not a major issue in the brief" (p. 37). It is, in short, a typical question of honor in keeping with the priority of politics over economics, and it has been completely distorted in Greif's interpretation. I leave the reader to draw his own conclusions from the original text.[5]

Things are no better when one leaves the Latin sources for those in basic Italian. A mysterious word—*podestàs*—appears frequently in chapter 8, as well as in the paper it is based on (Greif 1998, pp. 54ff.). Italian does not have any words that end in a consonant, and the presence of any letter after an accentuated vowel has no grammatical sense. But on further reading it emerges that *podestàs*, according to Greif, is the plural of *podestà*, which means the chief magistrate, usually a foreigner, chosen by the emperor or by the citizens to rule the Italian city-states. It is a little like stating that the plural of the German word *Haus* (house) is *Hauses* and not *Häuser*, or that the plural of French *cheval* (horse) is *chevals* and not *chevaux*. The problem is not so much that an unintentional comical effect ruins the thoughtful solemnity of statements like: "The idea of ruling cities through *podestàs* also reflects institutional learning" (Greif 2006, p. 238). Rather, one wonders how good a knowledge can be had of the sources if one lacks an understanding of such an elementary rule as the plural in the language of the place being studied, to the point of not thinking that it might be different from English.

## New Social Darwinism

Gregory Clark's book, *A Farewell to Alms* (2007), is a good example of another path being followed by the newer economic history. Clark emphasizes cultural beliefs as the driving force of the industrial revolution, and the root of the Great Divergence between the West and the Rest that

[5] "Quod si aliquis bis vel ter ad faciendum sacramentum Compagne specialiter et nominatim publice a consulibus vocatus fuerit et non fecerit illud in eorum ordinatione infra .XL. dies postquam appellatus fuerit, suam pecuniam, me sciente, per mare ad mercatum nullomodo portabo" (*Codice*, vol. 1, p. 352).

subsequently continued to widen. The shocking element is his claim that underlying this process is the Darwinian evolutionary mechanism. The Malthusian trap of preindustrial demography marks the watershed for Clark's reconstruction. Only those who inclined toward economic success were able to survive it. The culture of success thus passed from one generation to the next and apparently prevailed in the continual process of natural selection. Thus, the westerners of today are "for the most part the descendants of the strivers of the pre-industrial world, those driven to achieve greater economic success than their peers" (p. 16).

For his basic argument, Clark draws on an article of the economists Galor and Moav (2002)—fifty-eight pages of mathematics arguing that economic growth is a form of adaptation. But a more useful thing would have been a thorough discussion of the biological literature on which this argument is based. Claims that trespass onto the territory of other disciplines, especially the natural sciences, require an explicit mention of the results achieved in those fields.

All we find in Galor and Moav is an indirect reference to the concept of gene-culture coevolution expounded in works such as those of Boyd and Richerson (1985; 2005). Biologists and environmental scientists have noted that the capacity to digest lactose, which normally disappears in adult animals, is widespread in certain human groups originating in northern and central Europe and in western Asia, while it is found only in limited regions of Africa and not anywhere else. It seems to be closely associated with the fact that dairying was practiced in those areas, causing the organism to preserve the enzyme used to digest the sugar in milk (2005, pp. 191–92). From this, Galor and Moav conclude: "Evidence suggests that evolutionary processes in the composition of genetic traits may be rather rapid and even the time period between the Neolithic Revolution and the Industrial Revolution that lasted nearly 10,000 years is sufficient for significant evolutionary changes" (2002, p. 1136).

But which genetic traits are these? Clark maintains that the successful characteristics have something to do with English society, and specifically with WASP values—"the extraordinary stability of England back to at least 1200, the slow growth of English population between 1300 and 1760, and the extraordinary fecundity of the rich and economically successful. The embedding of bourgeois values into the culture, and perhaps even the genetics, was for these reasons the most advanced in England" (2007, p. 11).

The idea of genetically passing on these values has no scientific basis whatever. "Thrift, prudence, negotiation, and hard work" (p. 166) are characteristics that plainly differ from the capacity to digest lactose. First of all they are not fixed in the DNA (there being no such thing as a gene of thrift!), and moreover the time involved in bringing about any change in man's biological makeup is considerably longer than the duration of any civilization.

Bearing in mind that there is little sense in speaking of English society and culture before the Battle of Hastings, this leaves us with a period of a few centuries, or a time span that is nothing in comparison with evolutionary time. But even assuming that the successful characteristics are found in the universal psychology of human beings (or at least of certain privileged examples of the species), as Galor and Moav apparently do more politically correctly though equally wrongly, the neo-Darwinian argument leads to a contradiction.

To start with, overcoming the Malthusian trap did not take place gradually, nor did it filter out one or several cohorts of the elect, contrary to the assumption that these authors seem to make. Preindustrial population calamities such as the Black Death and the recurring shocks caused by the famines cannot be interpreted as events capable of selecting people with psychological characteristics that aided their survival. We know that English society as a whole escaped the Malthusian trap in the eighteenth century as successful attitudes and practices gradually reached a critical mass and became sufficiently widespread to condition collective behavior.

It cannot be substantiated that only specific individuals or families in each society are the depositaries of the "right values," otherwise within a few generations we would similarly find them spreading throughout at least the Euro-Asiatic societies on the principle of the natural selection cited by these authors. Thus, it is not explained how some of these societies did not experience the demographic transition until the twentieth century (though their history was even more dramatically affected by plagues, famines, and other natural calamities). Were there perhaps no entrepreneurial individuals on the shores of the Mediterranean or on the shores of the Yellow River who could have passed on their genes? Or are we perhaps to believe that for some strange reason they were less successful at reproducing themselves?

But the evolutionary argument does not hold true even if one starts from the assumption that successful psychological attitudes have something to do with the whole culture shared by a particular society. If one assumes there is a mechanism of transmission based on the enduring survival of human groups that possess qualities that are favorable to adaptation, how can the survival of the human race in the underdeveloped world be explained? Being rich is clearly not such a fundamental attribute from the point of view of Mother Nature after all.

Curiously, Clark seems to think that natural selection operates at the level of chosen individuals as well as within chosen societies—which is intrinsically contradictory, if only from a logical point of view. Clark's claim is so outlandish that it has been widely discussed in newspapers, from the *New York Times* to the *Sacramento Bee*. Some have written that *A Farewell to Alms* is the economic history book that has attracted most attention in and beyond academia since *Time on the Cross*.[6] It is not the type of notoriety to be proud of. Even the circle of cliometricians has dissociated itself from this book.[7] Deirdre McCloskey—who, by the way, has become increasingly skeptical about the profession itself—dubbed it a form of "eugenic materialism" (2010, chs. 30–32). However, what most cliometricians do not seem to realize is that Clark's is an exaggerated and extreme version of their own way of practicing economic history. The difference between Clark and North, or between Clark and Greif, is not so much substantial as of façade. On one side we have a biocultural interpretation and on the other a bio-institutional one. The emphasis is on different historical periods—the Middle Ages, the Glorious Revolution, or the industrial revolution—all cases that reveal a destiny that has already been written. Clark's more instinctive and direct narrative does not use the subtleties of rhetoric nor does it conceal his ideology behind the esoteric language of cognitive science or game theory. But it is no more unscientific than many others. It shares with them the same ethnocentric naturalism, which assigns a moral value to the differences in income, wealth, and development existing in the world and traces them back to a preestablished order. Such differences are a confirmation of the superiority of the order incarnated by the political and economic constitution of liberal democracies.

Like North and Greif, Clark gives us a crystallized image of the human experience. It is fixed precisely because it is path dependent, and any form of social change within a cultural reference system is inconceivable. For someone like William Graham Sumner, one of the fathers of nineteenth-century Social Darwinism, the inspiration for this type of theory of social evolution came from faith in Puritan predestination (Boldizzoni 2008, pp. 119–21). The credo of his modern followers is more secular, but it has common ideological roots.

[6] Among the scholarly reviews, see, for example, those of the economists Robert Solow in the *New York Review of Books* (November 22, 2007) and Samuel Bowles in *Science* (October 19, 2007) and that of the historian Kenneth Pomeranz in the *American Historical Review* (June 2008). On the other hand, biologists and natural scientists do not seem to have shown much interest in it.

[7] They discussed it in a session of the Social Science Association Annual Meeting, Chicago, November 15–18, 2007, whose transcript can be found at: http://eh.net/bookreviews/ssha_farewell_to_alms.pdf, and in a symposium in *European Review of Economic History* 12.2 (2008), 137–99.

## Materialism Triumphant

Unlike the new institutional historiography, the cliometric current associated with the theoretical contributions of the Chicago school does not describe the civilizations of the past and the non-Western ones as being second-best solutions. But it does see market phenomena everywhere, and extends the rational choice approach to branches of social behavior that would not normally be considered economic. A typical example is given by the economic history of the family, which draws its inspiration from Gary Becker's *Treatise on the Family* (1991).

Thirty years ago Becker had pointed out:

> The application of the economic approach to fertility, marriage, employment, and other interactions among family members continues to encounter open hostility. When the first paper in this section suggested at a conference on population that children could be treated as durable consumer goods, it was greeted with derision by many participants. However, studies using the economic approach to analyze fertility have steadily increased in number since then, and they are now becoming respectable in the economics profession. (1976b, p. 169)

In the meantime, the fortunes of this paradigm have grown out of all proportion, and it has extended to related disciplines. It has already been successfully argued that the *Treatise on the Family* offers a poor theory of marriage decisions, quite apart from its empirical weakness (see Procter 2000), and it is not necessary to go back to this point. Here I will simply show how misleading it is to apply it historically.

Dowries in Renaissance Tuscany are an interesting case study (Botticini 1999; Botticini and Siow 2003). They are seen as "marriage payment" as well as an "intergenerational transfer." Their value is inversely proportional to the value of the bride's contribution to the marital household. The latter is represented by the value of the labor she will carry out within the household in addition to whatever value is attributed to the following two characteristics: the "love and pleasure she will bring to her husband" and her ability to raise children. The value of her lifetime consumption is subtracted from this total (Botticini 1999, p. 109). Thus, for example, the parents of a bride who is no longer in the bloom of youth will have to pay a higher dowry to compensate for the fact that she is a "less valuable product" (p. 110) in relation to the first characteristic.

With regard to the function of intergenerational transfer, dowries serve to resolve a free-riding problem. By paying the dowry of the daughter, the parents remove her from the line of hereditary succession, preventing any competition with her brothers over the division of the family resources after their death. According to Botticini and Siow (2003, p. 1386), the free-riding problem arises especially in virilocal societies, where the married sons, unlike the daughters, live with the parents, and it is precisely in these societies that dowries are mainly encountered. If the daughters were not paid off separately, they would take possession of the fruits of the labor carried out by the brothers in the home and on the land of the parents. The brothers would thus have little incentive to work in order to extend the family wealth.

We can certainly assume that in the case of arranged marriages, which was very common, there were many couples who did not love each other in a romantic way, but it is by no means the same as assuming that women were merely assets valued for their individual characteristics and skills. The supposed inverse correlation between the value of the dowry and the "value" of the bride (using age as proxy) is not an empirical standard. Botticini (1999) states that she obtained the worth of the dowries from 328 matrimonial contracts (notarial deeds) drawn up in the town of Cortona between 1415 and 1436, and then cross-checked this against details on the ages of the brides taken from the Florentine census and property survey for 1427, the Catasto. In the contracts the names of the fathers endorsing the transfer of the dowry are found, while in the Catasto the names of the children in each family nucleus are also found. A spontaneous question arises as to how, for instance, she managed to combine both sets of information for the period before 1427. She says she looked "for the household under the name of the surviving wife or children" whenever the household head had in the meantime died (p. 112). But this is not where the problem lies. It lies in the fact that information is available only on the ages and identities of the brides whose marriages took place in the period immediately after 1427 (in the city of Florence, to give an example, in the following twelve months). And even this is highly fragmentary.

Lack of data is due to the nature of the Catasto, which is an occasional document giving a sort of snapshot of the situation of taxpayers. If a daughter was getting married and leaving the paternal home, the father or the older brother would remove her name from the list of family members, and she would be added to the family nucleus of the husband.[8] The fact is that cancellations and additions "reflect only the marriages contracted during the short periods of time when the Catasto was open to changes" (Herlihy and Klapisch-Zuber 1985, pp. 204, 207). Hence,

[8] Only the rich (who paid large dowries) had an interest in reporting to the tax office that a daughter was no longer a dependent of the family nucleus. This declaration made it possible to subtract the value of the dowry from the taxable goods of the family, but in return the lump-sum deduction previously associated with that family member no longer applied (Herlihy and Klapisch-Zuber 1985, p. 204).

one cannot see how the twenty-year sample on which Botticini's conclusion is based could have been made. It appears even more implausible if one bears in mind that she claims that her cross-checked investigation was successful for 224 contracts out of 328 altogether (Botticini 1999, p. 112). She does not publish her database of names and ages, nor does she provide precise references for the items she has consulted, merely saying that she looked at the files of the Florence Archives![9]

Moreover the virilocality hypothesis on which the free-riding problem is based is refuted for most traditional societies. If we confine ourselves to preindustrial Europe, the neolocal residence model associated with the nuclear family seems to be the rule (Laslett 1972). Tuscany in 1427 was no exception despite a more diversified situation compared to England. Of the households in Florence, 92.25 percent were single nucleus; in Arezzo, 90.8 percent; and in the surrounding country areas, 80.4 percent (Klapisch 1972, p. 279). Extended- or multiple-family households made up only 29 percent in the whole Republic of Florence. Average life expectancy was short, and consequently the period during which several generations could coexist was also short.[10]

Anthropologists have been making comparative studies of the phenomenon of the dowry for a long time now (Goody and Tambiah 1973; Goody 1983; 1990). They interpret it by tracing it back not to the market but to the action of gift and countergift, which is to do with asserting status and establishing bonds of solidarity between the families of origin (who play a leading role in the marriage). In short, it is anything but a problem of impersonal negotiating and free riding. It is sometimes associated with the indirect dowry, a transfer from the family of the husband to the wife, to act as a support for her in case she becomes a widow. The Italian medieval and early modern experience shows how the dowry system joined two family clans in a bond of mutual support, in accordance with a typically aristocratic ethic of honor. It originated among the elites and, after the mid-fourteenth century, spread to the rest of society. Dowries moved backward and forward over the long term between families of equal, or similar, rank, and there was a sort of circulation very much resembling a continual recycling operation (Cattini and Romani 2009). It has been argued that the continuing survival of lineages and the ruling class in Florence was made possible by means of a strategy of en-

[9] In fact, the data of the Catasto were transcribed by Herlihy and Klapisch-Zuber between 1966 and 1976 and have been circulating among scholars since at least 1981 (since 1996 it has been possible to find them online: http://www.disc.wisc.edu/catasto). Thanks are due to Cindy Severt, librarian at the University of Wisconsin at Madison, for providing me with this information.
[10] Barbagli (2000, p. 136). For a discussion of the variables that affected household structure, see pp. 137–38.

dogamous intermarriage, with a periodic return of the dowries (Molho 1994). Here, as in the rest of Europe, whoever paid a large amount did so to acquire dignity and prestige. Thus, the dowry could also act as a means of social promotion in contexts where there was a certain degree of social mobility (Padgett 2010). The role of the dowry as an instrument in the choice of bridegroom on the part of the bride's family should not be underestimated either. As has been pointed out, it is no accident that societies that carry out this practice, unlike others, consider prematrimonial virginity to be quite important because it is a way of preventing unwanted claims to the girl and her possessions on the part of suitors deemed unsuitable (Schlegel 1991).

Thus, a degree of calculation did exist, but it was a political and social calculation, and not economic. If the dowry was a price and marriage was a market, then we would not have witnessed the disappearance, but rather the reinforcement, of this institution in modern times when economic values have taken on such an unprecedented role. The goods that once made up the dowry have instead gradually decreased, to the point of becoming a symbolic exchange of presents in our own day. This testifies to the fact that marriage has become an essentially private affair, and that its importance as a means of social alliance has diminished (Chan 2006).

A second trend is to portray people as if they had no feelings. Avner Offer's book *The Challenge of Affluence* (2006) is a recent example, though it is not a typical cliometric product, Offer being a sufficiently eclectic author to escape mere attempts at cataloging him. His book conveys an authentically moralistic intention that is hardly compatible with the neoliberal ideology of the newer economic history and betrays a sympathy for nostalgic and slightly antimodern conservatism. After all, Offer only repeats and provides empirical support for the thesis on the divergence between wealth, happiness, and well-being in mature economies that Tibor Scitovsky (1976) famously put forward. However, Scitovsky is cited rather parsimoniously, but to make up for that, Offer is very adept at exploiting a copious repertory of fashionable mainstream models to make his arguments fresher and more appealing. The result is an ingenious but highly unstable construction precisely because of the heterogeneity of the theoretical building blocks, which at times seem to be simply held together by the rhetorical force of the narrative.

In addition to chapters inspired by the new institutional economics, such as the one on "The Economy of Regard," where the gift-exchange is described as "perfect price discrimination" (Offer 2006, pp. 78–79), there are others, such as chapter 13 entitled "Mating since the 1950s," that are more properly Beckerian. The title seems to suggest an exhaustive discussion on the reproductive habits of rodents, but it is actually on human beings. According to the author, who not by chance draws on evolutionary psychology, love is an illusion of the senses, and its accurate nature is that of an economic transaction: "Love is easy to perceive as a magical state of grace, but it has always been a market as well, with imputed values for personal attractiveness, social standing, and economic potential" (p. 304).

The subject under discussion here is not marriage, which as a social institution has also certainly had an economic significance in history and continues to do so: what is being discussed here is the *economic nature of a feeling!*[11] Yes, because in Offer's view mating, or its romantic veneer, is based on a calculation: an individual looks for the best object available on the market taking into account his personal objective limitations or, more optimistically, his exchange value (pp. 304, 308–9). He will fall in love with the most attractive person he thinks he can have taking into consideration his own personal qualities. Thus, a man who is unattractive, poor, and not even powerful will surely fall in love with an unattractive dull woman. (One feels like commenting that if it were so simple, the world would not be so full of disappointed lovers, but this we will disregard.) In "stable societies," mating choices essentially respond to this mechanism of constrained maximization in accordance with the precepts of neoclassical microeconomics. But in "fluid, affluent societies," such as postwar United States and Britain, "the pool of those eligible, their capacities and intentions, is imperfectly known, the cues can be ambiguous, and the search has to evaluate every candidate against the probabilities of finding a better one" (p. 308).

Economic growth increases the alternatives available, sending the brain calculator of the partner-seeking agent into a state of confusion. Women find interesting things to do outside the home, and the stability of living as a couple becomes a less desirable alternative; sexual behavior becomes less restricted. In order to make up his mind in this new context, which probability distribution will our agent use? Gauss's? Pearson's? It is impossible to say, as there is too much uncertainty. This leaves the way open to opportunistic and strategic behavior that is ultimately responsible for the instability of family life in the second half of the twentieth century. "Abortion, births outside marriage, cohabitation, divorce, single parenthood, infidelity" and in particular "homosexuality" (*sic!*) are all "tentative, short-of-optimal resolutions of the intractable dilemmas of choice" (p. 303). However, the idea of "myopic choice" is not an invention of Offer's, but is an upshot of various commonplaces in the literature on market imperfections and in the economics of information.

[11] The rational choice of emotions is introduced in Becker (1996). For a critique, see Archer (2000), pp. 41–42.

Quite apart from the questionable nature of certain deductions, is there really any need to construct a cynical model of human behavior, expressing it "in a pithy, almost surgical fashion" (Trentmann 2008b, p. 417) in order to explain it all? Why not instead reflect on the changes in values and social norms to which the economic transformations in the period under consideration have certainly contributed? In a society tending toward individualism and self-realization brought about by economic success, it is clear that an increase in number of possibilities in this field has provided an enormous incentive for divergent behavior patterns. On the other hand, it has also brought about some positive effects. The gradual emancipation of the intimate sphere has meant that men, and women in particular, are able to avoid choices of convenience. Today marriages may well be less frequent and shorter lived than in the past, but they are probably more liberated and motivated by personal and sentimental convictions.

The weak link in Offer's reasoning is precisely that he mixes up, or perhaps is not interested in distinguishing between, feelings and mating choice. But these two elements need to be kept conceptually separate. Indeed, the model is not able to explain how economic growth leads to changed feelings. If love is a market, then it has to be shown that an increase in the supply of substitute goods produces a qualitatively poorer feeling through the choice mechanism. Yet this is impossible because (*pace* Offer, and Becker) we do not choose whom we fall in love with. Underlying this particular phenomenon, there is unquestionably a process that is both biochemical and cultural, but there is no calculation, whether rational or myopic. After all, this is a characteristic common to many of the things that can bring authentic happiness, but also untold suffering, to human beings.

The third example of Beckerian narrative that I wish to mention is the economic history of religion as it is presented in Ekelund, Hébert, and Tollison's *The Marketplace of Christianity* (2006). It matters little that on the opening pages they inform us they do not wish to write a book of history (p. 2), perhaps thinking of history writing as a tedious and pointless exercise. Because in this work historical interpretations are formulated that aim to show how the economics of religion can explain the past better than other approaches, it will be assessed bearing this objective in mind.

Ekelund, Hébert, and Tollison set out to provide a convincing interpretation of the evolution of Christianity, from the medieval church to the proliferation of the Protestant sects and the "self-supplied" Christianity in the United States of today. (It should have specified that it is a study of the evolution of Western Christianity, as an Eastern Christianity has also existed since the fifth century but the book provides no trace of this.) To summarize the interpretation, changes in the form of religion take place as rational decisions determined by comparisons of benefits and costs. Individuals demand a Z-good, religious services, for which they pay some full price (monetary and time costs) and receive some benefits. . . . In societies that allow plural religions to compete with each other, religious entrepreneurs adjust product characteristics to match different sets of demands and, in the process, sometimes create alternative forms of religion. (p. 105)

In this account, the Protestant Reformation acquires vital importance as being "the first major break in the Roman Catholic religious monopoly" when the religious market came to discover the benefits of competition. In the Middle Ages this monopoly translated into forms of price discrimination, which allowed the church to extract rents. Since the twelfth century, tools of price discrimination had been doctrinal innovations such as the doctrines of purgatory, penance, and indulgences. Even the creation of new religious orders such as the Franciscans and the Dominicans were attempts to differentiate supply in order to protect the monopoly against potential heresies (pp. 108–9, 113ff.).

In the late Middle Ages the price of the services sold by the church became too high, and this was the moment when its barriers to entry could no longer hold. That is why they were broken down by Luther and the other reformers. Protestantism offered a cheaper way to redemption. By establishing the principle that salvation can be obtained only through faith, it swept away indulgences. This "low-cost alternative" to Catholicism was embraced by wealthy and industrious people in particular, who were concerned with regaining their consumer surplus (p. 119). Consequently, Protestantism gained a particular hold in "profit-seeking societies," while it was rejected by "rent-seeking societies" (p. 120), and it is not difficult to guess which societies these were. It had prodigious macroeconomic effects, because "the consumer surplus released made investments in capital possible and, in Protestant areas, economic growth was stimulated" (p. 190).

With the Counter-Reformation, the Catholic Church tried to regain ground by means of a strategy of "product differentiation" (p. viii), but it was particularly concerned with safeguarding its privileges by intensifying rent-seeking activities, which "took the form of nepotism . . . simony . . . and other financial abuses" (p. 155). This was supposedly reflected in the "trend toward Italianization" of the Vatican, which "has continued to this day" (p. 154). Why not cite *Angels & Demons* and *The Da Vinci Code* among the documentary sources as well? Indeed, it appears extraordinary that while this book declares that it aspires to an "unbiased analysis" (p. viii), Catholics are regularly described as obscurantist and retrograde ("the aim of the medieval church was to eliminate competition" [p. 108], the worst sin imaginable for a neoclassical economist), while Protestants always prove to be enlightened and modern.

The merits of such arguments do not bear discussion. To gain an idea of the real significance of what Ekelund and his coauthors consider means of price discrimination, one could take Jacques Le Goff's book *The Birth of Purgatory* (1981) as a starting point. The emergence of an intermediate place between salvation and damnation in the geographic imagination of the late Middle Ages corresponds to the break with the feudal order and the development of social mobility. The transformation of ultramundane space thus reflects the conquest of urban space by the bourgeoisie. In any case, a basic knowledge of the facts would be enough to know that the foundation of new religious orders was not the product of papal initiatives but instead grew out of the dialectic between social movements and the hierarchy. In order to gain recognition for his brotherhood, Saint Francis had to overcome the suspicions of the Roman Curia. A celebrated legend represented in Giotto's fresco *The Dream of Innocent III* testifies to the astonishment of his contemporaries at this approval.

The argument that a part of Europe had embraced the Reformation through economic calculation ignores the whole complex of cultural motivations and political power struggles that prepared the way for it. If the Reformation was a response, it was to the diversity of a Europe that the military and administrative might of the Roman Empire had managed to unify from Sicily to Hadrian's Wall, but where centrifugal pressures to assert the deeper identities of each ultimately, and logically, prevailed. Moreover, it ignores the great heterogeneity of the Reformation, which had not only doctrinal but also institutional features that in England differed radically from those in Germany and Scandinavia, or in Switzerland, Scotland, and the Low Countries (Hsia 2004; Rublack 2005).

Historians have long reached the conclusion that there is no sense in conceiving the Catholic Reformation purely as a reaction to the Protestant Reformation because it too contained autonomous elements of renewal and a response to social changes in Latin Europe (Luebke 1999; Hsia 2005). Finally, one cannot help smiling at the idea that because the removal of indulgences reduced "the average price of religious services" capital was released, investment increased, and growth induced (Ekelund et al. 2006, p. 190). Arguments of this type are not very far from Cipolla's joke about the aphrodisiacal power of pepper driving the economic development of the Middle Ages.

Nor is the authors' prose without its peculiarities. On page 117 they mention "the German Fuggars," who "became papal agents for the collection of indulgence receipts." I am certain they are referring to the Fugger family, and that "Fuggars" is a mere typo. But for other more exotic

names, like that of the Bavarian city of Augsburg, there seem to exist two
alternative versions. The "Augsburg Confession" on page 166, becomes
the "Augsberg Confession" on pages 173, 176, and 333, while on pages
81 and 346 the "Peace of Augsberg" is conspicuous. Ironically, Augsburg
was also the city of the Fugger family! The book was published by an
excellent press that carried out its own careful editing. Slips of this type
in a scholarly book inevitably raise questions as to the credentials of the
authors (not as historians but as intellectuals).

## Making Up Antiquity

In order to celebrate the virtues and efficiency of the market economy,
there is no better way than to show its existence in a distant past. Indeed,
American public discourse, as James (2006b) and Meckler (2006) have
interestingly pointed out, is particularly fond of classical antiquity for its
mythical potential in reflecting the political events of the nation.

Prompted by divisions among ancient historians, economists have now
been trespassing on the territory of antiquity for at least fifteen years.
Until the 1980s in this field Moses Finley's model enjoyed universal consensus. Historians such as A.H.M. Jones (1974) in England, and Pierre
Vidal-Naquet in France (Austin and Vidal-Naquet 1972) were working
in the same direction. In 1980 the English-speaking world began to see
attempts to destroy this "new orthodoxy" from within, which is hardly
surprising considering that among those who had been put in its shade it
had created a number of disgruntled people. It might also be added that
Finley was probably a unique example of a cosmopolitan scholar because of his New York background in close contact with expatriates such
as Franz Boas and Max Horkheimer, in addition to Polanyi (Whittaker
1997; Tompkins 2006). He thus had direct knowledge of the works of
the German historical school, of Sombart, and of Weber—which others
would read only through Parsons's lenses.

Within the historical profession, the first to go against Finley was probably Keith Hopkins (1980), one of his successors to the Cambridge chair.
He challenged Finley by producing a model of the Roman economy, the
so-called "taxes and trade model," resting on an entirely hypothetico-
deductive basis and taking up very few pages. Hopkins did not reject the
autarkic position of the small producers or the local nature of their activity, but he argued that the economy of the Roman Empire was integrated
at the monetary level. According to his analysis, the first two centuries of
the common era experienced economic growth driven by the tax-raising
power of the Roman government and by the luxury consumption of the
elites living in the metropolis, which was capable of stimulating long-

distance trade. The chain of deduction would make up for the lack of macroeconomic data, and for this reason a "minimum GDP" was obtained starting from an estimate of population, provisions, and seeds, so that a specific ratio between aggregate income and taxes and so on could be conjectured. But as has been pointed out, the argument gets weaker at each of these phases because the margin of error already implicit in the initial assumptions is multiplied in a sort of avalanche effect.[12]

The controversial work of Edward Cohen (1992) on credit in the Athens of the fourth century B.C. followed a decade later, on the other side of the Atlantic. The book questions the nonproductive-loans thesis and argues that in Athens a market for maritime loans was in operation and functioned in accordance with modern banking rules. Cohen based his argument on a single type of source, the Attic orators, and Demosthenes in particular. These texts are constructed in a deliberately ambiguous manner and lend themselves to various levels of interpretation, as anyone who happened to translate them knows. Even for an interpreter who is motivated by the best of intentions, it is very easy to twist their meaning (cf. Foraboschi 1995). Proof of this lies in the fact that Paul Millett (1991), who was working on the same sources in the same years, reached exactly the opposite conclusions and lent support to a view that credit in Athens was embedded in forms of reciprocity suited to creating and supporting *philia* (solidarity) among citizens. As Sitta von Reden (2002, p. 145) points out, "In Millett's account Cohen's examples are exceptions which were not sufficient in number and impact to make a difference to the economic process, while the ideological background considered by Millett is for Cohen no more than public rhetoric."

This opened up a breach that made it easier for economists to make their way in. The best-known exponents of the economic profession to venture into the terrain of ancient history are Morris Silver and Peter Temin. The former investigated the ancient Near East while the latter concerned himself with the Roman Empire. Neither is there any lack of student textbooks such as the one on Greek history written by the Stanford economist Takeshi Amemiya (2007).

Silver (1995) puts forward a familiar blend of the new institutional economics and rational choice theory. On the one hand he follows North and argues that the ancient economies are a product of maximization restricted by the imperfections in the market mechanism. One chapter, entitled "Gods as Inputs and Outputs of the Ancient Economy," contains some rather amusing lines, such as: "The economic role of the gods found important expression in their function as protectors of honest business

---

[12] Andreau (2002b, p. 39). An extensive critique of this model is in Duncan-Jones (1990, ch. 2; 1994).

practices. Some deities openly combated opportunism . . . and lowered transaction costs by actively inculcating and enforcing professional standards" (p. 5).

Thus, the gods (or at least the belief in them) existed in order to increase market efficiency! Taken to its extreme, this is what the new institutional approach leads to. The temples, Silver explains, acted "as relatively efficient financial intermediaries or (possibly) banks," so much so that "the natural reluctance of debtors to default on loans given by gods or priests," by resolving the problem of free riding, ultimately lowered interest rates (pp. 27–28).

On the other hand, Silver distances himself from North, arguing that the market played a dominant role in ancient economies. On what documentary evidence does he base this conviction? Not on any primary source, nor on any evidence of the ancients considered as a whole. But to those who, such as Renger (1994), "seek to delegitimize or preempt the research of professional economists" with similar observations, he replies that they are tedious pedantries. One might think that a knowledge of ancient languages at the very least is needed before venturing into studies of this type. But, according to Silver, "This is simply false and, in fact, the Internet has opened a treasure of resources for nonlinguistic scholars" (2004, p. 82).

Historians and archaeologists are warned: why waste time studying strange alphabets and looking through dusty dictionaries when you could quite easily get away with a bit of research on Google? A book on ancient mythology immediately catches the eye from among the products of this innovative method (Silver 1992). A survey of the most important Greek myths is made with a view to showing how they actually have an economic origin. With regard to the myth of the birth of Athena, we read, for example, that "the meaning of Athena's birth from Zeus' head is that an elaboration of her cult—new temple(s), a priesthood, landed estates, tax revenues—was financed by the cult of Zeus, possibly by means of coins bearing the imprint of his head" (p. 28).

Naturally, we find no such implications either in Hesiod's *Theogony* or in any other sources. But the most surprising interpretation comes a few lines later, when Silver sets himself up as a literary historian. Because the cult of Athena appears to him to be more important in the *Iliad* than in the *Odyssey*, he concludes: "The implication of this is that, contrary to the scholarly consensus, the *Iliad* is later than the *Odyssey*" (Silver 1992, p. 28).

With a high degree of imagination, even the torment of Tantalus is reinterpreted in economic terms. Tantalus had betrayed the trust of the gods, rather like Prometheus and Sisyphus. He had revealed the secrets of Olympus to the mortals, he had committed filicide, and he had deceived the gods by getting them to perform cannibalism. But Silver presents him as a kind of investment broker. According to his reconstruction, "Tantalus was an 'agent' of Zeus," and his seat on Mount Sipylus "was admirably situated to serve as a financial center" (pp. 69–71). The punishment inflicted on him is not a warning against the overweening pride (*hybris*) of mortals or the assertion of the principle that taboos are not to be violated. The stone that he is forced to hold over his head while he suffers eternal hunger and thirst is none other than the public emblem of a bank!

The second author, Peter Temin, is a well-known cliometrician. Evidently considering that the last 120 years of scholarship is irrelevant, he has recently argued: "Ancient economic history is in its infancy, both because few economists have learned much about the ancient world and because ancient historians have typically not incorporated economics into their analysis" (Temin 2006c, p. 133).

Determined to guide the specialists in the right direction, Temin started out in the field of classical studies with an article emphatically entitled "A Market Economy in the Early Roman Empire," where he claimed that "market exchange was ubiquitous" and "Rome had an economic system that was an enormous conglomeration of interdependent markets" (2001, p. 181). The argument is built up by isolating and emphasizing a few elements taken from secondary sources (the works of the historians who came after Hopkins). At the same time, in an article on "Price Behavior in Ancient Babylon" he applied regression analysis to some series of agricultural prices already published by the Assyriologists. The series cover the period from 464 to 72 B.C., though "the data contain many missing values because of the many lost tablets and the large number that are damaged or broken" (2002, p. 48). The conclusion is that because these prices "fluctuated a lot," and one can hardly see the utility of a regression analysis to point this out, a market economy existed (p. 59). In chapter 4, we will see how prices "fluctuated a lot" even in the feudal economy of medieval and early modern Europe, which was not a market economy, as Temin himself admits (2001, p. 172). In any case the wide and uncontrolled fluctuations in the prices of staple goods is more a sign of the marginality of the market as an allocation system and the poor functioning of its mechanisms.

The next steps were to argue that in the early Roman Empire there was a "functioning labor market" and a "unified labor force" (Temin 2004b, p. 514) that was sufficiently mobile to respond to economic incentives, as well as sophisticated financial markets "which had the potential to promote growth" (Temin 2004a, p. 705). They were "more accessible and flexible than much of the English and French eighteenth-century financial markets" (p. 728). What about slavery? According to Temin (2004b), it was a purely formal institution that left slaves mainly free to do what they wanted while waiting to be manumitted.

In another article, Kessler and Temin argue that the office of the prefect of the *annona*—the imperial official whose task was to guarantee food supplies for the capital—"functioned as an information-clearing house." In an astonishing passage, they liken the prefect to the chairman of the Federal Reserve Board:

> The issuing of certain public contracts could signal private merchants about expected prices and fluctuations in the market, as well as about shortages or surpluses in areas in which they did not normally deal. In essence, this information distribution is similar to speeches given today by individuals such as the chairman of the Federal Reserve Board, who, with a massive amount of economic information, take actions that signal market conditions to private businessmen. (Kessler and Temin 2007, pp. 322–23)

The rare fragments of Roman authors are quoted in translation, probably from the works of such reviled historians. But a knowledge of the languages in which the sources are written does not seem to be the only thing that the cliometricians lack. They also seem to lack a knowledge of elementary geography. In a work on market integration in the early Roman Empire, at a certain point we run into the curious statement that "the Po valley was linked to Rome by rivers rather than sea" (Kessler and Temin 2008, p. 140). As far as I am aware, the Po Valley is nowadays linked to Rome by an expressway and by high-speed train, but there are no traces of any rivers, and since the time it was known as Cisalpine Gaul this has not changed. Then as now, the Po Valley is separated from the Italian peninsula by the Apennines, a large mountain chain that cannot be crossed by rivers in common with all the world's mountain chains. Perhaps this is a negligible detail for someone who argues that the markets of the Mediterranean had been integrated since biblical times, "even before coinage was invented," thanks to the operation of the prodigious forces identified by the Heckscher-Ohlin model! (Temin 2006b).

The ancient historians certainly did not merely stand by. John Davies has listed the four main characteristics of ancient economies that make them unsuitable for the application of modern economic theory, whatever the type. These are the pursuit of autarky; the lack of ancient equivalents for "firm" and "state"; a social motivation for economic action; and a different psychology of choice and the lack of a price mechanism that is typical of competitive markets (2005, pp. 128–30).

Rigorous studies have been carried out on the Finley model, which has been clarified, perfected, and where necessary amended. These studies confirm that the economy of classical Greece was based on agriculture. Large and small tenant farmers, operating within a dense network of social relations, were not interested in wealth maximization but pursued strategies of "interpersonal risk-buffering" (Gallant 1991, ch. 6). As in most agricultural societies, land was not sold unless one was burdened with debts, which accumulated when there were recurring food crises. Within this context, exchange was an "exchange of surpluses" rather than anything else. It was not planned before a harvest but became necessary to make up for any unsuccessful harvests of specific crops (Burford 1993).

In contrast to the Homeric period, the emergence of the *polis* extended the close-knit social network of neighborhood and kinship ties to the dimension of citizenship, where political, social, and economic exchange formed an integrated whole (von Reden 1995, pp. 105–6). The structural inequality of Greek society—of which only a fraction was made up of citizens who saw themselves as part of the *demokratia*—was also reflected on the economic plane. In classical Attica, "about 9 percent of households owned around 35 percent of the land" and indirectly controlled a further 10 percent of it (Foxhall 2002, p. 211). Citizenship was necessary in order to own land but at times anyone who lost his land also lost his citizen status (Burford 1993, p. 50).

In the Hellenistic period, when the Mediterranean and the Near East had by now been unified by Greek culture, again there were no signs of market integration. Gary Reger (1994; 2002) has carried out a robust quantitative study of the prices of consumer goods taken from the temple accounts of the Delian sanctuary of Apollo in the third and second century B.C. From an analysis of this exceptionally rich body of documents, it does not emerge that general economic trends affected price formation on this much-visited island, but that prices for different commodities developed independently over time. "This strongly suggests that any explanation for a particular individual price history must be sought in the particularities of that good, and not in a general appeal to a common price-setting market for imported goods" (2002, p. 145), a sign of the "overwhelmingly local character of almost all economic activity in antiquity" (p. 137).

Research carried out on the Roman economy by Jean Andreau (1999; 2002a) confirms that productive loans were a minority, although difficult to quantify. He makes a basic distinction between elite financiers and professional bankers. Certainly, wealthy Roman aristocracy, senators and knights, did not disdain the loan of large sums of money in exchange for political favors. But "banking was something quite different": "Those who consider the knight Atticus and the senator Crassus to have been proper bankers do not have a clear idea either of how business operated in the ancient world or of the social and political roles played by the various kinds of financiers" (1999, p. 2).

Professional bankers (*argentarii* and *nummularii*, or *trapezitai* in Greece), far from being high-status people, fitted perfectly into the picture of marginality that Finley depicted. In order to make a living, they had no choice but to make interest on any money they received on deposit, and in some respects this put them below clerical status because they were close to living by expedients.

In his recent comparative study, Peter Bang (2008) underlined how misleading it is to associate the system of exchanges in Roman antiquity to the notion of the modern, capitalist market. Comparing the Roman Empire against the great Euro-Asiatic empires such as Mughal India, Ming/Ch'ing China, and the early modern Ottoman state, he argued that in all these contexts exchange was closer to the model of the bazaar. The Roman markets were subject to the unpredictability of supply and demand, highly volatile prices of commodities, very little transparency, and fragmentation or low and fragile integration. Sellers adopted all kinds of strategies ranging from clientelization to predatory practices—in short, everything but competition.

Whether or not the image of the bazaar is actually the most suitable for describing these heterogeneous types of exchange, Bang's work has the merit of highlighting the gulf between the Roman economy, which was organized according to the rules, values, and technical possibilities of Roman society and the economy (economies) of our own times.

However, it would be a mistake to think that the profession has joined forces against the aggression of economists. Scholars who share the representation of the ancient economy that I have outlined here are still a majority in Europe, but a minority in the United States. This is particularly true if we consider the generations of classicists who have gained their PhD since the 1980s. They are visibly fascinated by economics. The recent *Cambridge Economic History of the Greco-Roman World* (Scheidel et al. 2007) reflects this trend.

In the past decade two collections of essays with the same title, *The Ancient Economy*, have appeared almost one after the other. One represents the European stance (Scheidel and von Reden 2002), and the other the American (Manning and Morris 2005). Although both seek a balance between the contributions, the viewpoints are quite clear. With the latter, the majority of the younger contributors are willing to agree more or less passively to adapt their narratives to rational choice, new institutional, and law-and-economics models. For example, a paper on the Near East uncritically accepts the Ellickson and Thorland (1995) utility-maximization model without even being aware that it confuses rationality with utilitarianism. The chief premise is that if the economic agents of each historical epoch share the same degree of rationality, they cannot but act in conformity with neoclassical theory, regardless of any social and cultural differences between them. It proclaims the usual clichés, starting from the triumph of property rights and the free market, unless second-best solutions are produced by choice under uncertainty.[13]

There are studies on the "power of the market in early Greece," on "property rights and contracting" in Ptolemaic Egypt, and on "economic rationalism" in the following Roman period. All that is missing is that the "revisionist view" of Greco-Roman money attributes the invention of the credit card to the ancients, though the "elasticity of money supply" is already widely extolled.[14] This vision does not differ very much from the cliometricians' claim that the early Roman Empire formed "a single currency area like the euro zone today" (Kessler and Temin 2008, p. 159). Regardless of any exaggerations in the interpretation, the weakness in the arguments of the professional historians who endorse these visions often lies in the poor representativeness of the material studied. As Paul Cartledge puts it, "the modernizers focus . . . on the 2% of exceptions for whom macro-economic activity at a regional or international level was the sole or prime source of their wealth" (2002a, p. 14).

It is legitimate to wonder why people trained as classicists have this fascination for economics. The influence of the environment in which they operate as well as ideology undoubtedly plays an important part, and this is a serious limitation for historical research and the social sciences in general. The historian who is not sufficiently thorough investigates the past seeking what he wants to see there—that is, the attitudes, values, and practices that are familiar to him and therefore appear natural to him. Of course, there are also reasons of opportunity, if it is true that the adoption of certain paradigms "could sometimes lead to rapid career advancement" (Morris and Weingast 2004, p. 705n). There is no doubt that the ability to master academic politics explains at least in part the spread of the new institutionalism, which appears hardly justified by its intellectual power.[15] But I believe that a no less important element is the prestige that economics enjoys in American society, and therefore in American academe. The fact that ancient historians are driven toward modernism and improbable attempts to draw on Gary Becker's latest extravagant idea or the new growth theory as popularized by Lucas (2002;

[13] Bedford (2005), which is criticized in Granovetter (2005a, pp. 84–85).

[14] On archaic Greece, Tandy (1997); on Ptolemaic Egypt, Manning (2004), in contrast to the picture of von Reden (2007); on Roman Egypt, Rathbone (1991), which is disproved by Bang (2008, pp. 153–73); on credit money, E. Cohen (2008), Harris (2006; 2008a).

[15] Morley interestingly reports a view, held by his colleagues, that the new institutional economics "simply allows historians to carry on in exactly the way they had before, while using some economic-sounding language" (2007, p. 105).

cf. Saller 2005, p. 232), often reflects the feeling of isolation in a discipline that also wants to be relevant for the present. This is the sense of Ian Morris's exclamation that was prompted by what Samuelson and Nordhaus (1998, p. 7) wrote in their famous textbook for economics freshmen: "The history of economic growth explains differing standards of living in the past; and if we can explain why standards of living differed in the past, we may be in a better position to create institutions that foster continuing improvements in the future" (Morris 2005, p. 105).

The problem underlying the arguments of the "new ancient historians" is the assumption that economic growth is a sort of constant in the history of humanity, regardless of how strong it is. Instead, growth is a somewhat recent phenomenon that in the Western world was made possible by the economic development of the eighteenth century. In sixteenth-century Italy or seventeenth-century France, it makes sense to speak of expansion (increase in output without increase of productivity) but not of growth (systematic increase in output supported by an increase in productivity). Cycles of expansion and years or decades of crisis and famines often alternated unpredictably.

Growth and economic development are not synonymous, and to understand the former concept one necessarily has to understand the latter. For a European or an American of today, it is normal for the economy of his country to grow at an annual rate of 1, 2, or 3 percent in terms of GDP, and when it enters a recession, as at the time of writing, one is rightly alarmed. The rate just needs to fall below 1 percent to create a sense of anxiety (and the government or central bank typically has to take the blame). Yet in Asia some economies are growing at an annual rate of more than 10 percent, which is a growth rate of takeoff. The Western economies in the meanwhile proceed at a "rate of maintenance."

Neoclassical theory is not able to make this fundamental distinction, as it has nothing to say on economic development. Its models, starting from Solow (1956), merely establish a certain functional relation between inputs and output in a "state of the world" that is taken as given (exogenous, as it is said). Of course, the framework can be embellished with technical progress or human capital, but these are left unexplained, unless one is happy with rational choice explanations. Or the increased output can be made to depend on the efficiency of institutions, which are then considered right or wrong, and economic change is reduced to "performance" (North 1981). In both cases, we are faced with a physical or institutional engineering problem to be studied in a vacuum, as if time and space were totally insignificant.

Interpreting history in the light of an ahistorical theory leads to serious errors, as we will now see in more detail.

## The Perils of Playing with Numbers

Once the virtually inborn nature of the market economy has been proved, it is then necessary to measure its performance. Another obsession of our age is that of quantification pushed right back into the mists of time. In his statistical outlooks, the late Angus Maddison (2006; 2007) presented estimates of per capita GDP relating to two thousand years previously, not only for Europe but also for China and sub-Saharan Africa (famously lacking in written sources). How he managed to do this is a mystery for many people. In the European archives, series of prices and wages along with census records are found only from the Middle Ages onward. For the ancient world, we find the odd item of quantitative information in the texts of classical writers. But they are mostly incidental and are certainly not to be taken literally.

Though some cliometric work is based on Maddison's data set (see Acemoglu et al. 2005), cliometricians have become themselves generators of statistical information about remote economies. The recent works of Robert Allen provide good examples of these acrobatic calculations. In the first place, he compares European wages and prices from the late Middle Ages to the First World War (Allen 2001). Noticing that they are expressed in units of measure that are not comparable, he converts them into grams of silver. At this point, the data becomes the basis on which to calculate living standards. Purchasing power is determined by dividing wages by the prices of a basket of consumer goods.[16] Therefore, comparisons between European countries and between Europe and Asia can be made (Allen 2005).

Yet an underlying problem lies hidden behind the apparently innocuous operation of converting prices into grams of silver, and ignoring it shows a lack of clear understanding of the workings of monetary systems in the medieval and early modern period (Bloch 1954; Cipolla 1956; Van der Wee 1977).

Over this long time span, prices and wages were measured in pounds, shillings, and pennies (*lirae*, *solidi*, and *denarii*) throughout Europe (including the British Isles). They were units of account that corresponded to the extremely variable quantities of silver that was contained in the real coins. In the time of Charlemagne, the pound (*lira*) actually corresponded to a pound (*libra*) of silver, from which 240 pennies (*denarii*) of 1.7 grams each were obtained, the whole being equal to 20 shillings (*solidi*). But while the equivalence £1 = 20s = 240d held good for many

---

[16] An approach of this type, even though very much simplified, is also used by van Zanden (1999).

centuries—on the Continent until the Napoleonic era—by the late Middle Ages any link between the pound as a unit of weight and the pound as "ghost" money had been lost.

People made payments with real moneys (from the prized groats to the petty coins of copper alloy) whose content of precious metal fluctuated over time.[17] Thus, their value in terms of units of account was periodically fixed by edict and was reviewed each time any variations in weight or fineness were encountered. The exchange rate actually practiced on the market was different again. While the large silver (and gold) coins were relatively more stable and were thus used for long-distance trade, the small billon coins ended by becoming the main means of payment for everyday transactions. This type of coin was used to pay for the bread and wages of a bricklayer, for example. The emblem of the sovereign engraved on the billon coins guaranteed that they were legal tender within the state.

With this in mind, one can see how converting prices and wages into grams of silver—which is what comparisons like Allen's are based on—have no economic significance. Moreover, wages were largely paid in kind, at least in country areas. On the other hand, this method of calculating living standards assumes that the market was the main allocation system for the product and the factors of production, based as it is on market prices and wages.

There are potentially serious consequences of the technical problem we have seen. A mathematician once famously argued that the flap of a butterfly's wing in Brazil could set off a tornado in Texas. Something of this sort happens in economic history when calculations of this type lead to deductions that in Britain wages were higher than anywhere else in the world and capital and energy cheaper, and this becomes the cause of the industrial revolution (Allen 2009b). Or when, from improbable comparisons of skill premiums, empirical support is fabricated for the new institutional narratives on the predestination of the West since medieval times (van Zanden 2008; 2009).[18]

It is therefore appropriate to try and understand the exact reasons why these types of calculations are being made. Behind Maddison's tireless work there was very probably a genuine interest in statistics. In the

[17] After the thirteenth century, gold coins such as florins and ducats were added to the large silver coins, with similar functions.

[18] In short, one starts from the assumption that low interest rates are a proxy for institutional efficiency and the safeguarding of property rights; skill premium (the difference between the wage of a skilled worker and that of an unskilled worker) is used as proxy of the interest rate; and the proxy of the proxy is compared on a world scale (including those countries that did not practice loans against interest). Incidentally, for preindustrial Europe, information about interest rates is anything but rare. Their trends could be more usefully studied to reconstruct the economic conjuncture. See, e.g., De Maddalena (1982).

case of professional economic historians, there is often another aim that has more to do with the "naturalization" of the concept of economic growth. This trend also overlaps with trends in economics. While for economists the naturalization is total—they suppose that growth has always existed (Goodfriend and McDermott 1995; Galor and Moav 2002), economic historians trace its origins back to a variable point in the past, which generally coincides with the historical period in which they specialize.

Nobody likes having to deal with static situations. Sluggish economies appear tedious, even those that are by no means poor, and are ill suited to being studied using analytical tools that focus on performance (not to mention those that are underdeveloped). A historian who deals with starvation in early twentieth-century Calcutta is very unlikely to be invited to give a paper in the economics department of a top university (unless he argues that it lay in a problem of contract enforcement). Hence, historians have started to say that growth did exist to some extent in the times and places they were dealing with. This trend began in the 1990s, and its target was the so-called static picture of preindustrial Europe.

After the first rather feeble attempts, with declarations far outweighing actual analysis (K. G. Persson 1988), there followed a decidedly better-prepared offensive that went by the name of the "revolt of the early modernists" (de Vries 1994; van Zanden 2002). Taking advantage of the predicament concerning the concept of industrial revolution that was being called into question following Nick Crafts's (1985) new estimates of British economic growth, these early modernists set about tracing the start of modern economic growth back to seventeenth-century Netherlands (de Vries and van der Woude 1997). There is no doubt that the Dutch economy was extraordinarily productive. But it had objective limitations that made its industrialization impossible in contrast to what happened in England, despite there being a number of common elements. The problem arises when the growth of Dutch productivity is used as a general model and the concept of industrial revolution is replaced with that of "industrious revolution" (de Vries 2008). This will be discussed in the next chapter.

Then Philip Hoffman (1996), a cliometrician based in California, began to argue that even the economy of early modern France showed growth. France was a particularly attractive target because it represented the laboratory for the *Annales* school in which the "static picture" of the preindustrial economy had been formed. Studying it meant challenging the French historians on their own ground. Hoffman was reluctant to use the abundant direct data for production, population, and arable areas in the archives, which would have confirmed the traditional view, and he based his reasoning on indirect deductions such as total factor productivity (TFP). However, these modern indices make no sense if applied to other epochs where there was a different juridical framework for the use of the factors of production, which also affected their mobility.

Not just "at first," as Hoffman concedes, but as we investigate these estimates the more do they seem to be "a picaresque adventure in pseudo-statistics" (p. 82). In addition, there is the problem of the examples chosen. It is obvious that "certain farms could extract more output than other farms from the same amount of land, labor, and capital," but this does not mean "achiev[ing] economic growth." How many of these farms were there? And what relation did they have with the economic and social structure of the country? These are all questions that Hoffman does not ask.

Neither is there much sense in speaking about GDP (expressed in 1990 dollars PPP!) for polities and economies, such as early modern Italy, that were not integrated at a national level (Malanima 2003), quite apart from the fact that these calculations are often made by starting from one or two series of wages, possibly of large cities that have been arbitrarily chosen from among hundreds of series, each reflecting the distinctive particularities of the area in question. Whatever the case, the vogue for anachronistic quantification spread rapidly and found at least one supporter in each European country ready to venture into this type of speculation (see van Zanden 2001).

In the meantime, the medievalists also began to claim there had been economic growth in the Middle Ages, some even going so far as to locate it in Sicily (S. R. Epstein 1992; 1994; 2000). This growth, if not Schumpeterian, was at least "Smithian," and depended on the capacity of the "centralised states" to promote markets. The political economics underlying this interpretation was a form of do-it-yourself whereby certain elements of the new institutional framework were recombined and adapted. At this point the ancient historians came forward. If the Middle Ages were going to be upgraded, why not the Greco-Roman world too?

The idea of economic growth is at odds with the mentality of the ancients who, no differently from other preindustrial civilizations (Foster 1965), conceived of wealth as a cake of a fixed size. In their view the portions could be divided out differently, but the size of the cake could not be increased (Millett 2001). This is not a vision of a "primitive" world, unworthy of peoples who had codified the principles of logic and knew how to build ingenious aqueducts. For the Greeks and Romans, knowledge (*episteme*) and technique (*techne*) were still two separate planes and very far apart in the hierarchy.

Finley had warned historians not to take the few figures to be found in the classical texts literally (1985, pp. 24–25). However, I do not believe he ever imagined that these days quantitative history would be written without any figures at all. How can calculations be made without figures? By carrying the deductive method inaugurated by Hopkins (1980; 2002) to its extreme. Amphorae of olive oil are counted (Hitchner 2002), houses and the level of air pollution are measured, but bones especially are measured and used as proxies for economic growth. And where even these proxies are lacking they are obtained by analogy from figures relating to other places in other epochs. For example, Morris finds that house size in ancient Greece increased around five or six times between 800 and 300 B.C., and that is enough for him to state that "economic expansion was massive, sustained, and desperately in need of explanation" (2005, p. 123). But he is already certain that it "will turn out to be a surprisingly high level of economic growth," and naturally: "This calls for new models, probably owing more to economic historians like Douglass North . . . than to Weber or Finley" (pp. 124–25).

Each draws water to his own mill. For the specialists of Greece, "the Greek economy performed spectacularly well: in aggregate terms, it is comparable to the gains made in early-modern Holland" (Morris 2004, p. 736). For those of the Roman world, on the other hand, the growth of the Roman economy was a unique experience in the preindustrial period, at least until the rise of Holland and England. According to Jongman (2007), around the year 0 there was a peak in the number of Roman shipwrecks, in atmospheric metal pollution recorded from the glaciers of Greenland, and in the use of wood in western and southern Germany. In his view these three elements suggest an extraordinary expansion of long-distance maritime trade, of money supply, and building activity in the late republican and early imperial periods. But how can one draw conclusions on economic performance from these rather vague clues? (Scheidel forthcoming).

"Bone measurers" now make up a subfield of ancient economic history and would deserve a separate chapter. I do not wish to be misunderstood: bone analysis might well provide important information on the state of health and nutrition, and this could be fertile terrain for collaboration between history, archaeology, and the medical sciences. But to claim that bones can tell us something about economic growth is like claiming that blood can be drawn from a stone.

Even limiting oneself to the first type of analysis, good use needs to be made of bones. Calculating that the Romans were on average taller than 168 centimeters, Kron (2005; forthcoming) concluded that they were better nourished and healthier than any one else before the Victorian period. This estimate is certainly overoptimistic, based as it is on observations that are excessively dispersed (the sample is made up of Italian skeletons dating from 500 B.C. to A.D. 500), and indeed it has been questioned by several scholars. But, even allowing for its feasibility, that sort of stature is in itself compatible with a general context of relative malnutrition and low life expectancy.[19]

Then there are those who make calculations based on the system of national accounts. Richard Saller, who favors the application of the powerful tools of the new classical macroeconomics to account for the prodigious phenomenon of growth in the imperial economy, ultimately finds that it was "less than 0.1 per cent per year, and even that rate was not sustained" (2005, p. 231). Temin (2006a) has also become involved in calculating GDP. In his view, it can be estimated from both the expenditure side and the income side. Both ways require the assumption of integrated, competitive markets with price uniformity, but he does not consider this a problem, as we have seen. Neither does he see any problems in regarding the wage of an employed worker as being representative of average income in a system based on slavery. Finally, to put an end to the controversy, the classicists have called on Robert Allen to come to their aid. Using the prices and wages in Diocletian's Edict (A.D. 301) as his basis, he reassures them that "the Roman worker in Diocletian's time was doing about as well as most workers in eighteenth-century Europe or Asia" (2009a, p. 342). Allen reached this conclusion after applying the usual method, with one significant innovation. Because the price of bread, which was an essential element in the basket, was not available, he decided to reconstruct it with his "bread equation" (p. 336) from the price of wheat and the wage of a skilled worker (which are not even those written in the edict, but the product of conversions into grams of silver!). One thing is certain: whoever thought that cliometrics was an arid discipline that lacked imagination was mistaken.

[19] See the discussion in Scheidel (forthcoming). On malnutrition in antiquity, and in the Roman world in particular, cf. Garnsey (1999, ch. 4).

# Chapter 4 _____

## THE WORLD WE HAVE LOST

### *Microeconomic History*

IS IT POSSIBLE TO PRACTICE a different type of economic history from cliometrics, without lapsing into narrative history? The answer to the question is that it is. This chapter is the first of two that intend to show that a third way is possible and, indeed, was already being extensively applied in the second half of the twentieth century. It involves approaches that were molded in continental Europe but were not exclusive to Europe, and had the *Annales* school as their catalyst but were not coincident with it.

The following pages are concerned with an investigation of the past from a microeconomic point of view, with an analysis of decisions taken with regard to production, consumption, and exchange at the level of producers and households, and naturally of the consequences of these decisions. Chapter 5 deals with the macroeconomic framework, which includes economic cycles, money, price levels, the nature of growth, and the historical roots of underdevelopment. We will also see how the micro level is logically linked to the macro level.

Here we discuss the model that the Polish historian Witold Kula introduced in his *An Economic Theory of the Feudal System* (1962), a work of great analytical power. In fewer than two hundred pages, it demolishes the claims of neoclassical microeconomics to universality and shows how its theorems are not applicable to preindustrial eastern Europe. Starting from an investigation of this context, it creates appropriate alternative theoretical tools for explaining it. But the usefulness of this type of history also extends to the present, suggesting that the working of each particular economic system needs to be understood on its own. In this respect, far too often a simplistic approach is followed by current theorists and policy makers, and this applies to international development policies in particular.

Kula wrote his book at the height of the Cold War. It came out in the same year as the Cuban Missile Crisis, at the time when Walt Rostow's (1960) classic book on economic development bore the subtitle *A Non-Communist Manifesto*. Thus, the value-free nature of Kula's text, and its aspiration to be unconditioned by any ideology, stands out

all the more. If the comparison with Marxist scholarship is de rigueur
(the concept of "feudal system" itself is meant in that sense), he makes
just as many references to contemporary Western literature. They reveal
his continuous dialogue with the writings of his Anglo-American colleagues, starting with those of Arthur Lewis (1954) toward which he
was often well disposed (see also Kula 1960). Western scholars were
not so consistently open-minded. The book was translated into several
languages and met with considerable fortune on the European mainland. But with the exception of Eric Hobsbawm's circle it attracted very
little attention in the English-speaking world, despite being praised by
the leading Cambridge medievalist Michael Postan, who welcomed it as
"the most intelligent as well as the most independent of all the treatises
on the economy and the history of feudalism now available to readers"
(1977, p. 72).

However Kula's strongest sponsor west of the Iron Curtain was undoubtedly Fernand Braudel. On one occasion, Braudel went so far as to
declare that Kula was more intelligent than he was (Burke 1990, p. 95).
Considering how unusual it was for such a concession to be made by a
scholar for whom it was not enough to be the foremost French historian
but who also considered himself "the best Italian historian" (Le Roy Ladurie 1995), Kula must have made a great impression on his colleagues.
When after October 1956 Polish historians were once again able to travel
the world Kula was especially at home in France. The traditional friendly
relations between Paris and Warsaw were also reflected in the scientific
sphere. The beginnings of the *Annales* school at the end of the 1920s
had been closely watched in Poland where top-ranking economic and
social historians were working, and those relations were consolidated
by the French with an active academic policy, which continues to this
day through the initiatives of the Maison des Sciences de l'Homme.[1] It is
difficult to assess whether the influence of the *Annales* on Kula or Kula's
influence on the *Annales* was the stronger, and probably there is no sense
in even trying. What is certain is that he was an example of a free and
independent historian.

## Basic Assumptions

*An Economic Theory of the Feudal System* is built around an empirical
analysis of the Polish economy between the sixteenth and eighteenth centuries. These geographic and chronological references appear alongside
the title of the French and English editions, but they do not appear in

---

[1] Pomian (1978). On the intellectual context of interwar Poland, see Kula (1989).

the original edition, whose subtitle is simply *Próba modelu* (testing of a model). This is not a chance detail but a deliberate choice. It indicates Kula's wish to arrive at something more than a study of the economic history of early modern Poland—namely, an interpretation of the functioning of economies that are no longer primitive, but not yet industrial, in noncapitalist contexts.

The premises that Kula (1962, p. 26) starts from are the following:

1. Agriculture is of overwhelming importance in the economy of the country.
2. The factors of production (land and labor) are not commodities. They cannot be freely placed on the market, as the land belongs to the nobility, and labor is provided by serfs who are tied to the land.
3. Manufacturing and artisan activities, which make up the secondary sector, are carried out exclusively within the framework of the large estate or the town guilds.
4. The state does not interfere with the decisions of the nobles, and there is no such thing as a national economic policy; for example, duties are not applied on imports.

Ownership of the land (and of the villages on it) is thus the privilege of a very small elite. It is maintained and passed on intact from one generation to the next. Each estate is divided into two parts, one of which is the demesne (*folwark*) where the nobleman carries out economic activity for himself, whether directly or through his functionaries, while the other is subdivided into small plots entrusted to peasants who gain their subsistence from it. The peasants are obliged to perform services for the lord, and in particular to provide labor (in the form of corvées) on the demesne. The size of the peasant plot is fixed in relation to the size of the family, so that its bare necessities are assured (reproduction of the labor force). In such circumstances, the creation of any surplus is thwarted by the lord.

The lord's estate is profitable, at times very profitable from its owner's point of view. This is indicated by the Polish nobility's strong propensity toward the consumption of luxury goods. But this profitability is possible only because the factors of production are not acquired by means of the market. If the lord had to purchase even only the labor, his activity would run at a loss. And the situation would be even worse if he had to purchase the raw materials or invest any sums of money to replace investments in kind (Kula 1962, pp. 31–33).

This apparent paradox requires a comment about method. The profitability of a noncapitalist enterprise has to be calculated necessarily in "real" terms. The premise of the neoclassical theory of the firm that "everything has a price" proves to have little sense in an economic system characterized by a different juridical and institutional framework (pp. 43–44).

Connected to this aspect is the objection that Kula raised with regard to the problem of choice. According to Lionel Robbins's (1932) famous definition, what characterizes economic activity is precisely a problem of choice involving ends and scarce means that have alternative uses. But in the feudal system there does not seem to exist any problem of this type.

In the case of the demesne being a long way from any watercourses, how could the timber obtained from its woods be exploited? Often the only possibility was to burn it as fuel. As a result, a decision could be made to set up a glass manufacturing plant, if there was a local demand for glass. Of course, the activity in question does not become any less "economic" because the agent has no choice. Yet once again, if the agent had had to acquire the wood on the market, the consequences for his business would have been disastrous (Kula 1962, pp. 33–34).

> Calculating the expenses seeks to reconstruct the amount of losses encountered in the process of production. Taking into account the monetary value of the timber used in production (but not purchased) can rationally be regarded as a loss only if the timber could have been sold at that price. But could it actually have been sold? Similarly, including in the costs the value of labour supplied by the serfs would only make sense if, by foregoing their use, that labour could have been sold at that particular price. But could this actually have been done? (pp. 38–39)

The answer is clearly in the negative. Standard economics assumes that there is a uniform price for the factors of production, including labor. It assumes that all goods and factors have an economic value and a price that enables this to be measured. It assumes that the entrepreneur, or the owner of the means of production, is always in a position to decide whether to sell those means at market price or to utilize them in the production process, which he will do only if keeping up the business proves to be the cheaper alternative (p. 38).

Outside the capitalist system none of these conditions occurs. If the truth were told, "even the reality of laissez-faire capitalism is far-removed on many points" from the "full-blown possibility of choice" idealized in the theory of perfectly competitive markets (ibid., p. 34). The study of the feudal economy thus makes it necessary for the historian to free himself of the useless toolbox of received theory and to build up his own microeconomics that is compatible with the empirical evidence he is interpreting.

Kula's position has obvious points of contact with that of the Russian economist Alexander Chayanov (1924; 1925). Chayanov investigated the Russian rural economy of the late nineteenth and early twentieth centuries and was convinced that neither the neoclassical tools modeled on the capitalist system nor those of Marxist analysis could be applied to it. The Russian peasants were careful to maintain a proper balance between the drudgery of work and economic return. Having limited wants, they cultivated the amount of land needed to sustain the family but only for as long as was strictly necessary to guarantee a steady income. Hence, when there were small children around they worked harder, but as the children grew up and started to work themselves the toil of each member of the household was gradually reduced.

In other words, Chayanov's peasants acted on the basis of a different rationality from that of the West, and it led to evident paradoxes. Because it would have caused seasonal unemployment, they refused to adopt the threshing machine, even though it would have been more economical in bookkeeping terms. Similarly, they cultivated labor-intensive crops such as flax and potatoes, which were less profitable than other crops such as oats. They also paid higher rent for the land than any profit they could obtain from it, if calculated according to capitalist criteria (1925, pp. 39–40).

## Production and Consumption

Extensive cultivation was carried out on the demesne (Kula 1962, pp. 44ff.). On the large estate, the harvest was proportional to the cultivated surface area, and the number of serfs was commensurate with the size of the demesne.

The noble tried to maintain high labor intensity on the demesne, the aim here being to create a surplus. Short-term fluctuations in production, which were enormous, usually depended on noneconomic factors such as the climate, wars, epidemics, and other natural calamities. Surplus products exceeding what was needed to reactivate the agrarian cycle were used for direct and indirect consumption; namely, they could meet internal demand directly or do so indirectly by being commercialized.

An analysis of consumption of the demesne is of great interest. Direct consumption was considerable and made up most of the total consumption. It was made up not so much of the personal consumption of the noble and his family, which was in general rather modest. What really did have an effect was consumption for the court—the social rank of a noble depended on the rank of the clients he had to maintain. Indirect consumption, on the other hand, was "conspicuous consumption" in the sense of Veblen (1899) and was made up of luxury articles that the noble needed to assert his status. These goods generally came from abroad and were handled by only a small number of markets, principally in the great port city of Gdansk. They were exchanged for part of the surplus agricultural products, according to the terms of trade (the ratio between the prices of the articles sold and those of the articles bought).

However, Kula's first surprising discovery was that the investments of the feudal enterprise were independent of both the volumes of surplus produced and the terms of trade. In other words, deciding whether to sow more, to buy equipment, or to extend the cultivable area was not path dependent, nor was it sensitive to improved terms of trade. If there was a succession of good harvest years, the lord did not make greater investments but merely put greater quantities of product on the market, and in this way achieved a higher standard of living. When the terms of trade grew worse, the lord did not disinvest (because by doing so he would have spoiled his image) but on the contrary tried to increase production. This happened either by increasing labor intensity (i.e., the services demanded of the serfs) or by changing the ratio (always flexible) between the area of the demesne and that of the peasant plots, to the detriment of the latter. Either way, the lord acted on the distribution of social income—in other words, the sharing out of the cake—rather than increase its size.

Hence, the feudal enterprise did not follow market logic and, paradoxically, often went counter to market signals. The noble did not have profits to maximize. His one aim was to maintain (or not to lower) his status as reflected in his lifestyle. Choices relating to production were adjusted as a function of this requirement.

## Supply and Demand

The volume of agricultural products exchanged via the market was exceedingly unstable and depended exclusively on the exogenous factors that have been mentioned. Because the fraction of product for consumption was largely constant, the part that was commercialized was a direct reflection of fluctuations in the harvest and thus yet again the incidence of natural and human factors over which there was little control.

From a global point of view, or interpreted in aggregate terms, this is a valid way of reasoning. If, on the other hand, we take the economy of the small peasant plots, the quantity of surplus product left over after meeting domestic needs was always negligible. Relations with the market were sporadic and limited to the need for finding the money to pay state taxes, the additional levies on the part of the noble landowner, and monetary debts. Even these sums tended to be constant, so that whatever was sold (often to the detriment of consumption) was inversely proportional to the level of the prices. If market prices in year 2 were higher than in year 1, the peasant could simply sell a smaller quantity of products to meet his obligations. But if they were lower, he was forced to sell more (Kula 1962, pp. 43, 57). Very often the peasant went to the market to sell but did not make any purchases. In any case, purchases were mainly of non-indispensable goods and were thus postponable. In this connection, Kula speaks of "one-sided contacts" with the market (pp. 67–68).

In the feudal system, and in this case in peasant economic behavior, the speculative drive is absent once again (p. 43). And once again we come across a reversal in the connection between prices and economic decisions. Figure 4.1a shows this typical phenomenon of the feudal economy, which is unintentional and therefore independent of the agents' will. When prices increase—for example, following an outward shift of the demand curve from D to $D_1$—supply contracts (from S to $S_1$). The "anomalous" functioning of this market is particularly evident when compared with the prediction of neoclassical theory (figure 4.1b), according to which the shift of the demand curve and the movement along the supply curve are coordinated, with supply following demand. Indeed, the arrows in the graph have the same direction. In Kula's model, conversely, the process is uncoordinated, with supply moving independently of demand. This indicates that the producers do not respond to price signals. Another important element is the form of the supply curve. In the feudal system, it is vertical and indicates perfectly inelastic supply, a sign of the producers' complete disregard for the profit motive.

Thus, a correlation does exist between quantities and prices that gives rise to an empirical regularity, but there is not a causal link. The variation in the quantities exchanged is not caused by prices, following a logic contrary to that operating in the capitalist system; the link between the two measures is only indirect.

Underlying this correlation are two sorts of circumstances: cultural and material. Included among the former is the fact that status in this type of society cannot be achieved by means of economic acquisition. These societies are ascriptive and are characterized by a very low level of social mobility.[2] From the point of view of the nobleman, it does not count to have increasing amounts of money, and he is not anxious to become wealthier. What might count, on the other hand, is to have more than others. Wealth in general is thus a sort of "positional good," in Fred

---

[2] The "status ascription—status achievement" dichotomy was formulated by the anthropologist Ralph Linton (1936) and was the inspiration for the controversial book of the psychologist David McClelland (1961). We owe Richard Tawney this fine definition of acquisitive society: "Such societies may be called Acquisitive Societies, because their whole tendency and interest and preoccupation is to promote the acquisition of wealth" (1920, p. 29). The "achievement" of Linton does not necessarily imply "acquisition" in Tawney's sense, but the historical connection between these two aspects seems clear.

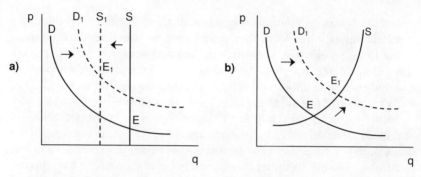

Figure 4.1. Price formation in a feudal economy (a) and the neoclassical model (b)

Hirsch's (1976, ch. 3) interesting concept. From the point of view of the peasant, once subsistence level has been reached the economic drive is even less important. His problem is to obtain what experience has taught him is enough to sustain his family and maximize his free time. Werner Sombart argued that preindustrial man worked to live and did not live to work. He "had towards economic activity the same psychical attitude as a child towards learning in a school, to which he would certainly not submit if he was not obliged to." Moreover, with labor "there was never any hurry."[3] In this type of context, if the labor supply curve had to be represented on a graph, it would very soon slant backward or would perhaps remain always vertical. Faced with the trade-off between extra hours of work and free time, preindustrial man did not find it difficult to choose (Kula 1962, p. 172).

The economic ethos of the serf is neatly summed up in this formula: "If a surplus was created, everything inclined the peasant to consume it all; if a deficit resulted, the peasant attempted to pass it on to the lord" (p. 63). The peasant always knew how to pass on any deficits to the lord. In a poor year he could keep his consumption at the same level as previously, at the expense of cattle or seeds, which the lord would have then had to replenish. The serf was an indispensable asset on the demesne, but if the peasant attempted to get rich, "the lord was an ever-present threat" (p. 62). It might be pointed out that this type of dynamic had significant analogies with the behavior of public employees in the Soviet bloc countries.

[3] Sombart (1913, p. 20). By "preindustrial man," I mean the ancestor of the *moderne Wirtschaftsmensch* (the "modern economic man"). In English, the expression "premodern man," which is closer to the author's terminology, would sound ambiguous. In any case, it is worth pointing out that Sombart traces the genesis of the "modern economic spirit" to a period that preceded the first industrial revolution by about a hundred years.

Material circumstances lie in the physical limitation to the productive possibilities of the feudal economy (p. 55). In the capitalist system, producers can opportunistically exploit price increases for two reasons: labor reserves can be found in one or another sector of the economy, and a credit market exists to make their use possible. In the feudal system, these two conditions do not exist because the quantity of available labor is always limited and credit does not have productive potential but is for consumption. In addition, constraints of an institutional nature (the secondary sector being organized in guilds) would in any case prevent the mobilization of reserves toward the primary sector. Besides in the feudal system the manufacturing producers are price makers, and in microeconomic terms the guild has a collective monopoly (p. 78).

But even if all these obstacles were removed, the most important aspect would remain: in the feudal system, cyclical price movements are not predictable. A strong fluctuation in one direction might be countered the following year by an equally strong fluctuation in the other. And because a rise in prices is typically due to a poor harvest, in the years when prices are high the meager supplies are soon exhausted long before the seasonal rise in prices occurs (pp. 57–58). This pattern, which is actually not exclusive to the feudal system, has made it possible to extend and adapt Kula's model to the economy of early modern Europe, as we will see.

## The Rationality of Agents: Overcoming Weber's Deadlock

At this point a question might arise. Was the economic activity that took place in early modern Poland rational? If by rational economic activity one means the minimization of means or the maximization of results, behavior could be considered rational when there is more than one possible solution for any given state of technique, and there is the possibility of comparing existing alternatives in order to choose the most economical one (Kula 1962, p. 168).

If we adopt this concept, it is clear that the world described by Kula will appear dominated by irrationality. Because from the physical point of view investments and results are expressed in different units of measurement, a comparison is possible only where there is a common denominator, which is the money price. This price, with a tendency to be uniform, has to be formed on a competitive market and to be applicable as much to products as to factors of production. Thus, for example, market wages will need to exist, and a labor market even before that (p. 165).

In the feudal system there is no free competition, there are numerous limitations to the freedom of choice of producer and consumer, and the overwhelming majority of the workforce is left outside the labor market, which in any case is rigidly regulated. To a certain degree, even the prices of goods are controlled and limited by public authorities. As to the possibilities of choice, it is clear they have proved to be wider in the capitalist system. In the first place, the possibilities for choice depend not only on the level of technology but also on the nature of the society; a society can refuse technically available alternatives as being contrary to its values, norms, or laws. The historical breakthrough of the capitalist system has been accompanied by scientific progress and by increased social mobility; the latter has replaced the acceptance of a destiny passed down at birth with the social approval of gain as a means of acquiring status (pp. 166–68).

However, some Western economists, convinced as they are that "the world in which they are living is the only 'natural,' 'free' world, 'the best of worlds,'" do not appreciate that in it there are also limitations to the freedom of choice (p. 168). The problem of rationality is thus a problem of quantity, not of existence, should one even wish to interpret rationality the way they do (p. 167).

In the modern Western world, technical improvements can be introduced to increase labor productivity, but it is not possible to trade in slaves and set them to work in factories, even though this would be profitable. Child labor is prevented by a general sensitivity, as well as by the law. However in the manufacturing plants of the early modern period it was allowed, though they might not have had the right to vary the assortment of articles to produce. The length of the working day (and week) depended on such arbitrary factors then as now. Industrial society agrees to the comparative publicity of consumer goods, which might turn out to be dishonest or even fraudulent, while it does not tolerate a pharmaceutical drug being advertised as a panacea. Centuries ago, the exact opposite happened (p. 168).

Hence, there does not seem to be much sense in disconnecting rationality from the values that orientate it. Choices are made in all socioeconomic formations. In no system, however, are they carried out in absolute freedom. This means that choices do not depend exclusively on economic calculation but are socially and culturally determined (p. 169). One might say that modern capitalist societies are more performative:

> Nevertheless, men in a pre-capitalist economy are also involved in making economic calculations, if only in their own way. Sombart was mistaken when he considered accounting an invention of the "capitalist spirit." It is possible that in pre-capitalist periods extra-economic elements enter into calculations more often—but neither are these elements altogether foreign to the calculations characteristic of capitalism. (pp. 34–35)

The confusion that Kula hinted at, and that still characterizes the debate on rationality in the social sciences, in fact goes back to Max Weber. Weber dedicated the last years of his life studying the evolution of Western rationality and introduced a dual concept of rationality: the "substantive rationality" and the "formal rationality" of economic action. The former involves seeking coherence between economic behavior and values, whereas the latter coherence between means and ends (Weber 1956–64, pp. 85ff.). This dualism was to lead to what we could call "Weber's deadlock," or the misunderstanding, in which economics is still trapped, between rationality and wealth maximization.

With modernization, in Weber's account, society frees itself from magic and superstition, authority is no longer the charismatic kind but has a rational-legal basis, and public affairs are no longer administered under the absolute discretion of a privileged elite but entrusted to a bureaucracy recruited on the basis of merit. But it becomes difficult for substantive rationality to survive in such a context. Because of the predominance of the economic (it should be said contractual) sphere, loyalty to religious or family values (kinship) turns out to be difficult in the modern world. Appropriation of the physical means of production, market freedom, the use of rational technology, calculable (i.e., predictable) instead of arbitrary law, free labor markets, and the commercialization of economic life are all phenomena connected to the development of formal rationality.[4]

Weber's idea of sociology as an "idiographic" science (i.e., historical and case specific) and his tendency to reason by ideal types naturally led him to focus on the only experience of modernization and rationalization that he could have observed—namely, the Western one. So it is not clear whether he would have acknowledged the possibility of other paths to modernization that did not involve the stages mentioned previously. It is a well-known fact that Weber's explanation for the Western transition from one type of rationality to the other was the triumph of the Protestant ethic (1920, pp. 123–24). Indeed, the values it conveys coincide with the conduct of "formal rationality," which translates into "world mas-

[4] The anthropologist Stephen Gudeman (2008) has recently suggested that the development of calculative reason might depend on the degree of competition in the economic context. The more competitive a system is, the wider the choice between alternatives, and our mind tends to operate in accordance with a formal rationality principle à la Weber. The sociologist Peter Wagner (2000, pp. 29–32), noting how rational choice theory is a typically American phenomenon, connects its origins to the quite exceptional circumstance of the settlement in the New World of individuals uprooted from their respective contexts of origin. Having lost their value commitment, they were left only with instrumental rationality. However, I believe that the latter does not exist in its pure state and that the condition of being uprooted has actually reinforced the radicalization of the prevailing values of Puritan inspiration.

tery." But this does not resolve the problem of the neutrality of the formal rationality concept that Weber had in mind.[5] It is identified with capitalism, the "iron cage" that survives itself and turns into the "mechanical foundations" of human action. Weber's deadlock arises from the illusion that this "iron cage" can *really* be separated from the value structure of the society that has produced it.

Sombart, who did not share Weber's emphasis on the Protestant ethic as the triggering cause of Western rationalization, maintained that economic calculation was basically alien to European traditional societies, and to back up this argument he used examples of misuse of calculation that had systematically been made (1913, p. 18). This imprecise use of calculation was not restricted to economic activity but extended to all areas of life. Sombart speaks of "imperfections of thought" (*unvolkommenheiten im Denken*) and even of "poor development of the intellectual skills" (p. 17). This claim cannot be generalized and has to be qualified. In his famous book on Rabelais, Lucien Febvre showed that in the sixteenth century people often had a vague idea of their real age and more generally did not consider that precision was important. The cyclical pattern of rural life, closely linked to the rhythms of nature and liturgy, left little space for novelty; hence, it was quite pointless to force oneself to measure things beyond a certain point (1942, pp. 150, 391–99). John Nef adds that the aptitude for quantification began to change in the following century (1958, p. 8). But these facts certainly do not suggest that early modern people had a cognitive defect: it was merely an attitude that matched the operative context. Indeed, large landowners, monasteries, hospitals, public institutions, and obviously merchants kept extremely sophisticated accounts. Our knowledge of Asia, which has grown enormously in the course of the twentieth century, offers an equally diversified panorama (Goody 1996, pp. 24ff.).

Polanyi (1944; 1957b) drew widely on Weber, whose *Economy and Society* came out posthumously in the early 1920s. Polanyi's definition of "economic" action perfectly reflects the Weberian formal-substantive dichotomy. But it is precisely his belief in this dichotomy that led him to argue for the disembeddedness of the modern economy. Just as for Weber modern rationality is disengaged from values, so for Polanyi the modern economy is disengaged from society. Even Marxist thought, with a few notable exceptions (Godelier 1966), has traditionally described rationality as a product of capitalism—a product that could of course be

---

[5] The concept of "formal rationality of economic action" is to do with the idea of "instrumental rationality." However, it has been pointed out that in Weber's theory of action "wants are . . . not merely given, but evaluated. . . . Instrumental rationality thus is involved in the selection of ends, not just means" (S. D. Parsons 2003, p. 66). See also Swedberg (1998, p. 37).

perfected, and indeed was destined to be made more efficient in the economic system that would take over from capitalism.

The Weberian interpretations miss a central point: neoclassical economic calculation is not the only type of economic calculation that exists. The aim of a public hospital, today as in the early modern period, is not to make a profit, yet this does not prevent it from operating in such a way as to avoid waste. But when it comes to defining what waste is and which constraints to abide by, values come into play and are decisive. In contrast, most modern firms are profit-oriented, but the pursuit of profit does not imply a special type of rationality: profit itself is a value. The Polish serfs' aversion to labor, just as much as the propensity of the workers at General Motors to do overtime, is value oriented. The "emancipation from magic" has little or nothing to do with these different attitudes.

## Extensions of the Model

*An Economic Theory of the Feudal System* had a very profound impact on European historiography. In the 1970s, the Italian historian Marco Cattini (1973; 1984) worked on a microeconomic model for northern Italy that ultimately showed interesting points of contact with Kula's. He gathered a considerable quantity of data on the production, consumption, and exchange of grain in the area between the River Po and the Apennines in the early modern period.

This was an area with very different institutional aspects from those in Poland. Whereas Poland was dominated by the feudal system, in the country areas of the Po Valley with the scattered towns that had formerly been free medieval communes, there was a system of widespread landownership. In the same region, small, medium, and large landowners could coexist side by side. The latter often let their land holdings to tenant farmers. However, agricultural productivity was significantly less than in the more fertile lands north of the Po. This was due to the physicochemical properties of the soil (which tended to be clayey) and to not having a dense network of canals such as those that irrigated the Lombard plain. Nor by any means could it be compared to the productivity of northwestern Europe.

In Cattini's model, society was obviously not separated into two distinct orders as in Poland. Though it was a long way from the large centers of European merchant capitalism, the context was not entirely immune from its influences. On the juridical and formal levels, there was a greater degree of freedom. Nonetheless, cultural conditioning was at work that produced similar economic effects. Theoretically a land market did exist, and nothing prevented land from being bought and sold, but in practice this happened only in exceptional cases. Land was the last resource to be given up and only in the case of overwhelming debt. The tendency was to keep it intact as long as possible so that it could be passed on to the future generations.

The behavior of households was oriented toward autarky, as in the models of Chayanov and Kula. The values of the small owners were similar to those of the Polish peasants; but the large owners were not disinterested in profits despite sharing the concern for status with the aristocrats of eastern Europe. Many were from the bourgeoisie, but there existed a variety of intermediate levels. The mid-seventeenth century saw the appearance of the field hand—the peasant who was left landless following a period of agrarian crises—but not even in this case did one see the emergence of what could be called a labor market. Labor was intermittent (seasonal), and wages, which were mainly settled in kind, were independent of labor supply and demand and apparently followed the subsistence level criterion.

Starting from the data on prices and quantities of wheat exchanged in the village of San Felice sul Panaro between 1590 and 1630, Cattini obtained the market supply and demand curves. The dots that form the scatter plot for demand have a particular pattern: they form an inverse logistic curve (figure 4.2). From a dynamic point of view, it is the product of the movement in opposite directions of a negatively inclined demand curve and a vertical, or at most weakly positive sloping, supply curve (Cattini 1984, pp. 111–13).

The state of technique prevented agents from governing economic fluctuations. As wide fluctuations in output took place from one year to another, it was impossible to predict the market prices. In a neoclassical world, when these prices rise, one would expect a drop in the demand for goods. But this correlation was not the case for the Italian economy, because the price increase was due to famine; and again famine was what forced the consumers to get from the market what they could not produce themselves. Similarly, supply did not increase when market prices rose. Instead, it reached a peak when prices were low. This correlation occurred because only when output was plentiful (and prices low) was there a surplus that could be sold on the market.

Therefore the same uncoordinated dynamics of supply and demand that we saw in Kula's model were produced. In this case as well, the peasants' aversion toward the market, which was already deeply rooted in popular culture, was further reinforced. On the other hand, as it was impossible for them to utilize prices as signals, the large landowners were discouraged from making opportunistic calculations or from making any investments toward producing a surplus for commercialization.

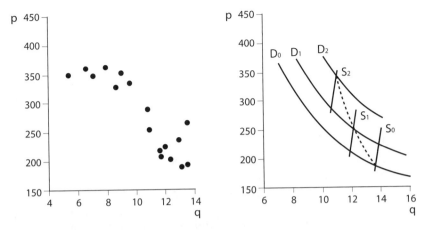

Figure 4.2. Market demand for wheat in the Po Valley
*Note*: quantities are expressed in thousands of *stari modenesi*; prices in *soldi*.
1 *staro* = 63.25 liters. *Source*: Cattini (1984, p. 110).

In his comparative analysis of subsistence crises in preindustrial Europe, which owes much to his previous works on Germany, Wilhelm Abel (1974) showed how the factors capable of causing famine were totally beyond control until the seventeenth century. Subsequently the rationalization and improvement of agricultural techniques in the northwestern areas gradually reduced the margin of fluctuation in cereal prices. This process continued and extended to central and southern Europe until the mid-nineteenth century when the problem of agricultural underproduction ceased, with some notable exceptions though.

According to the meticulous study carried out by Andrew Appleby (1978), the last nationwide famine in England dates back to 1597; in 1623 the country suffered another crisis, but this time it was limited to the North, and to Cumbria in particular. If local and regional food shortages certainly occurred in the early seventeenth century, in comparative terms the southern counties had an unquestionable advantage. The natural fertility of these lands and the ease with which they could be worked were hard to match in other parts of Europe.

It is somewhat misleading to use the term famine, which suggests a sudden and catastrophic event, to indicate the structural problems of many preindustrial societies. The subsistence crises or, as Jean Meuvret called them, "old-type economic crises," show a typical dynamic: they are marked by a rise in the prices of foodstuffs that then spreads to the whole economy (1977, p. 16). But they were often the result of a recurring series of small traumatic events—as happened in the 1590s (P. Clark

1985)—and human factors such as war were added to natural causes. Malnutrition and passing armies were sources of diseases in their turn, and so the spiral continued.[6]

In western Europe, self-sufficiency was a difficult target to reach no matter how actively it was pursued. This was all the more so for the lower layers of society, which were driven to resorting to the market by the chronic insufficiency of domestic production.[7] The peasants lacked the safety net that east of the Elbe was held out by the feudal lord, who was obliged to guarantee reproduction of the labor force working on his estate. In the context of the Italian communes, relief institutions that had been inherited from the Roman world did exist. These included public granaries, successors of the *annona*, whereby the public authorities took on the task of supplementing the needs of households in difficulty with the town's grain stocks. Their working was sophisticated, acting as a kind of forerunner to the welfare state (Corritore 2007; see also Marin and Virlouvet 2003). Wherever this level of social protection fell short, however, the market was all that remained.

Yet even in the West the relationship with the market was seen as a necessary evil. This is evident from observing the price-wage dynamics. It is unrelated, or at most divergent, as happens in northern France where market formation (as well as for labor) was historically much earlier.[8] When prices for foodstuffs were low, wages were typically high. On the other hand, when bread became dearer, wages went down. This small paradox suggests that the peasants sold their labor only in the years of poor harvests (as reflected in the price rises).

A similar argument applies to the wide range of occupations that complemented agricultural work and that included textile manufacturing and the putting-out system in which the peasants were occupied to supplement the family budget and procure the money they needed. They worked long enough to be able to balance the family budget, hence longer in the years of famine and less in the years of good harvest. In other words, they behaved like "target producers" rather than like "market producers" (Aymard 1983, p. 1398).

In his study of the region of Beauvais, to the north of Paris, in the seventeenth century, Pierre Goubert (1960) showed that food surpluses

---

[6] Comparative overviews are offered by Rotberg and Rabb (1985); Newman (1990); Ó Gráda (2009). For a comparison with the ancient Mediterranean economies, see Garnsey (1988); Hanson (1998).

[7] Aymard (1983, p. 1394); Meuvret (1987, p. 208). The phenomenon of selling cereals on the market to the detriment of domestic food consumption has also been documented in rural societies of West Africa and southern India and seems to be directly correlated with the degree of poverty of the household (Hill 1982, p. 51).

[8] Aymard (1983, p. 1396). On wage stickiness, see Meuvret (1977, pp. 37–38).

were produced systematically for export only in the southern part of this region, which was the nearest to the capital. In the northern part, households had something to trade only in the exceptionally good years, while in the normal years they were barely able to produce what was necessary for self-sufficiency, and in the poor years they risked malnutrition.[9]

Concerning the supply of labor, Goubert gave a warning:

> The wage in the seventeenth century appears to us as a sort of recompense in kind that could at times take on the form of money. . . . As for "wage earners" and the "wage system," the language of the seventeenth century does not have any knowledge of such nouns, and what we in the twentieth century name as such cannot easily be transferred three centuries into the past. Except for a small number of professions in some of the large towns . . . in this period I see no homogeneous groups of men without any property, whether moveable or real, or without any "means of production" that could permanently live on a monetary wage, whether it be their only income or even their main income.[10]

Taking works such as these as his starting point, Braudel (1979) would later produce his metanarrative *Civilization and Capitalism*. In this interpretive model of the preindustrial economy, three levels are distinguished: material life, market economy, and capitalism. The material life level is the one in which most of the population of the world and Europe was immersed between the fifteenth and eighteenth centuries. History was experienced as being seemingly immobile and characterized by repetitive gestures, habits, and routines. Terms such as "structure," "depth," or "unconscious" are often used to describe a history made by men and women but in a certain sense independently of their will. Far from being postmodern, this type of language depicts collective categories in which individual actions are objectively constrained and conditioned. At the material-life level, people lived in close contact with the land, within a system tending toward self-sufficiency. Their encounter with the market was occasional and almost never happened out of choice.

Above this level, there was the market economy, which could be of two types. The first type was a regulated market, or a "public market." Goods from short and medium distances generally converged onto these

---

[9] "Aux années de disette, les pauvres mouraient partout" (Goubert 1960, p. 105). In good years grain yields might reach 6:1 (or 900 kilograms per hectare), and the surplus that could be commercialized thus amounted to around a third of production. The quantities produced fluctuated considerably: between a good year and a bad one, the harvest more than halved (p. 104).

[10] Goubert (1960, p. 547). "The very diversified range of wages in the seventeenth century should lead the historian tempted by statistics to be very cautious; he would refuse to create a metaphysical type of rural waged worker without age or expertise, outside of time, the seasons of the year and especially of places" (p. 522).

markets, and the quality and prices of the products were controlled by the town authorities and made transparent. The second type of market, the "private market," on the other hand was for financial activities, luxury goods, and all the types of goods that lent themselves to speculation after being transported over long distances. Capitalism, which forms the third level of the scheme, fed on these types of transactions, operated in the short term of the particular economic situation, and pushed the system toward anarchy.

As Braudel puts it,

> To my mind, the fundamental characteristic of the pre-industrial economy is the coexistence of the inflexibility, inertia, and slow motion characteristic of an economy that was still primitive, alongside trends—limited and in the minority, yet active and powerful—that were characteristic of modern growth. On the one hand, peasants lived in their villages in an almost autonomous way, virtually in an autarchy; on the other hand, a market-oriented economy and an expanding capitalism began to spread out, gradually creating the very world in which we live, and, at that early date, prefiguring our world. (1977, p. 5)

In the Braudelian metanarrative, the three forms described by Polanyi (1957b)—reciprocity, redistribution, and exchange—thus coexist at the same time, though differing in importance. The particularly interesting aspect is the way in which they are combined in a dynamic model that is able to explain the change because it shows how the germs of modernity were already present in a context that was otherwise dominated by tradition.

## The View from Economic Anthropology

According to the development economist Daniel Thorner (1964), who in the 1960s reintroduced Chayanov's work to the West, the "double orientation" of household producers characterized most peasant economies of the twentieth century. They were autarkic as regards the production of essential goods for household consumption (notably cereals) but looked to the market for nonessential goods (fruit and especially raw materials). Under the definition of peasant economy, he included economies that responded to various criteria: the agricultural sector provides at least half the total production and occupies at least half the active population; there exists some form of concentration of political power at the state level; there is a certain degree of differentiation between urban and rural areas; at least half the agricultural production is produced and consumed by rural households, without going via the market.

Apart from India, with which he was directly concerned, Thorner believed that even in the twentieth century the concept of peasant economies involved a considerable part of the world population: Indonesia, China, Japan until World War I, Mexico until the interwar period, and naturally the tsarist Russia studied by Chayanov.

It was a rather restrictive definition, in that, for example, it excluded organizational forms of economic activity in Europe between the fall of the Roman Empire and the late Middle Ages (p. 420). However Thorner's objective was to construct a sufficiently homogeneous historical survey to enable him to infer theoretical tools for analyzing developing countries, because he was convinced that the models of neoclassical and Keynesian economics were not suited for this task. Gunnar Myrdal, the great Swedish economist, also shared the same conviction. His *Asian Drama* opens with this statement:

> Economic theorists, more than other social scientists, have long been disposed to arrive at general propositions and then postulate them as valid for every time, place, and culture. There is a tendency in contemporary economic theory to follow this path to the extreme. For such confidence in the constructs of economic reasoning, there is no empirical justification. . . . As long as their use is restricted to our part of the world this pretense of generality may do little harm.[11] But when theories and concepts designed to fit the special conditions of the Western world . . . are used in the study of underdeveloped countries in South Asia, where they do *not* fit, the consequences are serious. (1968, vol. 1, pp. 16–17)

To replace the tools offered by Western economic theories with concepts having sufficiently wide-ranging explanatory power to apply to the investigation of other parts of the world, it was necessary to go to the roots of economic behavior (Dalton 1971; Hill 1986). First, it was necessary to ask what was meant by economic action, and what its universal significance was in relation to human behavior. Since the times of Vilfredo Pareto (1906), the endorsement for neoclassical microeconomics had rested on the assumption that in human behavior an "economic" component (by definition self-interested, utilitarian, individualist, and maximizing) could be separated from a "social" component (altruistic, relational, and often irrational). Pareto knew very well that *homo oeconomicus* did not actually exist, but he did not realize that his approach involved an arbitrary operation to decide which forms of behavior to consider "economic" and which not. Why should we consider the egoistic forms of behavior economic and not, for example, the relational

[11] He had also written: "Throughout this book I am making the generous assumption that the Western approach is fairly adequate to Western conditions. This might be an overstatement" (Myrdal 1968, vol. 1, p. 16, n. 2).

forms? The result is a sort of cognitive utopia, for which there is economics on the one hand and sociology on the other, with both aiming at studying nonexistent subjects (undersocialized or oversocialized human behavior).

In the twentieth century, while Parsons and Smelser (1956) were still endorsing this system to some extent (cf. Harry Pearson 1957, p. 313; Hodgson 2001, pp. 184ff.), Pareto's scientistic dream was interrupted by results from field research carried out by the anthropologists. An analysis of the simplest forms of economic organization was necessary before it was possible to understand what economic action was. In the already cited *Argonauts of the Western Pacific*, Bronislaw Malinowski (1922) proved that humankind does not have an inborn tendency to pursue gain. During his stay in Melanesia in the years of World War I, he found no trace of the bargaining savages described by Adam Smith (1776, p. 27). While the natives appeared to him to be no more and no less rational than their Western contemporaries, their actions were oriented toward reciprocity and cooperation.[12]

Other phenomena were at odds with the idea of economic activity as understood by the inhabitants of the industrial West. One of these is the *potlatch* practiced by the Kwakiutl Indians of British Columbia, which was described by Franz Boas (1897, pp. 341ff.) and taken up by his student Ruth Benedict (1934, pp. 195ff.). Here the actors competed not by accumulating wealth but by depriving themselves of it. The more a person was able to show he could give, the more he rose in the social hierarchy.

But the most organic and influential analysis was Marshall Sahlins's *Stone Age Economics* (1972). Sahlins attacked the formalist conception of economics starting with its central postulate, that of scarcity: he argued controversially against the viewpoint maintained by Lionel Robbins that "scarcity is not an intrinsic property of technical means" but "a relation between means and ends" (p. 5). Using the quantitative evidence of fieldwork on the Australian aborigines and the Bushmen of the Kalahari to back up his argument, he noted that primitive populations spent only a few hours a day looking for and preparing food. The pace of work was extremely relaxed and allowed for days in the week that were entirely given over to resting. Despite this, these peoples were able to acquire ample food for their caloric requirements. From the nutritional point of view, the diet even proved to be quite varied (pp. 14ff.).

How was it possible for peoples who had never even experienced the Neolithic agricultural transition to be in a state of relative affluence? The

---

[12] The rationality of the "savage mind" is argued in the classic works of Boas (1911) and Goody (1977), who takes up Lévi-Strauss (1962).

reply is simple: they were characterized by limited wants (pp. 2, 39). "Limited" is to do with a spontaneous state of affairs, and should not be understood in the sense of "restricted." In other words, there was no "struggle of the hunter against his own worse nature," no "renunciation of an acquisitiveness that in reality was never developed," and no "suppression of desires" (p. 13). The range of a society's wants is culturally determined.[13]

In this connection one is reminded of what Tacitus wrote, around A.D. 98, on the subject of the "wonderful savageness" (*mira feritas*) of the Fennians, the Sami people of Scandinavia: "They consider this life happier than the life spent toiling in the cultivation of the land and in domestic chores, in the constant preoccupation of defending one's wealth and limiting that of others. Safe against men, safe against the gods, they are successful in the most difficult thing; that of having nothing else to desire."[14]

Taking characteristics they have in common, Sahlins defines the economic organization that typifies primitive economies, what he calls the "Domestic Mode of Production" (DMP):[15]

- These economies are nonintensive and underutilize the available labor force. The division of labor is not uniform nor is it aimed at seeking efficiency but is mostly gender based.
- Technology is produced by households and tailored to their requirements; hence, it is easy to use for those who make it (but which does not exclude it being sophisticated and ingenious). Knowledge of the natural world is adequate and extremely well developed for classifying edible species of the vegetable and animal kingdoms.[16]
- The economy is oriented to mere reproduction, or production for use, as opposed to production for exchange. "The DMP is intrinsically an anti-surplus system" (Sahlins 1972, p. 82).

Household production follows "Chayanov's rule," whereby labor intensity does not increase with the quantity of labor available: on the contrary, the greater the household's labor capacity, the less its members

[13] This aspect is fully taken up in Sahlins (1976a).
[14] "Sed beatius arbitrantur quam ingemere agris, inlaborare domibus, suas alienasque fortunas spe metuque versare; securi adversus homines, securi adversus deos rem difficillimam adsecuti sunt, ut illis ne voto quidem opus esset" (*Germania* 46.5, my translation).
[15] Sahlins (1972, ch. 2). This formula is obtained by combining the concept of the "closed domestic economy" (*geschlossene Hauswirtschaft*) of the German historical economist Karl Bücher (1901, p. 108) with Marx's idea of "mode of production," but leaving out the adjective *geschlossene*, which described a situation of total self-sufficiency.
[16] On this point, cf. Fowler and Turner (1999).

work (p. 87). Sahlins clarifies that precisely the tendency to underutilize the factors of production means that the household not infrequently misses the target of self-sufficiency, which would otherwise be easy to reach (in any case, in overall terms the ratio between product and population is still balanced). This is where redistribution and exchange come into play. With redistribution the central role of politics is brought in. Politics is often the trigger for intensifying production—whoever deliberately produces a surplus does so in order to redistribute it, thus acquiring power (pp. 130ff.).

Exchange can originate from an actual state of material need, and even take the form of a "frankly utilitarian trade," but it is still "oriented to livelihood, not to profits" (p. 83). In all other cases, in primitive societies exchange takes on the nonmaterial character of the gift, interpreted by Mauss (1923–24) as a means of social alliance. It is a vehicle for expressing the sociality of the human animal and is an efficient means for preventing conflicts.[17]

The interests of economic anthropology do not stop at societies of hunter-gatherers. In the 1960s and 1970s with postcolonial economies increasingly opening up to international trade, scholars recognized a fascinating terrain for investigation—namely, the problem of the encounter/clash of rural populations with capitalism and the market economy. The concept of "peripheral markets" used by Bohannan and Dalton (1962) to describe economic systems in which market prices have little or no feedback on production decisions can be usefully applied to the ancient and early modern economies as well. Their idea of "spheres of exchange" seems even more topical: goods are not universally commensurable even in our own society, and though we do not notice it, exchange is considered appropriate only within sets of goods perceived as homogeneous in some way (Espeland and Stevens 1998).

In the wake of Polanyi—and of Marx too, of course—others focused on the "moral" nature of peasant economies (moral in that peasants were tied by a bond of mutual obligation to the community, which also guaranteed them assistance in times of need). The breakup of this universe would produce a collective trauma and lead to social rebellion (James Scott 1976; Halperin and Dow 1977). These interpretations, regardless of their importance for historiography (see Hobsbawm 1959; Thompson 1971), were undoubtedly shaped by the years in which they were formulated and do not lend themselves to generalization.[18] But the idea of studying householding from the point of view of decision making as well

---

[17] Sahlins (1972, ch. 4). On the anthropological interpretations of exchange, see John Davis's (1992) excellent synthesis.

[18] For a balanced analysis of peasant protest, see Wolf (1966, pp. 106ff.) and Fassin's (2009) reappraisal.

as from the point of view of its connections with the social system is still something of a challenge for economic anthropology and cultural ecology (Wilk 1989; Halperin 1994, ch. 5).

In their study on the peasants of Colombia conducted in the 1970s and 1980s, Stephen Gudeman and Alberto Rivera describe a rural society dedicated to reproducing wealth, rather than to producing it. This society identified wealth with the cultivation of the land and animal husbandry. House and farm formed the "base," and any increases had to be put back into the "base." It is a very similar conception of the economy to that of the Physiocrats in eighteenth-century France (1990, pp. 30ff.; see also Gudeman 1986, ch. 4).

The entire economy revolved around the house, even from a symbolic point of view. The interesting fact is that the Colombian peasants worked harder, and for more modest economic results, within the confines of their house and farm than for any wages they could obtain by selling their labor on the market. What might appear to be irrational behavior is not if we bear in mind the values of the agents. Even in Panama in the 1960s, the peasants did not appear to be interested in establishing equivalences between the quantities of land, labor, and agricultural products. They used a specific measure for each thing, and there was no general unit of account: "No one was concerned that the food and work measures did not mesh one with another; the measuring rods were incommensurate" (Gudeman 2001, p. 14). Surplus product was managed in a similar way in this type of community: it was not invested on the market in accordance with profitability criteria but was saved to increase the "base."

This is also found in the study of Sheldon Annis (1987) on the Maya weavers in the highlands of midwestern Guatemala. The majority of the population, whose traditional values were rooted in Catholic syncretism, followed the "*milpa* logic," which led them to pursue self-sufficiency, with anything extra being used to enlarge the piece of land from which they gained their sustenance, or perhaps for ceremonial consumption. On the other hand, the segments of the population that had converted to Protestantism in the second half of the twentieth century as a result of the considerable missionary work of U.S. evangelical sects tended to have market-oriented behavior.

## Why Alternative Explanations Don't Work

In many aspects of life individuals are irrational, and that includes economic life. Impulsive choices, or choices based on incomplete information, on a distorted perception of the actual or expected cost-benefit ratio, and on dislikes and fears, even when they are patently unfounded, are the order of the day in decisions relating to consumption and investment, and are not even entirely absent in the sphere of production. Choices of this type form most of our day-to-day economic actions, as cognitive psychologists since the time of Herbert Simon (1955) and of Kahneman and Tversky (1974) have been pointing out. What is more, in situations of risk, even in noneconomic spheres, according to the arguments of social anthropologists and political scientists, trust is put in subjective perceptions that mainly depend on the compliance of imagined scenarios with established social norms (Douglas and Wildavsky 1982; Dake 1991). Last but not least, emotions, which play such a decisive role in orienting human behavior, cannot be ascribed to any rationality or irrationality standard (Williams 2000).

Because human beings are relatively poor decision makers, their behavior cannot be the product of cost-benefit decision making but depends on imitation and routine instead. It has been argued that this "cultural transmission" is a form of adaptation (Henrich 2002). In my view, the meaning of culture is not reducible in biological terms (see chapter 6) and the concept of *habitus* taken from social theory seems preferable to indicate the conditioning that influences our decisions.

But even when, by some remote chance, we had eliminated the cognitive limitations and cultural conditioning, rationality in any case should not be confused with utilitarianism. Whatever meaning we give to the word "utility," it is clear that the wealth maximization principle that informs rational choice theory has nothing to do with the concept of rationality.[19] The latter should be a neutral, that is to say, value-free concept, while the maximization of profit (or income) is value oriented; it is only a *particular* interpretation of the rationality principle.

In a society in which status was not correlated with profit but let us say with physical performance, the maximization of status would not go via the maximization of profit but via the number of hours spent in the gym. This would be a perfectly rational decision. We could go even further and criticize the very association of the concept of maximization

[19] I prefer to refer to wealth maximization rather than to utility maximization, because of the known tendency of economists to also include altruistic behavior in utility functions. This is generally obtained by resorting to the concept of "tastes" (Becker 1996). It has however been pointed out that "such an expansion interpreting all modes of action as rational as long as they are consistent makes the [neoclassical] concept of rationality a tautology and thus only defines the problem away" (Beckert 2002, p. 16). Amartya Sen (1977; 1987, p. 16) has criticized the association of "rationality" with "self-interest," a criticism that for the reasons just mentioned is often flatly rejected (Ross 2005, p. 149). Similarly, the ethical motivations of human behavior are affirmed in Etzioni (1988). In chapter 6, I return to this point. Here the question is not to establish the "true" nature of human beings, or whether there is actually any space for altruism in neoclassical economics, but rather to dispute the identification of rationality with acquisitive behavior.

with that of rationality. Let us imagine a Socratic individual whose ideal of life was to escape from earthly passions and pursue the right measure in all things. From his or her point of view, would being satisfied with a modest salary and/or a mediocre social position not be perhaps a rational choice?

Regardless of the problem of cognitive limitations and the other aspects that indubitably matter in the real world, to define the rationality of an action by starting from the premises of the values (and ideologies) of the observer and not of the agent is the main weakness of the rational choice narratives. The strength of an approach à la Kula lies in the assumption that the rationality of an action has to be evaluated with regard to its conformity with a given end, but that the end embodies the values held by the agent and is inseparable from them. Besides, the end is always socially determined to some extent.

Trivial confusion could at least be usefully avoided by reading *An Economic Theory of the Feudal System*. How else can one define the thesis that, because the seventeenth-century Bohemians "although paid in kind . . . could evidently distinguish between a wage of one-twelfth of the output and a wage of one-fifteenth," they were neoclassical maximizers? (Ogilvie 2001, p. 437).[20] And what is there to say about the curious attempt to show that peasants were familiar with the concept of profit through examples of this type?

> In 1616, when the community of Mildenau complained that their bailiff-tavernkeeper repeatedly "kept them into the night with all sorts of [manorial] commands, solely so that his beer would be drunk up," the court agreed "that the bailiff, with his commanding-in, seeks his own advantage [*Vorteil*] and keeps the poor people until midnight so that he may get rid of his bad beer." (p. 441)

However, Douglass North had read Kula's book. He found it "undogmatic," "scientific," "objective," and "thoughtful," and he could only conclude: "Kula . . . simply does not understand price theory" (1977b, p. 510). Indeed, when it does not dispute the evidence, mainstream economics maintains that nonmaximizing behavior is in fact maximizing behavior taking into account institutional constraints (Federico 2005, p. 182).

---

[20] Warde (2006b, p. 296, n. 27) seems to have sensed this confusion, but I see no point in his attempt to reach a compromise with the economistic approach. In his article on seventeenth-century Württemberg, it is clear that theory goes one way and the evidence another. In the space of a few pages, he argues that the peasants were "utility" maximizers (p. 293), that "market participation was visible everywhere" (p. 313), that wages were paid in kind (pp. 314ff.), and the economy overall was characterized by "underdeveloped factor markets; an orientation to a first and foremost, but not exclusively subsistence agriculture; and subjection to power-holders and rent-takers" (p. 316).

But this argument leads directly to the tautologies that have been examined in chapter 2 and to a definition of economic rationality that is so stretched as to lose any significance. For example, the conservative and risk-averse attitude of the rural populations of Southeast Asia described by James Scott (1976) becomes highly strategic behavior that readily responds to incentives in the study of Samuel Popkin. The peasant is presented "as a rational problem-solver, with a sense both of his own interests and of the need to bargain with others to achieve mutually acceptable outcomes" (1979, p. ix). Individuals not only plan their short- and long-term investments (including children and "insurance programs"), modeling them on the life-cycle theory, but freely decide to adopt some sets of norms while rejecting others, depending on the economic advantage (pp. 18–20). Yet the problem that Popkin does not seem to recognize is that the idea that a norm can be chosen contradicts the very concept of social norm.

A good example of the other tactic is the recent work of de Vries (2008). He has criticized what he calls the "idealist concept of the 'family economy'" in order to replace it with Becker's (1965) theory of the allocation of time. On the basis of this model, the family members practice a rational division between labor and leisure time with the aim of maximizing their returns opportunistically; this leads them to dedicate more and more time to occupations outside the household, attracted by the prospects of earnings and sensitive to the market-induced urge to consume. Any alternative vision is caricaturized: "There are certainly many scholars who remain locked in embrace with the lifeless forms of old ideologies, but the now-prevailing academic climate is inclined to celebrate the triumph of the will [sic!] of the self-fashioning individual" (de Vries 2008, p. 5). But is a *new* ideology any better than an *old* ideology?

The question is not whether preindustrial Europe was a "golden age" or not, as de Vries ironically puts it, dismissing a hundred years of historiographical debate. The question is the role of the autarkic culture of the household. De Vries makes a very selective use of the existing literature, citing as a canonical example the work of Louise Tilly and Joan Scott (1987), whom he considers affected by feminist bias. But are the promarket narratives that emphasize women's wage earning role (Ogilvie 2003) not perhaps also affected by feminist bias? As for the idea of the early modern peasants being pulled toward the market (or of households enthusiastically responding to market incentives, in the reformulated thesis of today), it is anything but new. In its underlying logic, the "industrious revolution" is a remake of the proto-industrialization theory, which explained urbanization and modern economic growth with the formation of a proletariat depending on the market in the country areas in the centuries preceding the industrial revolution (Kriedte et al. 1981). Naturally the term "proletariat" does not appear in the de Vries remake, in the same way it did not appear in Franklin Mendels's (1972) original version. Nevertheless, it shares a fundamental characteristic with its forerunners, whether Marxist or not: it is unhistorical.

*Pace* de Vries, it is not only the economy of "some remote and backward Russian village" (2008, p. 211): this was two-thirds of western Europe seeing nothing more than "strategies for survival" in resorting to the market. Certainly this is particularly evident in Mediterranean Europe (Sella 2008), but to judge from recent empirical investigations that we will look at in chapter 6, even the assertion that autarkic attitudes "must be located in a very distant, if not a mythic, past of England and northwestern Europe" (de Vries 2008, p. 211) seems excessive if nothing else.

Probably, the age of which we are speaking was not at all golden. On average people were unquestionably poorer in the preindustrial period, humans lived shorter lives, and they were at the mercy of nature much more than they are today. The concept of affluence described by Sahlins with reference to the societies of hunter-gatherers is of *relative* affluence, that is, it is dependent on their limited wants. Sahlins's argument was that "the market-industrial system institutes scarcity, in a manner completely unparalleled and to a degree nowhere else approximated" (1972, p. 4). While I certainly agree with the fact that in this new system the increase in wants is frenetic, I am inclined to think that scarcity initiates with the transition to settled agriculture in the Neolithic period. If we heed Ester Boserup (1965), the price of economic evolution, or of the structural change in preagricultural societies, to the advantage of future generations is paid by the generations that initiate it; they experience increased toil and a much lower quality of life.[21]

Elizabeth Cashdan, an anthropologist who certainly did not embrace the substantivist approach, summarizes the state of the question this way:

> We can . . . demolish with confidence the old stereotype that hunter-gatherers had to work all the time simply to get enough food to eat. A corollary of this mistaken view was that agriculture, being more productive, freed hunter-gatherers from their burdensome life and gave them the leisure time to "build culture" and enjoy the finer things of life. The data . . . indicate that this is not the case. Although the origin of agriculture is a complex problem, the prevailing view among anthropologists is that hunter-gatherers did not begin cultivating crops until decreased returns from hunting and

---

[21] As Jared Diamond points out, "Archaeologists have demonstrated that the first farmers in many areas were smaller and less well nourished, suffered from more serious diseases, and died on the average at a younger age than the hunter-gatherers they replaced" (1997, p. 105).

gathering—perhaps resulting from increased population density—forced them into it. (Cashdan 1989, p. 26)

The nearer we get to the industrial revolution, the greater the phenomenon of the pressure on resources appears. Before the gains in productivity resulting from the new intensive agriculture spread to the whole population, for a long time there were heavy social costs. Thomas More's dire prophesy during the enclosures of Henry VIII that sheep would end by devouring humans has to be interpreted in this sense (More 1516, p. 18).

Not even economic anthropology has remained immune from the rational choice and new institutional interpretations. The origins of the formalist approach go back to the 1930s (see Heath Pearson 2000, pp. 964ff.). Its initiators, the New Zealander Raymond Firth (1939) and the American Melville Herskovitz (1940), came under the influence of Robbins's research program.[22] These anthropologists argued that neoclassical microeconomics was generally applicable to the study of "primitive" economies. According to Firth, in primitive man economic rationality, intended as sensitivity to personal gain, was only latent and limited by social conventions, but it was ready to emerge on contact with Western man. Herskovitz thought that the theory was adequate but needed to be adapted to the context in some way. During the 1960s and 1970s, others followed the same path, eager to demolish the constructs of Polanyi or Sahlins, the best known perhaps being Scott Cook (1966) and Harold Schneider (1974).[23] The weakness of their arguments led Posner (1980a, b) to deal directly with the question, developing the model that we have discussed in chapter 2. However, he could not do without the scarcity hypothesis, moreover in a strong version. His economistic interpretation of the paradox of the *potlatch* also depended on this assumption (Posner 1980a, p. 14).

Recent quantitative research shows the continuing validity of Chayanov's hypotheses (Durrenberger and Tannenbaum 1992; 2002), and archaeological evidence suggests that even after the Neolithic revolution the long-distance exchange of goods had a merely ceremonial function and did not concern ordinary forms of consumption (Sherratt 1997, ch. 10). Despite this, in the English-speaking world, and in the United States in particular, though its supporters no longer present themselves as such

---

[22] This influence prevailed despite the fact that Firth had studied under Malinowski and Herskovitz under Boas. Firth, however, had been trained as an economist in New Zealand before arriving at the London School of Economics. Herskovitz's attempt at dialogue with economics was dismissed by Frank Knight (1941).

[23] Other contributors include Edward LeClair (1962), Frank Cancian (1966), and Percy Cohen (1967).

but rather as eclectics eager to supersede outdated contrapositions, formalist anthropology, now merged with the new institutionalism and ecological reductionism, continues to represent its maximizing peasants and the utilitarian foundations of culture.[24] Even with regard to the foragers, there are two alternatives: either they turn to the market to provide for their wants or, vice versa, they minimize some cost by staying away from it. Where a scarcity of resources cannot be assumed (Bird-David 1992), scarcity of time requires that the agents find the most efficient way to do things. But neither is time perceived in the same way in human cultures, in rural and industrial societies: one only needs to consider the astonishingly wide range of attitudes in the tiny area of the world between the Sahara and the North Sea.[25] As Rhoda Halperin used to say, anthropological generalizations under the influence of exaggerated methodological individualism lead to the unconscious projection of one's own values onto other cultures (1994, p. 22).

Openly disagreeing with these trends, Sahlins concluded the preface to the recent new edition of his *Stone Age Economics* with these words: "In the West as in the Rest, rationality is an expression of the culture, of its meaningful system of utilities, not the antithesis. To understand our economy requires the same kind of anthropological sensibility we bring to the study of others. We are one of the others. Forget economic anthropology. We need a truly anthropological economics" (2004, p. xiii).

The research program of anthropological economics could to some degree converge with the objectives of the new economic sociology.

## What Has Sociology to Say?

As we have already pointed out in chapter 2 in discussing the revised definition of embeddedness, in the past thirty years sociological research has shown how economic relations in the contemporary West are anything but separated from the social system and from culture. A particularly fruitful concept for analyzing economic relations has proved to be that of "network," initially applied to the labor market. Studies that have become classics have highlighted that even in the American situation people

---

[24] Acheson (1994; 2002); Gwako (2002). The starting point of this new formalism is probably Plattner (1975). The strategy followed in the past thirty years has often been to counter the "homogeneity approach" imputed to substantivism with a supposedly "heterogeneity approach" presented as a more complex and realistic vision of peasant decision making (Barlett 1980; Cancian 1989; Cashdan 1990). For a critique, see Chapman and Buckley (1997).

[25] Bourdieu (1963); Thompson (1967). On the evolution of the Western attitude toward time and its measurement, see Landes (1983).

find work not by turning to an anonymous job market but through personal contacts, and especially thanks to "weak ties"—namely, relations with people who have access to diverse sources of information from those shared with relatives or close friends (Granovetter 1973; 1974). Thus, it happens that a considerable number of jobs are not offered on the market, while others are given to people who have not actively sought them.

The network is not necessarily a more efficient alternative to the market. In a comparative study on Java, the Philippines, and Bali, where three different ethnic groups of entrepreneurs operate, Granovetter (1995) found that where a "moral economy" with bonds of solidarity dominated, enterprises were not healthier or more stable than in situations where opportunism prevailed. Hence, the network does not offset a problem of uncertainty and lack of trust that would make it more unfavorable to resort to the market. Perhaps the greatest efficiency could be obtained through some intermediate combination. The fact remains that hardly any such combination is present in any of the cases observed. In short, the existence of the network appears to be totally unconnected with the size of the transaction costs.

What distinguishes an authentically sociological approach from the approach of the new institutional economics is that sociology does not need to argue for the efficiency of social institutions. While "economic theories start with the premise that social institutions would not persist if they were not efficient," sociological theories are "usually agnostic or skeptical as to the ultimate effect of social structures on efficiency" (Fligstein 2001, p. 9). This is a very important analytical aspect, because disengaging the problem of the efficiency of institutions from that of their existence and survival blows apart the conceptual edifice on which the economistic interpretations of society are based and opens the way to a truly alternative theory (pp. 13–14). The works of Neil Fligstein (1996; 2001) show that the market is not a spontaneous phenomenon but, on the contrary, is a complex social construction involving collective processes, cultural factors, and even political elements. Thus, it cannot be taken as a state-of-nature benchmark for comparing other allocation systems, whether explicitly or implicitly.

Rational choice theory sometimes defends itself by saying that, though its model of self-interested maximizing actors might not be a realistic description of human behavior, it is at least valid from a *normative* point of view (Elster 1984, ch. 2; 2007, ch. 13), and this model describes the best of all the possible economic systems from the perspective of efficiency. The new economic sociology responds by showing that this is false in at least three fields, those of cooperation, uncertainty, and innovation, where the application of standard axioms produces suboptimal results (Beckert 2002).

It is a new way of looking at an old problem that became prominent in the 1930s with the controversy between Oskar Lange and Ludwig von Mises on economic calculation under socialism (Kula was well aware of this debate).[26] Whether the economy needs society *even* to be efficient and whether the world imagined by the economists is a "first best" or not are certainly fascinating issues, but from the point of view of economic history only one thing matters: the compliance of theory to the facts. The moment economic theory declares it does not deal with "what is" but rather with "what ought to be," it is by definition of no use for our aims, and at the same time rational choice interpretations of the past prove to be discredited.

Sociology shows that buyers and sellers on a market are never identical, while anonymity and true product homogeneity (from the point of view of perception) exist in a relatively restricted set of transactions. Status is still an important motivation, and influences the behavior of economic agents in many ways. Consumers or firms will be reluctant to start a transaction with suppliers of lower status if their image is affected negatively in so doing. For example, in the United States, high-end jewelers do not sell semiprecious stones even if there is a considerable demand for such goods. Taking up the hypotheses on signaling formulated by the information economist Michael Spence (1974), Podolny's (2005) explanation is that status signals are the most effective means for facing market uncertainty—consumers resolve the usual problem of transaction cost minimization by seeing a proxy for quality in the status of the producers. However, it seems to me that people go to Tiffany's spurred by the gratification they will receive, which is associated more with the brand than with the intrinsic quality of the products. But a more realistic use of the very concepts of "status" and "signaling" can be made.

In the light of these categories patronage has been reconsidered in a recent work on Italian Renaissance art by an art historian and an economist (Nelson and Zeckhauser 2008). Powerful families, but also the rising social groups, competed to signal their status, and the most visible means for doing this was through works of art. They were commissioned from the most gifted artists, and in the struggle to assert status innovation and creativity were encouraged. Patron and artist gave life to a principal-agent relationship, and a similar relationship was set up between the "creative duo" and the public. In this case, the payoff was status per se, an unmistakably noneconomic motive: "Beyond carrots and sticks, a major element that kept artists faithful to their patron-principals was their own professional pride, the desire to produce outstanding works

---

[26] Among those taking part in the debate were Enrico Barone, Friedrich A. Hayek, Abba P. Lerner, and Fred M. Taylor. See Hayek (1935); Lippincott (1938). Cf. Kula (1962, p. 166).

and achieve high status. This motivation was apart from and in addition to the material rewards that a fine reputation would bring" (p. 27). Here it is not just "taste," as in Bourdieu (1979), that sets off the "distinction" but also and especially the "magnificence" incorporated in the works of art (Nelson and Zeckhauser 2008, pp. 68–69). Indeed, taste is a message that only the cultured public of the elites could decipher, whereas magnificence applied *erga omnes*. It involved huge "differential costs" that were social as well as financial for whoever was not up to the level. If the patron commissioned a work of art that was out of proportion to his hierarchical position in society, society would be ready to stigmatize him, which would have had a counterproductive effect. The fact that the patron-client was aware of these costs made his signal credible.

In this second model, not status signal but the cost of the signal is thus the means for overcoming the problem of uncertainty or, as the economists would put it, the "information asymmetry problem" between the patron and the public (Nelson and Zeckhauser 2008, pp. 73–81). To argue however that such a problem exists seems to be rather twisting the truth, more suited for justifying the application of Akerlof's (1970) theory than for explaining an actual situation. Unlike the famous "lemons," the works of art commissioned by Renaissance patrons spoke directly to their well-practiced and well-informed rivals. In this sense, it would be more useful to see a resemblance between the conspicuous consumption (and the conspicuous investment) of the Italian nobles and the *potlatch* of the Kwakiutl (Burke 1987, ch. 10). In other words, palaces, chapels, and tombs were the confirmation of what everyone already knew, including the ordinary public. Finally, did the credibility of the signal really need to be guaranteed by a system of individual incentives in a world where the public authorities regulated the appearance of the social orders through sumptuary laws? (Roche 2000, pp. 203–4).

One could be more audacious and argue that the art market in the early modern period was not a market because of pervasive power relations, the extremely personalized relationship between patron and artist (hardly fixable in an anonymous scheme of supply and demand), the nonreproducibility of goods, and price variability (once again hinging on personal relations).[27]

Regardless of the limitations that I have tried to highlight, these models are interesting as they show how a key concept of sociological analysis—status—influences both costs and prices and the process of industrial concentration; even the "spread" of financial products is influenced by

[27] Goldthwaite's (1993) idea of supply-and-demand markets can in my view be applied only to the serial production of mediocre artworks, or of copies, which was, however, an important phenomenon (Labrot 2004). The best analysis of the role of power in economic life is still that of François Perroux (1973).

the status of investment banks (Podolny 2005, pp. 63–75). These results still apply when status is considered an end in itself, emancipating it from economistic interpretations. In this regard, it is significant that other non-economic elements (from social relations to the mechanisms of emulation) have been brought in to explain price volatility, by network analysis as much as by the French "economics of conventions" current (Baker 1984; Orléan 1990; 1992). Finally, taking precisely the complexity of the present-day world as its starting point, anthropology is slowly progressing toward an "ethnography of price" to interpret phenomena that escape the mechanistic explanations that economics has slavishly derived from physics (Guyer 2009).

# Chapter 5 _____

## THE WORLD WE HAVE LOST
### *Macroeconomic Perspectives*

IN THE MIDDLE OF WORLD WAR II, a few months before his tragic end, Marc Bloch wrote his historical testament:

> It is sometimes said: "History is the science of the past." To me, this is badly put. For, to begin with, the very idea that the past as such can be the object of science is ridiculous. How, without preliminary distillation, can one make of phenomena, having no other common character than that of being not contemporary with us, the matter of rational knowledge? On the reverse side of the medal, can one imagine a complete science of the universe in its present state? . . . the object of history is, by nature, man. Let us say rather, men. Far more than the singular, favoring abstraction, the plural which is the grammatical form of relativity is fitting for the science of change. (1949, pp. 19, 21–22)

Only thirteen years had passed since he had founded the *Annales* together with Lucien Febvre. In 1929 in Strasbourg the conditions for an intellectual revolution to take place were all there.

There was the dissatisfaction with narrative history, the *histoire historisante* that was more concerned with the chronological reconstruction of events than in understanding human behavior, and events that were nonpolitical and did not deal with "great men" were all being excluded from the accounts. As far back as 1900, Henri Berr and his *Revue de synthèse* had already expressed their uneasiness at this.

There was the heredity of Durkheim and the *Année sociologique*, which had provided the conceptual tools for analyzing society. Before Durkheim, it had been simply impossible to decipher the profound sense of social practices without losing sight of the whole, and the only option was to set up relations of cause and effect between individual phenomena.

Finally, even though it was more indirect, there was the influence of the German historical school (Steiner 2003). It had taught the need to contextualize economic phenomena in historical time, but had also acknowledged the importance of the economic dimension as a subject for historical research.

Bloch claimed a place for history among the social sciences; history was not "the science of the past" but rather "the science of men in time" (1949, p. 23). The enormity of such a definition is clear not only for the times in which it was written but also for the present time. How many of those who are currently working in the humanities and social sciences think of historical research in these terms? It suggests that the message of the *Annales* has still not lost its innovative force and even at the start of the twenty-first century could be a source of inspiration. An attempt will be made in the present chapter to show its potential for economic history and, more in particular, for dealing with macroeconomic questions. The best way to do so is to reassess the central problems confronted by the French approach in the years of its expansion and the methods that it developed.[1] Let us start then from the moment in which it all started.

## The Birth of Social Science History

There is no doubt that the crisis in traditional historiography in France came about largely because of the development of a scientific sociology. It can hardly be overestimated how important the economist and sociologist François Simiand was in promoting an attitude toward the past that was not just the usual reconstruction of battles, treaties, and the deeds of kings and statesmen.[2] In the footsteps of Durkheim, Simiand (1903) attacked the three "idols of the tribe of historians": the excessive importance attributed to diplomatic and military questions, which he baptized the "political idol"; the obsession for the actions of "great men" (the "individual idol"); and, finally, the preoccupation with the study of origins and particular cases (the "chronological idol"). Likewise, he conducted a strenuous campaign against the ahistorical economics represented by marginalism, and strongly advocated the analysis of economic decisions using a social psychology approach. Simiand (1912) mainly believed in induction rather than in deduction, and for this reason he maintained that history and the social sciences (including economics) were inextricably linked.

These principles found immediate application in three spheres of research: money, prices, and wages. Drawing on direct observation as much

[1] The intention here is not to provide a historiographical account, for which there are the excellent studies of Burke (1990) and Burguière (2009). Stuart Clark (1999) has gathered a vast collection of essays devoted to specific aspects of the *Annales* from many different perspectives, while Daileader and Whalen (2010) offer individual profiles of some of the authors mentioned in these pages.
[2] On the lasting influence of this author, see Day (1999, ch. 8).

as on the work of his anthropological colleagues, Simiand (1934) demonstrated the social nature of money and the implausibility of the utilitarian theories regarding its origin. Money was not the product of a coldly stipulated pact to facilitate exchanges between individuals with incompatible wants, which was a retrospective and misleading interpretation. Barter was found only in societies that already used money but were forced to do without it during emergencies, such as wartime hyperinflation. The origins of money were to be sought in collective representations such as faith, belief, and magic. The precious materials with which it was directly or indirectly associated (whether gold or shells) took on a sacral or totemic significance, vestiges of which were found even in modern secularized societies.[3] As Mauss wrote,

> The purchasing power of primitive money is first of all, in our view, the prestige that the talisman confers on the person who possesses it and who uses it to command others. But is it not a phenomenon that is still very much alive with us? . . . Does not the essence of faith in the value of gold perhaps lie in the belief that thanks to it we could obtain the services from others . . . that the market allows us to demand? (1914, pp. 111–12)

There are evident associations with works such as Bloch's *The Royal Touch* (1924), but Simiand, despite being held in great consideration by the founders, remained outside the movement. The young man who was to bring Simiand's approach *inside* the *Annales* was Ernest Labrousse, though he was more interested in studies on prices and wages.

As to this direction of research, the originality of Simiand's contribution (1932a, b) clearly did not lie in the subject matter, which was rather typical during the Great Depression, but in the unconventional way he dealt with it. The long-run evolution of prices since the sixteenth century, as well as the dynamics of cyclical movements, was interpreted through a sophisticated theory of action and expectations that included noneconomic motivations. Even the interpretation of wage fluctuations in more recent times was put down to categories such as social mobility and social conflict. Soon afterward, statistical quantification would become a cornerstone of the *Annales*, which until then had expended its energies on cultural history, psychohistory, and geohistory, and this evolution was by no means accidental.

---

[3] The term "money" comes from Latin *Moneta*, an epithet of Juno, near whose temple money was coined in republican Rome. This marked its divine nature and, at the same time, its inviolability on the part of humans. Speaking of temples as if they were "entrepreneurial" institutions (M. Hudson 2010, p. 16) means to have confused ideas as regards both the ancient world and entrepreneurship. In the late Middle Ages, it was still considered a grave sin to falsify money, as Dante shows (*Inf* XXX, 46–90; *Par* XIX, 118–20).

Ernest Labrousse received his training in economics from Albert Aftalion, but he very soon turned to history, attracted by the ferment that was transforming it. He explored the French archives in depth and gathered an abundance of data on prices, wages, and rent in the eighteenth century. He regrouped prices by categories of goods and studied their patterns from two complementary points of view, making of them the distinctive mark of French-style quantitative history: structure and conjuncture (see Braudel 1974). Structure reflects elements in social organization, such as mental habits, environmental constraints, and the state of technology, that are constant over the long term. Conjuncture refers to the dynamics of the economic cycle, which was highly unpredictable in the preindustrial period, as the results presented in chapter 4 show, as well as its impact on society.[4] Labrousse (1933) found that cyclical and seasonal fluctuations in prices were more marked for the consumer goods on which the subsistence of peasants and laborers depended, while they were less marked in the case of raw materials and finished manufactured products. On the other hand, rent remained stable and, over the long term, even showed a tendency to rise, overtaking growth in prices and wages. He concluded that the groups most exposed to the negative effects of economic instability were the peasants and laborers. Thus, the main explanatory variable in this model is social structure, conditioning the distribution of income.

The revolt against the "old history" came with a cost, in the form of obvious exaggerations that were not due so much to Labrousse's Marxism, which he generally managed to contain, as to his strong wish to reduce the weight of political aspects. In *La crise de l'économie française* (1944), the protracted economic recession in 1778–87, the so-called intercycle, was seen as the cause of social friction leading to the Revolution of 1789. Such an explanation can hardly be thought of as being exhaustive, of course, yet this influential work accustomed historians to thinking that an event—and the French Revolution was the event par excellence!—always had structural causes. Michel Vovelle (1972) and François Furet (1978) learned the lesson and were able to go beyond that.

## Quantification and the *Annales*

Underlying the use of the quantitative methods pioneered in France during the 1930s and developed in the postwar period was the rejection of the *histoire événementielle*, the idea that the historian should deal with

---

[4] This simplified view of Labrousse's schema, originally articulated on three levels ("long duration," "cycle," and "seasonal variation"), is found in Chaunu and Chaunu (1955–60).

unique and individual events, which were interesting because they were "extraordinary." Pierre Vilar has successfully captured this spirit: "The historian, like the judge, rejects isolated testimony. In his eyes, only frequent repetition confers a degree of objective meaning on the subjective document" (1964, p. 449).

The procedure envisaged constructing long time series from out of archival material and breaking them down into cycles and trends. In the "regional monographs" that sought to achieve the *histoire totale* of a portion of territory, it reached very sophisticated levels with the combined study of several sociohistorical variables. Simiand's influence was gradually being replaced by that of the development economist François Perroux, who was emphatic about reducing the importance of prices and monetary movements as indicators of economic performance (see Richet 1968, p. 763). In Baehrel's (1961) innovative work on Basse-Provence in the seventeenth and eighteenth centuries, a combined study was made of economic indicators (prices, wages, rent, tithes reflecting production levels, and taxation) and demographic indicators (baptisms, marriages, and burials); a further procedure was the analysis of the evolution of variables that included the structure of landownership, distribution of wealth and inequality, and social structure by age group. There were also examples of global history, such as Pierre Chaunu's *Séville et l'Atlantique* (1955–60).

The amounts of data to deal with and the calculations they required (from moving averages to standard deviation) were so huge as to create an enthusiasm for computers in the young generations. At the end of the 1960s, Le Roy Ladurie stated: "The historian of tomorrow will have to be a programmer or he will not be one at all" (1968, p. 14), but this prediction was disproved by a strong antiquantitative reaction in the 1970s and 1980s that was linked to the gradual loss of interest in economic history, and a return to the origins of the *Annales* and the terrain of the history of mentalities. But it is still emblematic of the climate of a particular period.

In the 1960s the American cliometricians knew little or nothing about what was happening in France. Reading only in English, they remained in splendid isolation until the end of the 1970s, when works of the *Annales* school were first made available in their language.[5] On the other hand, the French historians had known about cliometrics right from its inception. Braudel was already citing Simon Kuznets, following Kula's (1960) suggestion, and 1964 saw the encounter and subse-

---

[5] The first discussion of the French approach took place at the Thirty-seventh Annual Meeting of the Economic History Association; see Forster (1978) and North (1978). Drukker speaks about a "language problem" of the cliometricians (2003, p. 73).

quent dispute between the two opposing conceptions of quantitative economic history. In the same year the French economist Jean Marczewski attacked the *Annales* school, arguing that it was too limited in its use of statistics. Instead of the descriptive methods, he put forward an American-style reconstruction of historical national accounts, which he was trying to launch in France on the strength of a grant from the Social Science Research Council.

The historians' response was to argue that extending Kuznets's method to the eighteenth century or even further back meant distorting the facts. They maintained that "retrospective econometrics" gave only an "illusion of precision" that was achieved through rash interpolations and extrapolations; they defended "serial history," which was built up from data that had been painstakingly gathered, critically evaluated, and above all interpreted with historical intelligence.[6]

According to Vilar the use of a mathematical model to deduce data not found in documents would not lead to more objective history but would increase the margin of uncertainty in the quantitative representation; nor can a figure be considered objective just because it is written in black and white in a document. It is up to the historian to understand whether it is representative or reflects the individual perceptions of the men in the past that produced it (1965, pp. 304–5). This was a point that Furet also insisted upon. Unlike the case of econometricians who entrusted the task of interpreting to statistics, serial history left the historian free "to suggest internal relationships" (1971, p. 153). Indeed, the computer left to itself would generate only "truisms" (Le Roy Ladurie 1968, p. 11).

The other flaw that was found in the method of Marczewski and his colleagues lay in comparing what was not comparable. The meaning of the economic categories forming the national income identity changes over time; and, in any case, it is not possible to compare the living standards of societies that are structurally different. Setting up a quantitative hierarchy and speaking of "levels" make sense only if the contexts, or the "lifestyles," being compared are qualitatively homogeneous: how is it possible to determine, for a man of the sixteenth century, an equivalent satisfaction to that given by the possession of a television set? (Vilar 1965, pp. 305–6).

The econometricians would leave the task of explaining the "exceptional facts," the ones that did not fit in the time series, to the historians. Vilar's reply was that the econometricians had rather antiquated ideas about history; the historian was interested in the series, and no facts existed other than the social processes taking place in time (p. 302).

---

[6] Chaunu (1964; 1970); Vilar (1965). The debate has been summarized in Bourdelais (1984, pp. 180ff.).

## The Myth of Motionless History: How the *Longue Durée* Works

Interestingly enough, the expression *longue durée* has economic origins. Labrousse had come across it in the course of his university studies and enhanced its sociological significance. But with Braudel it took on a new meaning. It has rightly been written that Braudel was never shackled by words (Aymard 2009, p. 559); from Febvre he had taken the taste for geography, and from Lévi-Strauss the taste for structural anthropology and linguistics; he had undoubted gifts of abstract reasoning and his genius lay in combining all these elements.

In the *Mediterranean*, published for the first time in 1949, and then again in the first volume of *Civilization and Capitalism* of 1967, the image of a long duration was associated with the *part du milieu*, the physical and geographical frameworks lasting millennia. The technical solutions dictated to a civilization by the environment in its early history, such as whether to base the diet on maize, wheat, or rice, also condition its evolution and fix "the limits of the possible." The same thing happens with climate: living among the polar icecaps, in the savannah, or in a temperate climate clearly requires different strategies of adaptation.

But this is only one side of the coin. "Civilization" is not something passive, at the center of a field of forces, but continually creates and re-creates itself through cultural production. "A civilization," wrote Braudel, "is a set of cultural traits and phenomena" (1959, p. 256). In an article of 1958 setting out his program, he stressed the role of mental frameworks in forming the long duration. These frameworks, called *représentations* or more often *mentalités collectives* in the lexicon of the *Annales*, also ultimately condition human behavior and give rise to a *histoire inconsciente*. History is "unaware" of itself, not because agency and intentionality do not play any role in it; but over long periods of time, the shared *outillage* impresses regularity on individual actions. It orientates thought and circumscribes its horizons, which is what Febvre (1942) had intended to demonstrate with his somewhat extreme thesis of the impossibility of unbelief in the sixteenth century.

The *longue durée* makes the past intelligible to the present, and the present intelligible in the light of the past. In *The Historian's Craft*, Bloch referred to this phenomenon with the expression "solidarity of the ages" (1949, p. 36). "The past explains the present," and likewise "the present explains the past," Braudel would not tire of repeating. But what exactly does this formula mean? Does history perhaps make it possible for us to predict the future?

By observing the present it is possible to understand *why it is coherent* with the past. Bloch tells of his arrival in Stockholm and how Henri

Pirenne, the great medievalist, wanted to take him round the city starting from the newly built city hall, saying, as if to justify himself: "If I were an antiquarian, I would have eyes only for old stuff, but I am a historian. Therefore, I love life." The present reflects an image of the past, yet there is no single path that leads from the present to the future. If we look at the present, it is possible to say what is not plausible to expect from the future: for example, it is very unlikely that France will become a federal republic in fifty years' time, or Sweden will start to produce nuclear waste, or that labor unions will flourish in the United States. But it is not possible to photograph the future of any of these countries, the reason being that the long duration does not exist independently of other shorter times of history, namely the conjuncture and the event. Moreover the dividing line between structure and conjuncture is uncertain, and there is not always a qualitative difference between the two orders of phenomena. This dialectic relationship implies that history is only *nearly* motionless (*presque immobile*) and assimilates the changes that irremediably transform it gradually. Though he was convinced that none of them was decisive in itself, Braudel was clearly attracted by the sparkle and flicker of events. Above the structure *l'histoire bouge*, as Le Goff would say (1988, p. 55), "history moves."

When in the 1980s the cliometricians invented "path dependence" to make up for failings in the rational choice theory, they replaced an ahistorical way of reasoning with an unhistorical one. Not only in these models is historical continuity reduced to a device for transaction cost minimization ("change is costly," they say). More importantly, the assumption that the development of a historical process is contained in its origins leads inversely to the same error as that of the antiquarians, who consider "history as if it were an unending scroll with all the parts appearing to be identically fixed" (Simiand 1903, pp. 167–68).

Let us take Avner Greif's question: "How did the events that transpired in the Roman Empire shape the process through which modern economic growth has developed?" (2005, p. 242). Does it really make sense to ask the question in these terms? The innovations of the Roman period that he thinks have set us on the right path, and whose fruits were gathered in the nineteenth century, are the waterwheel, a common language (Latin), and the Roman legal tradition. But of the three, the first "invention" was made totally independently in the first century A.D. by the Chinese, who were already using it extensively in metallurgy (Needham 1965, pp. 366ff.), while the second and the third left very little trace in what would become the first industrial nation. Are we to refer to one or two millennia of history as an interlude?

Simiand was writing at a time when Heisenberg's uncertainty principle and bifurcation theory were not yet in the air, but his words appear to us today as being more modern than ever.[7] This is a yet another example of the nonlinearity of humanistic knowledge.

## The Character of Preindustrial Economies

With *The Peasants of Languedoc* (1966), Le Roy Ladurie freed himself from the Labroussian standpoint and sought to write a reasoned history that more closely resembled Braudel's. The protagonist was the "great agrarian cycle"; it extended from the end of the fifteenth century to the beginning of the eighteenth and was articulated in phases. It opened with the population rapidly recovering after the Black Death and starting its continuous increase throughout the sixteenth century. There was a general increase in overall output but not in per capita output, and productivity stagnated. It was not that the peasants were unable to extend the intensive margin of cultivation: but they did so by sowing wheat at the expense of olive groves. They obtained more food this way, but they lowered the nutritional value of their diet. Mentalities were what hindered the introduction of technological and agronomical innovations. "The people of the time had other things to think about than gross product" (p. 634); both Catholics and Huguenots were focused on gaining salvation in the next world, whether their religiosity was based on superstition, or whether it took on the aspects of mystic fervor. The ecosystem finally reached the saturation point in the seventeenth century. Wages decreased, properties were broken up, indebtedness increased, there was greater disparity of wealth, and social conflict broke out. The safety valve for the system was increased mortality.

The main accusation made against Le Roy by many cliometricians is that he put forward a rigidly Malthusian model. He was guilty, they say, of not having learned a series of important lessons:

> We have learned well from Ester Boserup that population pressure could and did drive human societies to greater intensity of work effort and the concomitant technological modifications suited to natural resource scarcity and labor abundance. (McCants 2002)

Of course, it *could* happen, but *when*? Has it always happened, everywhere? How can a fortunate intuition explaining the transition from a nomadic society to a settled one be extended to all periods of human history? Yet the true reason for their antipathy very soon emerges:

> We have learned from Adam Smith and his many followers the productivity advantages of specialization, encouraged as it was by the rise of urban

[7] This parallelism has been suggested by Aymard (2009, p. 579).

places and the increasingly dense networks of trade among them. . . . And of course, we also know from the body of theory built up over the last century in mainstream economics departments that markets are capable of clearing an amazing range of commodities, and that they often did so even in the somewhat murky pre-industrial past. Finally, the "New" Institutional Economics has taught us that social and political institutions had a lot to do with how well markets were actually able to perform their pure function. (McCants 2002)

In short, the historians are berated because they did not allow themselves to be indoctrinated into the school of (neo)liberal economics. Indeed, North wrote of Le Roy that "because he misreads Ricardo . . . much of his economic analysis does not make sense," and of the *Annales* in general, that "they have seldom learned price theory" (1978, p. 80). This was apparently a judgment he passed on anyone not sharing his own convictions.

In fact, Le Roy does not "apply" either Malthus or Ricardo. He starts from an analysis of the empirical facts and proceeds to interpret them autonomously; in so doing, he finds some connections between his own conclusions and the theories of classical economists. But it is logical that the similarities are only partial, seeing that these theories were developed in a very different context (the England of the early nineteenth century). What can be said about the notion that Le Roy allegedly "confuses rent with profit" (North 1978, p. 80), which North's devoted followers are fond of repeating ad infinitum? If the distinction were not important, why would a whole chapter of *The Peasants of Languedoc* be entitled "Wages, Rents, Profits"? Perhaps they have no clear idea of the meaning of the indicators he uses to study trends in profits.

There would actually seem to be nothing outrageous in French empirical reality confirming "the model which Malthus discovered and made immortal at the very moment it ceased to be true" (Furet 1971, p. 163). Frankly it would seem strange to me if the preindustrial economy resembled Romer's (1990) model. It is clear that it was the shock Malthus felt over the unprecedented demographic explosion following the English agricultural revolution that led him to predict the extreme tension between population and resources and to fear an imminent catastrophe. In early modern economies, usually the birthrate did not reach its physiological maximum thanks to countermeasures such as delayed marriage, with fewer conceptions as a result. But this does not mean they were on the path to growth: per capita wealth remained unchanged.

The idea of the prevalence of "culture" over "nature" in determining population patterns was one of the conquests of the historical demography founded in the 1950s by Louis Henry and developed by *Annalistes* such as Pierre Goubert and Jacques Dupâquier through family reconstitution based on parish registers.[8] This research was to inspire Peter Laslett and Tony Wrigley, who in 1964 formed the Cambridge Group for the History of Population and Social Structure. Thus, classics of British quantitative history such as *The World We Have Lost* (1965) and *The Population History of England* (1981) have their roots in Paris.

Anyone who thinks that the *Annales* described the early modern economy as an unevolving and undifferentiated mass would be quite mistaken. Instead, there were periods of expansion and contraction (which Simiand had already called "A" and "B" phases). For example, his study of different variables enabled Baehrel (1961) to prove that the agricultural economy of seventeenth-century Provence experienced a cycle of expansion that ended only around 1680. Le Roy Ladurie (1966) confirmed this result for Languedoc. These were conclusions that went against the current at a time when historians were discussing the "general crisis" of the seventeenth century.[9] In the second half of the century, French foreign trade showed an increase that was well documented by the growing volumes of goods leaving the Atlantic ports and Marseilles (Delumeau 1966); but it was still increased production and not increased productivity.

Vilar (1962) observed something different for eighteenth-century Catalonia. Here agricultural production was growing more than population, which brought about a significant rise in per capita consumption. He related this fact to improvements in irrigation techniques, but by now this was the eve of the modern period. It was also clear to the French historians that in northwestern Europe around 1650 a process of structural change in the economy, and even more so in mentalities, had started, and in his textbook, Pierre Léon (1970) would thus speak of an "acceleration of history."

Jack Goldstone (2002), after Eric Jones (1988), refutes this view of preindustrial "non-growth" as well as the rival thesis according to which the West experienced a single path of growth over centuries or perhaps millennia. He argues that economic growth was a frequent phenomenon in past societies and appeared everywhere after the Neolithic period; he calls these recurrent episodes "efflorescences," with each efflorescence involving both Smithian growth (based on the division of labor) and Schumpeterian growth (based on technological change). The first industrial revolution was nothing but the latest efflorescence. According to Goldstone, there is no qualitative difference between modern growth à la

---

[8] Fleury and Henry (1956); Goubert (1960); Dupâquier (1968). See also Rosental (2003).
[9] Aston (1965). For a restatement of this view, see Parker and Smith (1997).

Kuznets and the preindustrial efflorescence. The former is distinguished only by being "self-reinforcing." This ingenious rhetorical construction is prompted by the noble intention of making history less Eurocentric, and it implies that the primacy of the West is a very recent (and transitory) fact, largely due to the application of science to industry since the late nineteenth century. The expression "rhetorical construction" is used here because it is an argument with an artificial flavor. It is a fascinating theory but is constructed without any regard to sources.

Important technological innovations undoubtedly took place as much in medieval Europe as in High Qing China, but can Goldstone demonstrate that they increased factor productivity and that this was translated into a continuing increase in aggregate income? Can he point to new archival evidence to confirm it? Slicher van Bath collected more than eleven thousand figures on seed-yield ratios from the whole of Europe from the ninth to the nineteenth century (1963b; see also 1963a). The ratios varied from region to region in relation to the quality of the soil and climate, but they do not show significant evolution until the end of the seventeenth century, with change taking place in the Northwest; it is difficult to contradict the overall sense of these figures. Another indicator of productivity is the tithe. Until its evolution over time can be superimposed on the population curve, there is certainly no evidence of an increase in productivity. Once again, the data we have for Europe indicate that this situation changed only in the eighteenth century (Le Roy Ladurie and Goy 1982). There is certainly a noticeable difference between productivity levels in the eleventh century and in the seventeenth century, but even an enthusiastic supporter of medieval technological progress like Cipolla admits "they were still abysmally low" (1993, p. 77).

The reference to agricultural production is not a chance one. The focus on the rural context that dominates the *Annales* is fully justified by the fact that the primary sector in preindustrial societies contributed around 80 percent of created wealth and absorbed a similar fraction of the active population (Bairoch 1973, p. 469; 1997, vol. 1, pp. 103–4). Moreover, studies such as the one carried out by Deyon (1967) on Amiens successfully highlighted that manufacturing production (in this case, textiles) was largely influenced by the agrarian cycle.

The second-generation *Annalistes* were particularly interested in understanding what held back the early modern economies from takeoff, but they rarely moved beyond the *ancien régime*.[10] This has aroused the imagination of American reviewers, who have even attempted to provide

---

[10] Pierre Léon (1954) is one of the exceptions. Jean Bouvier (1961), a distinguished banking historian, and François Caron, the leading expert on French railway history (1973; 1997; 2005), belong to the third generation.

psychoanalytical explanations for it. One wrote: "The prestatistical world . . . is a more congenial world to French historians brought up on the artisanal-rural utopia of Babar's *Célesteville*" (Forster 1978, p. 60). Perhaps the same thing could apply to the Russian-born Michael Postan (1966; 1972), who is almost prohibited reading today: could he be a victim of the complex of Anna Karenina?

At the cost of disappointing these censors, it was not nostalgia for the past that influenced the chronological horizon of the *Annales*, and if anything it was just the opposite. The *ancien régime* in fact represented "a period which is neither totally identical with nor totally alien to our own," and hence it was the ideal laboratory for experimenting the "dialectic of the past and the present" (Aymard 1972, p. 21).

## Industrial Revolution and Underdevelopment

In the field of modern economic history, Braudel's hopes were pinned on Paul Bairoch, a young economist and historian. Like Kula, Bairoch was an outsider and had a rather independent mind.[11] His debut came in 1963 with the publication of his doctoral thesis, *Révolution industrielle et sous-développement*. Bairoch's powerful intuition was to study the industrial revolution as a structural process in the perspective of the world economy. He dismissed the European horizon, partitioned by traditional historians into first-comers and late-joiners, and instead adopted the perspective of a social scientist interested in understanding the imbalances between preindustrial and modern economies and making sense of the process of economic development—hence, the complementarity between the destiny of Europe and that of the Third World, as reflected in the title, and the need to trace their joint economic evolution. This view would remain with him for the whole of his academic career.

After a critique of the "pseudo-factors" of economic development, that is to say, its apparent causes (technical progress, demographic transition, rise in the price level, and capital accumulation), the book then considers its deeper "mechanisms." From a comparative analysis of successful experiences, Bairoch drew what he deemed to be a necessary condition for modern growth, namely the production of an agricultural surplus. Where no agricultural revolution takes place, no wealth exceeding the subsistence requirements of the system can be devoted to the secondary sector; this makes an industrial revolution impossible (see also Bairoch 1973). It is no chance that the population in prein-

[11] For a biographical profile, see Etemad and Batou (1999).

dustrial Europe, as well as in the Third World, is mostly made up of agricultural workers.

When and why does the leap in agricultural productivity take place? Bairoch's mistake here is not answering the "why" question. Although the last part of the book describes many barriers to development, the increase in productivity is still assumed as being exogenous. At the beginning of his career, Bairoch was reluctant to look into the black box of cultural change due to his rationalistic mindset as an economic statistician. We will see how this attitude would gradually change.

In two subsequent works, Bairoch (1971; 1975) focused his attention on the economic history of underdevelopment. He concluded, in contrast to the dependency theorists, that the wealth of the West was not created at the expense of the Third World. First, he noted that British takeoff in the eighteenth century preceded the advent of the colonial era. Second, by comparing GDP growth rates across Europe in the nineteenth century, he showed that the noncolonial countries were the ones that grew faster. Colonial powers such as Britain, France, the Netherlands, Spain, and Portugal experienced slower income growth than Germany, Switzerland, Belgium, or the United States. The U.S. economy had reached its peak before World War I, when a U.S. "neocolonial empire in the Third World was almost nonexistent." Moreover, it was largely self-sufficient in raw materials and could rely on a vast internal market.

However, even if the West did not profit from colonialism, Bairoch was equally firm in stating that colonialism was detrimental to the Third World. Because "the laws of physics do not work in economics," the effects of colonialism on traditional economies were disastrous, and postcolonial policies even more so. He particularly criticized the system of capital loans for fueling the vicious circle of accumulated interest.[12]

The study of underdevelopment led Bairoch to deal with urbanism, to which he devoted a number of books over the years, including the overall account *Cities and Economic Development* (1985). This covers an impressive time span (from the Neolithic period to our own day); it might appear to be a rash enterprise, but the type of problem-oriented history that Bairoch had in mind required it to be so. Indeed, an examination of the history of urbanism from any later stage would not make much sense, as it would not allow for regularities to be detected or big questions to be addressed.

When and how did cities spring up for the first time? Do urban models depend on cultural variables and models of civilization? What has been the weight of urban population in traditional societies? Is the urban

---

[12] Quotations are from Bairoch (1971, pp. 158–61).

explosion in the Third World an obstacle to development or an opportunity for it? Does urbanism foster innovations? What was the impact of colonialism on cities? Did the industrial revolution take advantage of urbanism? Bairoch's argument is first of all that cities are not the cause but the consequence of economic development. When this is a spontaneous process, it starts from the countryside. At this point, he rephrases his original thesis: cities normally spring up where an agricultural surplus exists, as in the case of Mesopotamia and ancient Rome. If they grow to enormous proportions in an underdeveloped context, they merely multiply poverty. But is this not a contradiction of the model? Why are there such big cities in the poorest areas of the world? Here is where the cultural explanation comes into it. The context of the Third World has become severely denaturalized from both a social and a cultural point of view, and urbanism is the expression of an underlying pathology. Cities act as a (deceptive) refuge for local populations, who feel deprived of their own identities after the destruction of the traditional social fabric in the encounter with Western colonizers.

Bairoch worked on two projects during the last decade of his life before his untimely death in 1999. They were quite different in scale and style though linked through being a synthesis of the author's thoughts, which by then had fully matured. The first book, *Economics and World History* (1993), examines and disproves twenty myths about world economic history. One half deals with left-wing narratives, dependency theories, and views that the West's wealth is based on the exploitation of the Third World. The other half examines the right-wing interpretations of the nineteenth century that emphasize the role of free trade in fostering economic growth. Bairoch shows that Britain only turned to liberalism a century after the beginning of the industrial revolution and that in other Western countries protectionism prevailed everywhere until the 1860s.

The second and more important work is the three-volume account, *Victoires et déboires* (1997), which is an economic and social history of the world since the sixteenth century, with emphasis again on the long-run dynamics of structural change. While the introductory chapter on the great discontinuities in history recalls Cipolla's *The Economic History of World Population* (1962), for the industrial revolution is described as the only change comparable in magnitude to the Neolithic revolution, the narrative here follows the pattern of complementarity between world regions. The first volume is devoted to the European traditional economies and British industrialization. The second tackles the issues of nineteenth-century Western development, turning then to the economic history of the Third World from 1492 to 1913. The third volume compares the performance of developed and undeveloped countries during the twentieth century.

The novelty of this last work is the weight attributed to cultural variables, which are readily made explicit. They are not taken as being the only key element, of course, but they nonetheless stand out among the others within the framework of a multifactorial explanation. As for the first industrial revolution, Bairoch's interpretation is now based on a consideration of four clusters of factors: business-oriented religion and mentalities, compatible political institutions, endowment of natural resources, and existence of a big city. Only in England were they all present at the same time. Were culture enough, the Netherlands would have been the first industrial region, but it was prevented from being so by its lack of natural resources. Conversely, in the chapters devoted to explaining why the industrial revolution did not spread to the Third World, some very interesting pages point out the "non-transmissibility of modern techniques." It is simply wishful thinking, Bairoch says, to suppose that a country could turn from Stone Age to High Tech; a set of economic policies cannot fill a cultural gap of centuries. If Japan and China, unlike sub-Saharan Africa, have eventually succeeded in finding the path to development, this is because the gap was not so wide. The fate of the other countries is a major tragedy of our time.

## Taking Stock

The experience of the *Annales* shows that collaboration with economics is possible and fruitful where economics relinquishes its deductive approach and bases itself instead on inductive methods, as in the period of French institutionalism from Simiand (1912) to Perroux (1983).

In the weighing process, the intellectual movement needs to be distinguished from the paradigm. The development of the paradigm was linked to the growing self-confidence of French culture in the postwar period. It is no coincidence that it formed in the years when France's geopolitical influence was at its greatest, and the inextricable link remains. The great *enquêtes collectives*, with the huge accumulation of data they required, could undoubtedly benefit from the French administrative experience and the special relationship traditionally linking Paris with the provinces. But it is also true that a great deal of the research that was carried out in the 1960s, and some of its most original outcomes, materialized without all that.

Rather than to any intrinsic weakness of the model, the crisis of the French-style economic history in the past twenty years is due more to

French historians transferring their interest to cultural history ("from the cellar to the attic," it has been said). However, abandoning quantitative history in favor of the *histoire des mentalités* does not imply there is no room for economic history alongside the new political history and other aspects such as the history of the body and the history of death that were once considered eccentric (Burguière 2009, pp 163ff.). Duby's (1973) analysis of medieval economic mentalities is an example of how both perspectives can be integrated, and even the "thick descriptions" of microhistory have unexpected economic implications (see P. Hudson 2010).

Two books such as *Carnival in Romans* (1979) and *Jasmin's Witch* (1983) might seem a far cry from Le Roy Ladurie's earlier economic interests as regards both subject matter and method. The former is the account of a massacre, while the latter deals with witchcraft. In fact, the bloody reprisal against the peasants of Romans who had satirized the town oligarchs in February 1580 depicts the problem of the polarization of wealth in the *ancien régime*. Tax privileges and structural inequality are reflected in this microcosm and precipitated an "event." In the second case, the interpretation of culture throws light on the link between the material conditions of society and collective representations. Le Roy shows that the people accused of being witches by the other members of the rural community had violated the taboo of wealth; in other words, those who enriched themselves in a context of limited wealth were suspected of doing so at the expense of others. Carlo Ginzburg's book, *The Night Battles* (1966), on agrarian fertility cults in northeastern Italy can also tell us a lot about the economic preoccupations of the early modern period.

In short, the history of the movement does not coincide with that of the paradigm. The former existed before the latter and survives it. Though for obvious reasons today it would be unthinkable to adopt the model of economic history developed by the *Annales* in the "institutionalized" phase of its venture again as it stands, it still teaches a fundamental lesson for the future: that one cannot write economic history that is not at the same time social and cultural history. The careers of scholars have been transformed by their enthusiasm for the *histoire totale*, and it has become possible for the same individual to tackle themes such as heresy and economic crises. Serial history, which requires evidence to be representative, has promoted the continual investigation of sources, methods, and disciplinary languages that have made French historiography an exciting laboratory for the avant-garde. Where there is a lack of specialization, there are obviously implicit risks, but they have proved to be far fewer than the advantages of mental elasticity; after all, the history of the movement provides examples of economists who have become historians and of historians who have become economists.

The revisionist interpretations of the preindustrial economy have to reckon with the *Annales* whether directly or indirectly. Heated articles contesting this or that thesis of Labrousse continue to appear every now and then.[13] This unusual fury against ideas that are seventy years old arouses the suspicion that perhaps the French were indeed on the right path.

[13] For instance, Cullen (2005). For a more balanced reappraisal, see Morineau (1996).

# Chapter 6

## BUILDING ON THE PAST

### *The Creative Power of History*

ONE COULD SAY THAT in economic history there are, or have been, three coexisting approaches. The first relates to the traditional vision of the historical disciplines belonging to the humanities rather than to the social sciences. It gives mainly descriptive narratives that tend to be more source oriented than problem oriented. The second is apologetic and conceives history as an instrument for validating economic theories or assumptions about human nature. Ideas taken from economics and sometimes adapted from the natural sciences are then assumed as the starting point for historical research. This is the path followed by practitioners affiliated with economics departments, especially in the United States, and known as cliometricians. The third approach is what I would call the "creative" use of history and forms the subject of this chapter.

In this approach, the fertilization process goes in the opposite direction, from the terrain of history to that of economics. Historians are aware of their capacity for building models and ideal types from which their theoretical neighbors can infer generalizations on economic behavior and practices. Naturally, there are no universal models but only interpretive schemes. Their role is to identify uniformities and differences in human experiences in order to make meaningful comparisons in time and space. Those who have adopted this perspective have often emphasized the interplay of nature and nurture in determining economic outcomes. Along with their colleagues in the social sciences, they have not treated networks, norms, institutions, and culture as epiphenomena of economic action but rather as explanatory variables (Granovetter 2005b).

Taking this standpoint does not mean dismissing the importance of economic theory. Here, by building on the twentieth-century foundational contributions to our field, what is being argued is that it should not be a one-sided relationship. Once again the practical relevance of history in establishing an *active* relationship with theory is worth stressing. Unless they have given up any hope of producing generalizations grounded in reality, economists cannot but interact with historians. And what benefit can theory gain from a history that does not question it? As Robert Solow once observed: "If economic history turns into something that could be described as 'The Occurrence of an Overlapping-Generations-like Legend among the Seventeenth-Century Neapolitans,' then we are at the point where economics has nothing to learn from economic history but the bad habits it has taught to economic history" (1985, p. 331).

## History and Theory

The relationship between history and theory has been one of the most debated and controversial questions in the development of the social sciences. On the one hand, it is natural there should be mutual reticence: the feeling of the irreducibility and complexity of history is at odds with the ambition of making sense of human actions on the widest possible scale. On the other hand, neither of the two can afford to pay the price of a "dialogue of the deaf" (Burke 2005, ch. 1). In the case of economics, with its aim of explaining such particular phenomena as wage formation or the relationship between inflation and unemployment, there is an additional problem that stems from the fact that its principles do not have general validity but closely hinge on the social and institutional context (Solow 1985).

In the 1960s and early 1970s, when cliometrics was a minority approach still awaiting legitimization, the new economic historians firmly maintained that it was not possible to interpret historical data without applying some theory, and if this was not openly expressed then it risked remaining implicit and untested (Lamoreaux 1998, p. 59). Yet this argument has the flaw of regression to infinity. If the historian needs a prefabricated theory to interpret empirical data, how has it been possible to arrive at the construction of this theory? If the reasoning is taken to its natural conclusion, then every theory ought to rest on some preexisting theory, which is patently absurd—that is, unless it is supposed that theories are the product of the free imagination of economists (which in certain cases might even be true) and have no connection with the observation of reality, as Clapham (1922) famously suggested. But in that case, delving into a repertory of tools constructed at random will produce an almost zero probability of finding something to fit the specific historical situation being investigated.

In recent decades, this attitude has hardly changed. As Mokyr puts it, "economic historians are overwhelmed by data and facts. . . . Theory builds the connections." Yet because no single theory can fulfill the task, "the best we can do is to choose a particular issue and then search for a theory that seems most applicable to help us sort through the evidence and build a model" (2005, pp. 196–97). In the desperate effort to find fresh instruments of persuasion, the repertory of applicable "pieces of theory" has increased out of all proportion. We have seen how today, besides mainstream economics, it includes natural sciences such as biology and cognitive science.

A variant of this procedure is known as "analytic narratives" (Bates et al. 1998), where the point of departure is not even actual reality ("data and facts") but an a priori idea of how the world functions. It is assumed that there are certain laws of nature, echoing Hempel's "covering laws," that can be represented in a mathematical relation, and to find confirmation for this, the past is investigated in a manner resembling "cherry picking."[1] Avner Greif, for example, supposes that the superiority of economic individualism is sanctioned by game theory, and he goes in search of elements from the past to endorse this conviction. The principle of transaction cost minimization performs a similar function in Douglass North's system, except it does not allow for any type of empirical proof.

These approaches share a rather poor conception of history. They all suppose that history is "blind" and needs to be guided from outside so that it can arrive at some form of explanation. But history is not blind at all and has its own methods to attain knowledge (Braudel 1955; Kula 1963).

In my view, what the economic historian needs is a *metatheory*, not any specific theory. A metatheory is not a "theory of economic history," as intended by John Hicks (1969). There is no need to go vainly after "laws of motion," be they in stages or in the evolutionary style, as in any case they would turn out to be a philosophy of history. Whatever the specialty, the historian simply needs a framework for finding the bearings but one that is general enough not to be constricting. This includes knowledge from the social sciences and other branches of historical inquiry that can be reworked in total autonomy (cf. Kocka 1984, p. 173).

Let us apply this principle to the case of social historians. They should certainly take account, among other things, of the existing approaches to modernization theory; that done, it is up to them to establish the workings of the specific society being analyzed. When the research has been published, the resulting feedback will be useful for improving, or correcting, the general assumptions made by sociologists and political scientists. Thus, for example, Putnam's (1993) emphasis on civic engagement as a legacy of the medieval and early modern commune will be confirmed, but he will be disproved on the assumption he makes about Western-style democracy being a gold standard. Doubts on the usefulness of the concept of "social capital" will also be raised, as history shows that all societies

---

[1] Grenier (2001) provides additional criticisms and comments.

have social capital, even those that channel it in the form of "amoral familism" (Burke 2005, pp. 72–73). This all forms part of the modern division of intellectual labor.

An economic historian's metatheory should include at least economic, social, and cultural theory, as well as social, cultural, and political history. It should pay particular attention to what Schumpeter put under the label of "economic sociology" to indicate the study of mostly nonmaterial motives that influence the behavior of economic agents—in other words, the spheres that lie over and above economic activity but condition its operation to the point of influencing its endogenous mechanisms, at the same time shaping economic institutions and systems (1954, pp. 20–21). The new insights being gained in economic history could in their turn serve to remold and enrich economic theory, correct its spatial and temporal distortions, and consequently increase its explanatory power. It is by no means coincidental that Schumpeter, *as an economist*, declared that if ever he had had to choose between practicing only history or only theory, he would have given priority to history (p. 12).

Other economists have highlighted the importance of metatheories. Let us take Walter Eucken's book *The Foundations of Economics* (1940). Written during World War II, it attempts to form a synthesis between the principles of German historicism, which advocate the specificity of human experience in time, and the unavoidable need for generalization. These two problems make up the "great antinomy" that economics has to contend with.

Joan Robinson's *Freedom and Necessity* (1970) is a further example providing a great deal for reflection. It is a splendid book on the human condition, which all students of economic history should read. The economic life of each animal species consists in the adaptation of population to resources and food. But the inception of conceptual thought in the humans, together with language, has created a surplus out of all proportion to the requirements of their physical existence. Conceptual thought has brought with it the capacity to solve problems. But it has also brought rational speculation and moral dilemmas. Freedom gradually gained the edge over necessity, and it has become articulated within the system of values we call culture.

The concept of "cosmology," the highest of the planes that form a civilization, cannot be ignored even by such a fervent supporter of the universal spread of capitalism as Deepak Lal. A cosmology is concerned with the ultimate meaning that members of a particular human group give to their lives and that guides their daily actions. Lal's (2008) metatheory, like Joyce Appleby's (2010), envisages the compatibility of the profit motive with different cosmologies, which is a very debatable point. But he admits that the contemporary notion of "rights" is a latecomer even within the Western cosmology, . . . there is nothing universal about the notion. Nor is there anything universal about egalitarianism. . . . Nor is democracy essential for development. After all, hereditary monarchy has been the most common form of government through human history, and it, not democracy, delivered the Industrial Revolution. . . . These aspects of Westernization, though contingently tied with the West's modernization, are not necessarily so: it is possible to modernize without Westernizing. (Lal 1998, p. 177)

Such reasoning leads directly to the problem of defining precisely what culture is and what role it plays in economic life.

## The Foundations of Culture

Throughout this book I have firmly rejected the black box of "cultural beliefs" that is so popular in present-day economic literature and which is a jumble of unexplained unknowns that supposedly explain why there is a deviation in reality from the "rational" behavior predicted by the standard model. The need for an organic concept of culture is here called for, and the moment has come to clarify this concept.

Clifford Geertz and Pierre Bourdieu, who draw on Weber, both define culture at a deeper level as a "web of significance." According to Geertz, culture is "an historically transmitted pattern of meaning embodied in symbols, a system of inherited conceptions expressed in symbolic forms by means of which men communicate, perpetuate, and develop their knowledge about and attitudes toward life" (1973, p. 89). Bourdieu adds that it "gives regularity, unity, and systematicity to the practices of a group" (1972, p. 80). The first definition indicates the close relationship between culture and matters of ultimate concern, whereas the second emphasizes consistency within this set of "mental tools" that are shared by the members of a society, as well as its practical implications.

Cultural attitudes, values, and mentalities can be thought of as the collective responses of society to questions arising out of the interaction between the agents and the environment. Values stemming from the higher levels of this interaction also shape the lower-level responses (Sahlins 1976a). The cosmological level is at the top of the hierarchy (religion helps deal with the question of relating to existence itself); then come the level of norms (an initial reference guide for identifying right and wrong behavior), the level of status (defining the position occupied in society), and the material level (the way people relate to things, including resources). The most important vehicle of cultural transmission is probably primary socialization, which usually occurs in the family, as even adults tend to regard the behavior stigmatized by their parents as wrong. It is noteworthy that cultural transmission begins well before people fully develop the faculty of reason, but throughout life these maps become adjusted by means of the internal conversation.

Looking at this "forest of symbols" (Turner 1967) from within, an operational definition can be outlined whereby culture is said to be the attitudes, values, and mentalities expressed, embodied, and represented in artifacts, performances, and everyday practices.[2] Performances and everyday practices, in the sense of Braudel's *structures du quotidien*, do indeed include economic practices. Because the economic behavior of the agents belongs to the material level, it is easy to see how it is influenced by considerations regarding religion, morals, or status. Examples of this vertical integration of culture in the sphere of economics can be found in the wide variety of attitudes, across societies and throughout time, toward wealth and poverty, consumption, savings and investment, the pursuit of profit, the use of money and its yield, inequality, and so on.

Critics of cultural explanation such as Eric Jones (2006) argue that economic factors transform cultures, and in their turn cultures interact and influence each other. The first argument, in fact, restates Marx's old thesis of the dialectic between "base" and "superstructure." From a materialist point of view, it could be conceded that the former (the development of "productive forces") contributes to some extent to the formation of the latter (values and social norms). But once this has come about, a relatively stable framework is created, which will certainly continue long enough for the "superstructure" to be considered constant for the analysis of particular facts or problems.

Let us take an example. Today western Europe and North America are the areas of the world with the highest per capita income, the outcome of a process of development lasting two centuries. Yet, while some European nations from Spain to Sweden have become largely secular societies, in the United States religious sentiment with its strong Puritan component has remained practically unchanged (see Zuckerman 2004). It is clear that there cannot be an economic explanation for this continuity.

The question of the interaction between cultures is fascinating, though it is to be considered not as a challenge to the cultural explanation but rather as an enrichment of it. Indeed, the issue of compatibility between cultures, which is a prerequisite for their "merging," should be emphasized. Cultures do tend to be impermeable but only when they are incompatible. The history of Brazil shows how neo-Latin cultures have happily amalgamated and even merged with indigenous cultures, and a great many examples of "cultural hybridity" could be cited (Burke 2009). The

---

[2] I am indebted to Peter Burke for suggesting this definition.

industrialization of Japan, as interpreted in Morishima's (1982) classic study, is explained by the compatibility of autochthonous values with Western capitalism (Macfarlane 1994; 1998). The latter has, however, been profoundly reworked and adapted with the result that doing business in Japan and in the West are still two very different things. As distinct from Latin America, the history of North America shows how groups divided by language or ethnic origin have kept themselves separate, with some showing a tendency to have control over symbolic production.

Naturally, there are no one-way links. The environment, even the physical environment, which influences scarcity to a greater or lesser extent, population density, and the existence of natural constraints, forges the way people think, so that any change in these conditions might end by triggering off social change. However, culture evolves very slowly, one reason being the effect of what the French sociologist Maurice Halbwachs (1925) defined as the "collective memory." A sudden change of mentality could lead to the loss of the map of symbols and meanings and leave people disorientated; hence, ways of stopping and resisting it are instinctively activated. This strategy prevents society from finding itself in a state of anomy (or the absence of normative standards) and explains why any changes in this sphere occur only very gradually and with an enormous struggle. But the collective memory is the product of constant manipulation and also has the function of repressing unwelcome memories through what the anthropologists following Evans-Pritchard (1940) and Barnes (1947) have termed "structural amnesia." In Mary Douglas's happy formula, "institutions remember and forget" (1986, p. 69).

In the previous chapters the importance of distinguishing between rationality, self-interest, and wealth maximization has been recalled several times. Because they bring human nature into it, these categories cause very heated controversies (Wilk 1993; P. Hudson 2006). The question can now be dealt with in depth; there is no point in steering clear of it, by advocating a practical, case-by-case approach. In chapter 4, it was seen that on an abstract plane rational behavior does not imply self-interested behavior, nor is the latter necessarily wealth maximizing. Besides, in the real world, with which economic history is concerned, the rationality of decision makers is somewhat weak and imperfect.

Self-interest, though not in the economic sense, informs many of our actions, while many others are not self-interested, whatever this term is taken to mean. With regard to the first category of self-interested actions, it might be useful to refer to a Maslow-like hierarchy of needs.[3] Individual or collective self-interest comes into play at the lowest levels of the hierarchy when it is a question of satisfying certain physiological and

[3] The original reference is Maslow (1943).

safety needs; but most economic activity does not fall into this category and is not carried out for this aim. Even human relations can become instrumental if the payoff is of a political or social kind, as in the case, for example, of spending time in the company of members of the French Academy in the hope of being elected among the *immortels*. But, quite paradoxically, in acting this way one seeks to improve those very relationships, because the desired "good" is thought to guarantee the respect and consideration of others.

It is also true that we do not normally go to a party among friends prompted by ulterior aims (Granovetter 2002, p. 38), and just as we are not economic calculators, neither do we maximize our political and social objectives, which makes the application of microeconomic tools pointless in this sphere. Utility functions do not exist: our objectives are local, and our preferences systematically violate all three axioms on which consumer theory rests: completeness, transitivity, and the nonsatiation assumption.

Yet people are also capable of completely disinterested actions, and in particular they are able to understand their significance. These generally regard the spheres where "ultimate concerns" are involved: "When we seek to be loved, regarded and respected, not only are these things not for sale, but also they are something like a terminus in that they do not lead on to further ends which could be achieved by an additional dose of instrumental rationality."[4]

Even Dawkins admits it when he sees that his theory of the selfish gene clashes with the behavior of humans "deliberately cultivating and nurturing pure, disinterested altruism" and is forced to introduce human reason from on high, like a foreign body in his evolutionary theory: "we have the power to turn against our creators," he says. "We, alone on earth, can rebel against the tyranny of the selfish replicators."[5] What has been chased out of the door comes in through the window!

Dawkins's solution, which Huxley (1894) had already excogitated, has an artificial character and is justified only because of the need to resolve an otherwise irreparable conflict between brutish nature and moral humans. The primatologist Frans de Waal (2006) has criticized this "Veneer Theory," showing that the bases of altruism are firmly anchored to animal cooperation, as are empathy and the emotions. But even the most sympathetic observer of the animal world cannot ignore the fact that conscious and genuinely moral altruism associated with the idea of justice is alien to nonhuman species. This is because the development of reason in humans confers on them the capacity for abstraction and "normative

---

[4] Archer (2000, p. 54); on ultimate concerns, Archer and Tritter (2000, p. 6).
[5] Dawkins (1976, p. 215). For a restatement of this view, see Stanovich (2004).

self-government" (Korsgaard 2006). As an example of this, if a person decides to donate blood, he could do it for the psychological gratification he will gain from it (a subtly utilitarian argument), but he could also do it because he knows that the action is a good thing in itself. At this point, the doubt arises that we decide what the "good in itself" is on the basis of a template forged by evolution, which rewards cooperative behavior. But the very fact of wondering why we act in a certain way and fearing that possibility is an index of self-awareness. We have come back to the *logos* that Aristotle spoke about, meaning not only "speech" but also "reason." The exercise of this faculty implies an abstraction from impulses of any sort—hence, the reflection on ethics. As Kant wrote in his *Critique of Practical Reason* (1788), the moral law is a "categorical imperative": it is inscribed in reason, but is independent of the will.

## Continuity, Change, and Diversity

In some Western countries it is a widespread practice to put the money into an envelope when paying cash to a professional, such as a lawyer or doctor, to prevent the gesture from seeming offensive. It is not the money itself that is considered offensive, but the fact that the service is being reduced to a commodity. Thus, the money, which shows the equivalence between the service and the agreed fee, has to be hidden. This rule does not apply to ordinary transactions such as those taking place in shops. There goods are being sold, and professional services are not being called upon. In Japan, though, the passing of money from one hand to another is considered an act of ill manners in all cases, and the cash is deposited in special trays. The Roman emperor Vespasian's maxim *pecunia non olet* (money does not smell) would be incomprehensible even today in what is probably the most technological society in the world.

Let us return to Geertz's bazaar, which is an interesting laboratory for examining the interaction of the economy, society, and culture. Some of the practices observable in a bazaar may be linked to a state of uncertainty; but this does not mean that by reducing uncertainty through some technical expedient (e.g., by standardizing the products, though even technology is a cultural variable) these practices would disappear and make way for contractual and competitive behavior. In a bazaar are sellers grouped by type of product to make it easier to compare the goods or to increase the social control exerted by the category over its members? Certainly in the eyes of the public, specialization is a sign of competence, but in the first place competence is something that increases the pride of the vendor. Clientelization, reputation, and the personal relationship that is established between client and vendor can all be instrumental or disinterested or can be a combination of both components. One can talk to the vendor to gain more information or to gain the time to check the product personally, but this is also because both the buyer and the vendor form part of the same community. And it is also quite possible for a friendship to arise out of a commercial transaction.

No more and no less than they are today, instrumentality and disinterest were largely present in human behavior a thousand years ago. In all this time, human nature has not changed; something else has changed. Nowadays in the West people are more individualistic and unlikely to put the requirements of the group before those of the individual. This is because Western society rewards people for what they are able to do and not for their rank. In addition, there is a tendency to erect a barrier between what is public and what is private. With regard to the concept of privacy, nobody would want to give it up, yet in the sixteenth century it was virtually unknown. It is much more difficult to socialize in a grocery store—let alone build up a personal relationship—starting from an economic transaction than it was in a medieval market or it is in a Middle Eastern bazaar. At the same time, in the modern West, society exerts less social control over the life of individuals. These things are to do with values and, hence, with culture. Over a thousand years Western culture has changed. The modern market economy reflects the new values and the separation of what is public and what is private. In his works, Adam Smith theorized this separation of spheres and their interdependence at the same time. With regard to nineteenth-century England, even Polanyi and Arensberg admit this interdependence, when they ask whether it was "historical accident alone that a 'free enterprise,' a free and equal democracy, an 'open' class system, a free choice of religious and associational membership, and a free choice of mate in a small, ego-reckoned family structure, should all have historically coincided" (1957, p. ix).

Thus today, in one way, the economy is embedded in Western society as in the past, but this must not lead us to think that it has always been the same. The economy is different. It is different not because it has divorced itself from society but because the society that produces it has changed, and the language of society is culture. Sombart rightly said that the "modern economic spirit" is essentially different from the premodern spirit. For the past two centuries, a previously unknown social prestige has been attached to economic activity. One of the reasons undoubtedly lies in the Protestant—or, better, Calvinist—ethic, as Weber indicated. On the other hand, one-half of Europe and the Americas does not share the Protestant culture, whatever the meaning of this adjective. Yet those countries have also undergone a similar phenomenon, albeit more slowly and less obviously. Emulation does not seem to offer a satisfactory explanation.

A more general explanation than the one offered by Weber is to do with social dynamics (Sombart 1913). In a society like that of the early modern period when power and prestige were acquired by birth, the only tool of differentiation for anyone who wanted to emerge out of nothing was wealth. Clearly, this was possible because the European aristocracy also recognized the utility of wealth, though subordinating it to other values. In the fifteenth century, the Florentine bourgeoisie started to overturn the aristocratic maxim that expenditure should exceed income, and a virtue was made of parsimony. Economic calculation *in the sense of a lifestyle oriented toward accumulation* made its appearance thus. But for many centuries the "acquisitive spirit" remained connected to the original motivation that had produced it. The aristocracy was still the model to imitate, and the money that was accumulated was used to buy land and to rise in the social hierarchy. Then the aristocracy was done away with and, where it survived itself, adopted bourgeois features.

This transformation of mentality, which was experienced for the first time in northwestern Europe in the mid-seventeenth century, spread to other places here and there at different times and at different rates. In England it was well in evidence by the end of the eighteenth century if Edmund Burke complained that "the age of chivalry is gone—That of sophisters, oeconomists, and calculators, has succeeded" (1790, p. 238). But the new tendency did not become generalized in the West until the end of the nineteenth century.

Has the self-regulating market taken the place of the regulated market, and has the latter taken the place of reciprocity? It would be more correct to say that what has changed is the predominance of one or the other in the combination. For centuries the ingredients that form the combination have been the same, though in varying proportions. The continuing practice of the gift-exchange is evidence of this (Carrier 1995), and the reference here is not to what happens in homes at Christmas, but the gift-exchange as a public ritual. In certain circumstances when somebody needs to be remunerated and a money payment might seem vulgar and offensive, this instrument is resorted to. Nowadays these cases are more circumscribed than in the past, but they do still form part of day-to-day living. Yet that is still not enough. As we will soon see, using money in a transaction does not in itself imply that it entirely loses its character of "reciprocity," and it is not enough to make it "anonymous." The instruments of the economy are molded and remolded by society.

Furthermore, the dominance of the self-regulating market over the regulated market is not absolute and differs in intensity from one place to another; even the role assigned to the market differs. This is because there are different degrees of individualism in Western societies.

As already mentioned in chapter 2, in Europe nobody would think of entrusting health care or social security to the market, whereas in the United States it is the norm. In Europe cars are insured against theft, homes against fire, but not people from sickness, or at least it is not compulsory to do so. The French, Germans, and Swedes like the state to take care of its citizens, while the Americans see the state as a potential intruder and are constantly vigilant that it does not deprive them of their individual freedom. Watching a television debate on a network such as Fox News Channel produces a "culture shock" in a European, to whom the conservative view of the tasks of politics seems as exotic as the "Wild West."

People make different choices with regard to savings and investment, and this is culture related. Italy, for example, has one of the highest homeownership rates in the Western world. Many Italians are owners not only of the house they live in but also of one or two others, whether by the sea, in the mountains, or simply bought as a source of income. They have a tendency not to trust the financial market. Of course, Italians also hold stocks and bonds, but by no means to the same extent as the British and Americans, and in contrast Italians have always had an extremely high savings rate. This means that they do not need to take out loans; an Italian almost never makes a purchase against credit (except for the first home of a young person when the parents lack the means to help or have no house to offer). Even in the North, until a few years ago it was considered despicable to go to a bank to take out a personal loan, a practice that is quite normal and routine in other countries. Only those who were driven by need did such a thing, and one was very careful not to talk about it. People who borrowed on the credit market were considered penniless, or as squanderers who were unable to manage their own affairs: in their folk culture, they were mercilessly dubbed as *poveri diavoli* or "people to pity." Yet this is not the case of a backward country but of one that was the fifth largest economy in the world twenty years ago, and today is the seventh largest, according to the economic statistics.[6]

This savings structure has the effect of creating a lack of investments with the result that the productive system is rather rigid and static: it is no surprise that with regard to all the so-called G8 countries the Italian economy has the lowest growth rate. Yet what many considered a very great weakness proved to have its positive side during the 2008 crisis. Compared to other countries, whose experience of the downturn was dramatic, especially in terms of its social consequences, Italy was

---

[6] By nominal GDP, year 2008. See IMF, World Economic Outlook Database, October 2009: www.imf.org; World Bank, World Development Indicators Database: www.worldbank.org.

relatively untouched. It also undoubtedly entered a recession, as is inevitable in a globalized world (James 2009), but it was spared the depressing scenes of employees being laid off en masse and leaving their offices carrying cardboard boxes, or of mothers of families in tears because, in addition to their homes being seized, the washing machine was also taken away. This does not mean that the Italian system is any better than others, or that it would be a suitable environment for Silicon Valley; it is simply the system produced by a society that is more concerned with welfare than with performance.

According to Paul Krugman (2010), European-style social democracy shows that social justice and economic progress can go hand in hand, and this view can be personally endorsed. However, it is not the task of history to give lessons or suggest paths to imitate. Economic history has to give an account of the extraordinary variety of solutions provided by past and present human societies to the problem of livelihood. It has to help us understand why such different economic systems coexist in the world, and even in the same part of the world. This is why cultural history is so necessary.

## A Manifesto

Of the significant elements introduced in chapters 4–5, some can now be utilized to outline an alternative framework to the one that was the object of criticism in the first part of this book. Naturally, there is no infallible recipe, and all that can reasonably be done is to put forward a manifesto for the renewal of economic history, which needs be based on the following five points:

1. *Adherence to the primary sources*. Economic historians cannot rule out a direct relationship with the primary sources. As wide a combination of sources as possible should be used and selected in a way that is not instrumental to the desired outcome.
2. *Historical background*. Economic historians should have a thorough background in the fields of social, cultural, political, and institutional history. This would prevent them from producing the patent anachronisms and oversimplifications that abound in the works of the cliometricians. The *histoire totale* advocated by Braudel is not a choice but a cognitive requirement. As John Nef put it, "A knowledge of general history is bound to change man's outlook on economic history, and in all probability on the other separate channels into which specialized research has divided the study of history during the past hundred years or so" (1958, p. ix).

3. *The careful choice of friends.* There is no reason why economic history should entertain a special relationship to economics. There are other disciplines, such as economic sociology and economic anthropology, that investigate economic life from a more holistic perspective and whose theoretical results are thus particularly useful to historians. Besides, sociologists and anthropologists are more likely to be genuinely interested in the historical work, as this provides them with an extraordinarily rich workshop; they can infer tentative generalizations from differences in time as well as space. It is not by chance that both economic history and economic sociology emerged as autonomous fields of inquiry after the German *Methodenstreit*.

4. *A different use of quantitative techniques.* Regression should not be a substitute for interpretation. That a technique can automatically generate a historical explanation is a fiction for conferring an illusory patina of objectivity on the results. The techniques of descriptive statistics are preferable to methodologies based on probability. The use of deductive reasoning should be avoided, because the work of the historian is inductive by definition. Furthermore, the principle of Occam's razor should be constantly borne in mind: there is no sense in resorting to heavy mathematics where it is not necessary or to obtain trivial results.

5. *A different relationship with theory.* We should develop a relationship with theory that finds expression in what I called the "creative" use of history. As figure 6.1 shows, cliometrics starts from a theory (generally an economic model) and applies it to a historical situation in order to show the explanatory power of that theory. For a historical phenomenon of a quantitative type, it resorts to specific techniques (such as a regression or a statistical test) to make the facts conform to the model. For a qualitative phenomenon, it resorts to other techniques (such as game theory) and to largely hypothetico-deductive procedures (e.g., lemmas, theorems, predictions).

The method I suggest (figure 6.2) consists rather of an inductive procedure that starts from the empirical evidence relating to a problem, or set of problems, that attracts the historians' interest. Once the sources have been collected and analyzed, historians will not allow themselves to be led by some prefabricated theory, nor will they grope forward blindly and helplessly, but will follow the general coordinates of their own metatheories. A metatheory is a much more general, flexible, and open construction than a specific theory. It is something similar to a *Weltanschauung*. It is used in the first instance to discard implausible hypotheses that are not consistent with the general picture that the scholar has made of a specific context, epoch, or problematic point. A background in the other

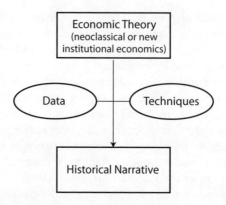

Figure 6.1 Cliometric method

branches of historical research, as well as in the social sciences, will help in building up this picture.

Once they have passed through the filter of metatheory, the historian's ideas are converted into hypotheses that are assessed using appropriate techniques. These techniques can vary very widely: from the construction of index numbers to the linguistic analysis of a medieval text, to the semiotics of an advertising campaign in a magazine from the 1920s. Providing that the available sources are sufficiently varied, it is preferable, wherever possible, to crosscheck the different techniques, whether they are qualitative or quantitative.

When it has been confirmed, specified, and refined, the hypothesis then takes the form of a historical model. By historical model is meant a synthetic interpretation of the facts whose explanatory power is limited in time and space (a model of the formation of pepper prices in twelfth-century Samarkand will differ from one of the grain market in Rouen in the same period or, even more so, in twentieth-century Oklahoma).[7] At this point, the historian's task is over, and if economists wish to learn from the results of the historical research, these will be used to revise the structure of their theories and generalizations. If not, an opportunity for dialogue will have been lost. In the former case, the concepts of a more realistic economic theory based on facts can be included in the interdisciplinary pool of metatheory and provide the historian with feedback. Otherwise, the historian will have every reason to suspect the conceptual tools that economists have devised.

---

[7] "The more elements we introduce into the model, the richer will be the theory we construct; but the number of societies to which this theory could be applied will decline commensurately" (Kula 1962, p. 20).

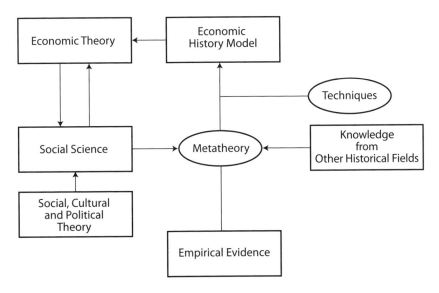

Figure 6.2 Historical method

## Trends and Prospects

In present-day economic historiography, some of the previously listed elements are already widely in evidence, while others need to be further developed. The edifice built up by our predecessors still stands and is renewed each day with work of scholars from a wide range of backgrounds. The most interesting element is perhaps that not only are historians contributing to this enterprise but that social scientists are also making an active contribution. It is to be hoped that the profession will soon institutionalize this fruitful interaction of recent years. The main directions of research that are making headway are presented in the rest of this chapter.

### Rethinking Europe, Globalizing History

Apart from convergence with regard to ideal principles, there is no agreement among cliometricians on almost any question when it comes to the task of explaining concrete things, which is what historical phenomena are. Mokyr (2008), for example, rejects the new institutional interpretation of the industrial revolution based on the role of property rights (North and Weingast 1989). At the same time, like many humanistic historians, he disagrees with the gradualist views and emphasizes the discontinuity between the preindustrial period and the industrial period.

The most obvious problem in proceeding by means of a bricolage of theories is that they lack coherence, which makes any explanations put forward short-lived. One particular element, be it technology, knowledge, or "the Enlightenment" (Mokyr 1990; 2002; 2009), is indicated each time as being the decisive one. An organic picture can, however, be obtained only from the systematic study of the sources, and there is no eye-catching idea that can substitute for it.

In chapter 5 it was argued that the most convincing framework for understanding the industrial revolution was the one offered by Paul Bairoch focusing on the concept of agricultural surplus. Starting from this material fact it is possible to go in search of the causes, but it is especially important not to lose sight of the global perspective. What happened in Britain two centuries ago should be "provincialized," to paraphrase Patrick O'Brien (2010).

In his latest synthesis of world economic history, Bairoch calculated that at the end of the seventeenth century there was a disparity of no more than 10 percent above or below between the wealth produced by Europe, North America, Russia, and Japan together (the future developed world) and the rest of the world (1997, vol. 3, p. 1036). It is clear that these estimates cast doubt on the doctrine of early modern economic growth. The same conclusion is reached if one looks at Europe from an Asian perspective. Pomeranz (2000) in his rightly acclaimed work has shown that the Great Divergence is a recent phenomenon, and until the eighteenth century East and West displayed similar levels of material progress. In that case, the rhetoric of path dependence, which maintains that the roots of "European primacy" lay in medieval institutions or in other specific circumstances dating back to remote times, is pure myth, precisely what Jack Goody argues in *Capitalism and Modernity* (2004).

Global history and historical anthropology have much potential for throwing light onto the past. The idea pioneered by twentieth-century historians (Bloch 1928; Bairoch 1963; Braudel 1987; Chaudhuri 1990) that the history of one part of the world cannot be written ignoring other parts is now more topical than ever.

Within this framework various points will need to be clarified. Why did Europe produce an agricultural surplus before others? The capacity for manipulating the environment should be investigated, and on this terrain help will hopefully come from a new history of science focusing on tacit knowledge rather than on Newton's apple.[8] And why did the

---

[8] The connection that is still made between the scientific revolution and the industrial revolution (Jacob 1997; Jacob and Stewart 2004) is simplistic and unsatisfactory because until the late nineteenth century there is no evidence of a direct link between the two phenomena. The emphasis of these accounts on the contribution of northwestern Europe to the birth of modern science is also hardly tenable.

agricultural revolution take place in Holland and England? We will need to reassess geography and culture, the quality of the soil, the climate as well as religion. And why did these two countries have such different industrial destinies? At this point other factors come into play, from the size of the country to natural resources. The interplay of chance and necessity extends well beyond the availability of coal underlined by Wrigley (1988) and demands a multifactorial analysis all the more.

Historical research should neglect none of the many possible paths to economic development. Free trade and protectionism have proved to be equally legitimate means as shown by the economic modernization of France, whose path of slow growth, achieved with totally different strategies, ultimately produced a regime of material well-being that is certainly not inferior to that of countries experiencing more traumatic takeoff (Minard 1998; Horn 2006). Thanks to the studies of the past few years, we have a more sophisticated knowledge of corporatism, which is no longer seen as a premodern residue destined to be supplanted by more efficient systems, assuming there is a univocal way of measuring efficiency (Kaplan and Minard 2004). Even the image of the triumph of contractual liberty in the Western labor market soon fades when actual labor relations are looked at comparatively (Stanziani 2008a, b).

It is also particularly urgent to increase our knowledge of the preindustrial past. Keith Wrightson's *Earthly Necessities* (2000) is an excellent guide to the economic transition of Britain from the sixteenth to the eighteenth century and shows unequivocally that the emergence of a market economy took place in that period. As we will see, studies on continental Europe place this transition more recently and suggest that in some places it has never been fully completed. The competitive market thus appears to be an extremely circumscribed allocation system and closely associated with a particular culture (the Anglo-Dutch). In Wrightson's words, in that context it "became not just a means of exchanging goods, but 'a mechanism for sustaining and maintaining an entire society'" (p. 23); that is why it is possible to speak of a "market society" (or of a "commercial society," in the language of the late eighteenth-century authors).

The global and comparative perspective is therefore expressed not so much in the subject of study, which does not need to be exotic, as in the approach. In other words, as Goody (2006) wished, it is possible to produce a non-Anglocentric history of Britain or a non-Eurocentric history of Europe.

## Consumption

Until not long ago, economic historians had a partiality for studying the processes of production, while today one of the most dynamic sectors of research is consumption. This change of perspective is partly due to the slowdown in growth in the developed world and to the consequent emphasis in public debate on the quality of life. But it is also partly to fill a large gap in knowledge, especially if we bear in mind the impact that demand has on the supply of goods and services in the modern world.

The history of consumption is a largely interdisciplinary field in which interaction with social history and cultural history has now reached a very high level. For example, for social historians the history of housing is naturally interwoven with the history of the family (Sarti 2004). It is impossible to take account of all these articulations, but their significance for the economic historian is obvious because they enable the evolution of society to be monitored throughout time, looking through the keyhole so to speak, which is a decidedly privileged standpoint.

In Daniel Roche's wide-ranging work, *A History of Everyday Things* (2000), consumption is the mirror reflecting the transition from a subsistence economy in which four-fifths of the population was rural and most of the household income was spent on bread, to a modern economy where luxury becomes standard. Roche innovatively recombines elements from the repertory of the *Annales* school, starting from the Braudelian concept of "material civilization," to show how *choses banales* have a lot to say about the structure and dynamic of an economic system. Through the history of housing, lighting and heating, water and its uses, furniture, and clothing, trends can be reconstructed, and qualitative differences that are quite compatible with the macroeconomic picture of the *ancien régime* can be appreciated. Not even the potential repercussions of the "base" on the "superstructure" escape this type of history from below, if it is true that the "morality" regulating the preindustrial economy relates to the sense of scarcity that pervades all agricultural societies, while the utilitarian attitude toward wealth develops in contexts of plenty. Roche's perspective makes it possible to link the features of traditional societies into a coherent whole: "reproduction of society in the same form, with little social mobility; primacy for redistribution of wealth, with capitalisation and accumulation rejected; luxury kept within the hierarchical conformity of the social authorities" (p. 73).

Luxury was certainly not lacking in preindustrial Europe, as long as it was commensurate with status. In the same way as the gift, the "expenditure of large sums of money on lavish public display" (Shepherd 2007, p. 47) was a way of making wealth circulate in a world in which avidity and hoarding were viewed negatively. Indeed, "liberality" and "magnificence" are two key concepts of the mentality of the Renaissance courts (Guerzoni 1999). It was only with the eighteenth century that luxury took on the different partly hedonistic meaning that we are more familiar with (Berg 2005; Berg and Clifford 1999; Berg and Eger 2003). However, the conquest was anything but simple if, as Malthus warned, "an efficient taste for luxuries, that is, such a taste as will properly stimulate industry, instead of being ready to appear at the moment it is required, is a plant of slow growth" (1820, vol. 1, p. 359). Steven Kaplan (1996, p. 577) cites the eighteenth-century economist Ferdinando Galiani and reminds us that in France in the 1770s bread still belonged "to police and not to commerce."[9] Historians are generally careful not to project the features of modern consumerism onto the past (Burke 2008, p. 70).

But the history of consumption also provides an important analytical contribution for understanding the operation of microeconomic structure. From an investigation of a considerable number of grain transactions on the marketplace in mid-sixteenth-century Ferrara, it has been observed that each day there was a significant range between the highest and lowest prices paid for the same quantity and quality of product. Even the formation of the price of fungible goods like cereals does not seem to follow a standard logic. This gives the measure of how much the pre-industrial market differs from our image of the market as a mechanism for consistent price formation, because "every single deal was an almost unique negotiation and . . . every price was the result of an individual transaction influenced by non-economic factors" such as personal ties and social connections (Guerzoni 2007, p. 86). Thus, as Evelyn Welch puts it, "finding out what something 'cost' turns out to be as much a cultural issue as a question of economics" (2007, p. 71).

A great deal of research has focused on consumption in the modern world, and there is now an abundant literature (see Trentmann 2006). It goes beyond the paradigm of the mass consumer society that was formulated in the 1960s and 1970s and the more recent postmodern narratives of the "active consumer" in order to observe the "making of the consumer." Historians, sociologists, and anthropologists show that modern consumers have not automatically arisen with the expansion of markets but have also been the product of state policies and the mobilization of the civil society in certain critical turning points of political and industrial history. The First World War, the New Deal, the construction of Nazi Germany, or postwar Japan were all moments in which models of consumption were molded by the national interest.[10] But the relationship between consumption and politics can be construed in yet another way, as Victoria de Grazia (2005) has done in her study of the Americanization of postwar Europe and the partial inversion of this process that started in the 1990s. The next frontier seems to be an authentically

[9] Cf. Judith Miller's (1999) thoroughly researched study of state intervention in the grain trade.
[10] Among the more representative contributions, see Daunton and Hilton (2001); L. Cohen (2003); Hilton (2003); Trentmann and Just (2006).

global history of consumption spanning the centuries and continents and making cross-cultural comparisons through time and space (Brewer and Trentmann 2006).

## Market and Obligation

The role of the market in the preindustrial period is one of the subjects of historical inquiry whose interpretation most lends itself to being distorted by ideology. For Marxist historians, regardless of what Marx actually wrote, the end of the feudal system in western Europe is the moment for primitive accumulation. The peasants were dispossessed of the means of production that had been at least de facto previously available to them (hence the tendency to minimize the importance of feudal constraints), and the conditions were created for capitalist development (Wickham 2007). Subsequently, early modern history for this school of thought, which has now fallen from grace, has become a tribunal where the injustices of the present can be vindicated. But "modernizing" the past is also equally useful for anyone writing from a liberal point of view, with conclusions reached by the former often being welcomed by the latter (e.g., Campbell 2005).

Long before the Middle Ages became the cliometricians' *pièce de résistance* (McCloskey 1989; G. Clark 1998; Volckart 2004; Greif 2006), there had been no lack of historians with a literary background portraying it as the crucible of the Western-style market economy, the most notable example being undoubtedly Roberto Lopez. Lopez had held a deep-seated aversion for the corporative economy of Fascism. He was forced to leave his native Genoa in 1939 because of the racial laws of Mussolini, settled in the United States, changed his name into Robert, and dedicated the rest of his career to making the Italian merchant the prototype of modern economic man (see Lopez 1971). History represented for him a sort of lost paradise that was able to make up for the harsh reality of the present.

However, unbiased investigation into early modern markets suggests that they functioned very differently from modern markets. Let us begin with the least regulated exchanges that were closer to capitalism (in Braudel's model, the "private market"). Paul McLean and John Padgett (1997; 2004), two social scientists with a sound command of quantitative methods, have shown that in Renaissance Florence competition was not perceived as a key element of the market. The banking sector was neither anonymous nor deconcentrated, while manufacturing industries such as wool were deconcentrated without being anonymous. Others, like cloth retailing, were relatively anonymous but were concentrated. In choosing commercial partners, the unwritten rule was to "first pick from one's own family, then from among close neighbors, and then from further afield only if need be" (2004, p. 204). In addition, partnerships were short-lived, and it was not uncommon for the actors to leave economic life for administrative or legislative offices (see also Padgett and McLean 2006). Civic duties with their political involvement always took priority over commercial activity. In short, the merchants of Florence did make huge profits but only for ostentatious purposes and for thereby cultivating their clientele, in line with Leon Battista Alberti's observations in his *Libri della famiglia* (completed in 1441).

In his recent study, Richard Goldthwaite has confirmed that what he calls a "competitive instinct" was absent from Florentine capitalism:

> The market process by its very nature consists in competing in the search for gain through exchange, but in Florence this process can be understood as operating only at the general level of the collectivity, for example, to explain the rivalry between Florence and Venice. . . . At the level of the individual entrepreneur, so well documented for this city, it is difficult to detect much of a competitive instinct, certainly nothing like the kind of competition that is an ongoing process of discovery, searching for opportunities for gain or for furthering other economic goals. (2009, pp. 588–89)

But let us consider the other type of market, the one that was closer to people's everyday lives, where food surpluses were exchanged, where the money to pay taxes was obtained, and where tools and consumer goods were bought and sold. According to Craig Muldrew (1998), though the fraction of created wealth that went through the market was greater in England than elsewhere, the market was still a regulated one with transactions being based on a "common estimation" of price that was made public by magistrates and other market officials. Muldrew speaks of the "social rationality of trust" underlying market behavior, which was based on credit, but not credit in the sense of the simple transfer of property rights against some future payoff. Rather, it was reputation in the least economic sense of the term. Trustworthiness did not depend on any abstract calculation of probabilities but was based more generally on the standing an individual had in society and on the social relations binding him to the community: "It was through these numerous small, personal, face-to-face acts of credit that agents interacted within the market, and given the ubiquity of such actions, the mutual interdependence of such agents was stressed and formed a much more comprehensive means of social interpretation than the private desire for profit" (p. 124).

Muldrew stresses that although contractual relations grew in importance during the seventeenth century, until the end of the eighteenth century the contract carried a different meaning, and he provides abundant evidence that the pursuit of self-interest was disapproved of as being covetous and miserly. This fundamental work not only offers a solid picture of preindustrial England but also allows Adam Smith to be read with greater historical sensitivity and to understand why the *Wealth of Nations* was preceded by the *Theory of Moral Sentiments*.

This vision is gaining wide consensus. Laurence Fontaine (2008) and Martha Howell (2010) have reached very similar conclusions for the European mainland, while other studies have explored the reciprocity mechanism that until recent times often lay hidden behind the ins and outs of credit (Finn 2003). Another compelling work on early modern England has explored the gray area below the level of market transactions, showing how during the whole early modern period the gift-exchange maintained its fundamental importance as a means of "informal support" and as a "status signal," despite the much-celebrated exceptionalism (Ben-Amos 2008).

### The Social Life of Money

The cultural historian Natalie Zemon Davis (2000) has made a study of the relationship between gift and market in sixteenth-century France in the light of the question of whether the spread of market relations was responsible for the progressive erosion of reciprocity mechanisms. She examined specific sectors such as the burgeoning industry of the press and relationships between university professors and students and between doctors and patients, showing that the two systems actually coexisted but with different functions: furthermore, that social relations were able to model market transactions. What restricted the sphere of the gift economy were the transformations in family life and politics, rather than any effect of the market.

Money provides a good test. In her investigation of England between 1640 and 1770, Deborah Valenze (2006) highlighted that the idea of money as a neutral means of exchange struggled to make headway even in one of the most precociously monetized economies. Money was loaded with different meanings, depending on the use that was made of it and on the social circles in which it circulated.[11] In taking on such symbolic connotations, it was as if it was invested with its own personality. At the end of the eighteenth century, the Quaker reformer John Bellers denounced "money's mischief," namely its capacity for acting as an instrument of accumulation, and he proposed that the *numéraire* should be used in such a way that income could be distributed according to the amount of labor that each individual actually provided. At the height of the financial revolution, Bellers's moralist point of view could still exist side by side

---

[11] For a comparison with Mediterranean Europe, see Boldizzoni (2003).

with the liberal stand that Bernard de Mandeville would take only a few years later.

Because of the sources on which they are constructed, literary studies have much to offer in understanding these ways of thinking and should not be dismissed by economic historians. They have proved to be particularly useful in understanding ancient money (Kurke 1991; 1999). Economic relations have a qualitative component with many nuances, and they cannot be reduced to numbers. However, in this field it is sociology that is owed the greatest debt.

Research carried out by Viviana Zelizer (2005; 2010) has shown that the idea of the "cash nexus" dominating modern society (a bias equally common to neoliberal and Marxist historians) is a misleading one. Zelizer (1979; 1994) investigated how difficult it was for life insurance to make headway in the United States because of the strong moral taboos it had to conquer, and she later concerned herself with the long and tormented process of money standardization in the late nineteenth century. When at the beginning of the twentieth century Congress finally managed to impose a single national currency by law, people still continued to create all kinds of monetary distinctions. These "social earmarking" strategies, which Thomas and Znaniecki (1918) and Mary Douglas (1967) had already found in other contexts, consisted in "restricting the uses of money, regulating modes of allocation, inventing rituals for its presentation, modifying its physical appearance, designating separate locations for particular monies, attaching special meanings to particular amounts," and so on (Zelizer 1994, p. 29). The social taboo of death is a good example of an extreme case: burial moneys were earmarked by the poor as a sacred expense and were considered absolutely untouchable, however urgently they were needed. Similarly, widows who had been paid their husbands' life insurance policies used them only in exceptional circumstances, preferring to resort to Social Security income for their day-to-day expenses. Even gangsters distinguished between honest money and "dirty money," and it was very unlikely they would draw on the second type of income to make offerings in a church!

## Capitalism

More than two decades ago, Simon Schama's *The Embarrassment of Riches* (1987) opened up a new phase in the study of the transition to modern capitalism. This monumental reconstruction of Dutch culture in the golden age gave a thorough picture of the innermost anxiety that lay behind the actions of the Protestant capitalist. Far from intentionally setting out on the path of utilitarianism and selfishness, he was uneasy about the contradiction between the possibilities that affluence offered him and the ethic that had produced it: "At the center of the Dutch world was a burgher, not a bourgeois. There is a difference, and it is more than a nuance of translation. For the burgher was a citizen first and *homo oeconomicus* second. And the obligations of civism conditioned the opportunities of prosperity" (p. 7).

The perspective of microhistory is also suited for investigating this delicate transitional phase of European history. In her study on the Tulipmania, Anne Goldgar (2007) highlighted the ambiguity of the relationship between society and economy in the Holland of the 1630s. It is misleading to interpret the tulip bubble as if it was the result of cold stock market speculation. Instead, the episode brought to the surface the conflict between economic individualism and the particular communitarian ethic on which it was nurtured. All in all, the crisis had only modest economic repercussions, but it left a profound impression on society and gave rise to a myth that would be propagated over generations: it "rendered unstable the whole notion of how to assess value" and threw people into a state of bewilderment. "What is value? And why is it so scandalous that it grows beyond what seems reasonable?" the citizens of Haarlem must have wondered. Questions of this type would have little sense if we simply assumed that value was the product of natural forces. But, as Goldgar argues, value is "a cultural construct, whether we are talking about the value of a painting, the value of a tulip, or the value of a person" (p. 17). When the economic *value* is upset, society's scale of *values* is also thrown into doubt.

One of the advantages of this type of approach is that it re-creates history that is rich and vibrant, in much the same way as when we look at a painting we are shown the thoughts and psychology of real people. Similarly, promising results have come from the study of "self-perception." Under the editorship of Jacob and Secretan (2008), historians have explored the image that the early modern capitalists had of themselves through the study of a collection of diaries, letters, pamphlets, portraits, and engravings. Once again, the stereotype of self-satisfied businessmen pleased with their achievements is far from the truth, and on the contrary these people appear to be ridden by anxiety. The anxiety stems from continually setting their actions against society's moral standards; these were introjected by the *nouveaux riches* despite their being deviants. For a long time, merchants and financiers lived with a sense of sin, and they tried to ennoble themselves by emulating landed gentlemen, and it was not uncommon for them to invest in education.

Significant results have also been obtained from using the techniques of network analysis. The work of Van Doosselaere (2009) on the Genoese traders, which was mentioned in chapter 3, successfully shows that the activity of the medieval merchants on the northern as much as on the southern shores of the Mediterranean was based on a system of social alliances whose focus was the community they belonged to. The fact that this type of network was still important even in recent times indicates that it was not a response to market imperfections. In his study of equity trades in early eighteenth-century London, the historical sociologist Bruce Carruthers (1996) made a powerful case for the way politics influenced economic behavior. One would expect the London stock market to be the nearest thing to a pure market on which the actors operated for purely economic motives. But this was not so. From his analysis of individual shareholding and trading in Bank of England and East India Company shares, Carruthers found that only the Bank of England shares were bought and sold on the basis of impersonal exchange. In negotiating the East India Company shares, traders who where Whig supporters tried to sell them to those who shared the same political views, and the Tories did likewise. But why did this not happen with the Bank of England shares? It was because it was firmly in the hands of the Whigs, and there was no risk of the situation being overturned. On the other hand, power in the East India Company was always in the balance. The shareholders' primary motivation was thus political, and this was expressed through the network.

Going even further, it can be seen how kinship has played a decisive role in the economic history of the modern West. The traditionally strong link between capitalism and the family in continental Europe comes to mind. Since the industrial revolution and until today, the business history of countries such as France, Germany, Italy, and Sweden has shown that individual families tended to control not only the small enterprises but also big business. The business was almost a projection of the family, ensuring its biological and affective continuity. Harold James (2006a) rightly argued that this family capitalism is a form of "relationship capitalism." It mirrors the culture of these countries, which rewards loyalty to the group rather than individualism. It has nothing "anonymous" about it, yet this has not prevented it from creating wealth any more or any less than a system where ownership and control are separated. The comparative method that James applied in the analysis of this subject led him to reject the view that it is an immature and less efficient form of business than the Anglo-American model of the public company. Whereas some claim that common-law societies have produced more efficient enterprises than societies with Roman law traditions because the rewards and remuneration are more closely linked to the company's performance, this book demonstrates that this view is distorted and suggests new lines of research in extending comparisons to Japan, China, and India. The varieties of capitalism are manifold, and none is necessarily better or destined to prevail over others.

## Public Actors and Public Policies

In the 1990s, under the direction of Richard Bonney, the European Science Foundation promoted a monumental research project in three thick volumes on the contribution of public finance to the process of state formation over the very long term (Bonney 1995; 1999; Ormrod et al. 1999). Far from being a mere superstructure, it emerged that the state contributed to molding the character of economic systems. There was a symbiotic correspondence between the type of political culture and the forms of taxation. In addition, the transition from "domain state" to "tax state" was not linear but went through various overlapping phases. The taxation model (such as the prevalence of direct or indirect taxes, exemptions and their amount, the distribution of the tax burden between the social orders) reflected the level of centralization of political power as well as the social structure.

Fiscal history can throw light on various aspects related to the workings of the economy. It shows not only that in the early modern period the European economy was not integrated but also that individual countries appeared economically fragmented at the regional level. Until the late eighteenth century, internal customs barriers survived more or less everywhere. On the other hand, regions that were politically separated but that still had cultural affinities were also linked through commercial relations. In short, this type of history based on close analysis of the contexts and able to combine several dimensions has nothing to fear from the assaults of those who isolate a dozen price series and think that highlighting some statistical correlation is enough to argue for the existence of common markets *ante-litteram* (K. G. Persson 1999).

It is hoped that in the future research will be carried out on preindustrial welfare systems and on mechanisms of income and wealth redistribution especially at the local level. How did welfare culture develop in Catholic countries, and what methods were envisaged to manage social conflict in northwestern Europe? The differences might be rooted in the completely different ways of viewing poverty in these two contexts, seen on the one hand as an outcome of bad luck and on the other as a sign of laziness and ineptitude.

With regard to the modern period, the work of Martin Daunton (2001; 2002) on the politics of taxation in Britain is masterly in the way it exemplifies not only how the past explains the present but also the capacity of historical knowledge to modify and rectify how an economic phenomenon is understood theoretically. A phylogenetic approach can make sense of institutional and legal arrangements that would appear incomprehensible in a "rational reconstruction"; in addition, investigating human behavior holistically makes it possible to explain how in different contexts similar policies have different effects. Daunton shows that what really lay behind the firm stability of the fiscal state in Britain between the mid-nineteenth century and World War II was trust. British subjects were ready to accept tax burdens that fluctuated in intensity because they were confident that other taxpayers as well as the government were fulfilling their obligations responsibly. When the foundations of this model of civil society started to erode in the second half of the twentieth century, the fiscal system also entered a crisis.

Contrary to assumptions of public choice theory, the relationship between state and individual is not necessarily antagonistic or coercive. The logic of the stick and the carrot is not the only way of understanding politics. It would be interesting to conduct a systematic comparison to ascertain the reasons for the stability, or instability, of taxation regimes in the modern experience of other countries. The first steps in this direction have already been taken (Nehring and Schui 2007) and indicate that a great many paths were followed, with each society pursuing those that reflected its values and attitudes. This type of analysis can also be useful in helping to avoid the mistakes that regularly occur when attempts are made to transplant the fiscal system produced by the economic culture of one country to another one.

## Facts and Ideas

The preeminence of "passions" over "interests," which informed Albert Hirschman's (1977) analysis of early modern capitalism, was not alien to the nineteenth-century British economy. Its distinctive feature, free trade, no longer appears as driven by opportunism and calculation so much as an instinctive response dictated by widespread values and attitudes. Frank Trentmann (2008a) reached this surprising conclusion using an eclectic approach drawing on political, cultural, and intellectual history to interpret an economic decision. It would have been difficult to arrive at a similar result only twenty years ago, if only because of the impossibility of bringing apparently irreconcilable disciplinary languages into a dialogue.

The first attempts to overcome the dichotomy between "history from below" and "history from above" were made in the 1970s and 1980s. On the one hand, general developments in intellectual history had made it mandatory to contextualize ideas, a requirement that had emerged in the study of political thought since Laslett (e.g., Pocock 1975). On the other hand, and this has to be stressed, it was a need that economic historians felt autonomously in their wish to link the evolution of ideas with the materiality of the facts and economic processes.

Economists had up until then maintained, rather superficially, that economic thought evolved by itself, or at best that the ideas of some thinkers had the power of molding history, as J. M. Keynes famously argued. But some scholars put forward the opposite hypothesis, that in fact it was the observation of concrete economic situations and their transformation that conditioned the way theories were formulated. In France, this approach was pioneered by Jean-Claude Perrot (1992); in Italy, by Aldo De Maddalena (1980); and in Britain, by Phyllis Deane (1978), Maxine Berg (1980), and Donald Winch (1978), one of the founders of the "Sussex school." The more recent contributions of Winch and O'Brien (2002) on modern Britain, Tribe (1995) and Tooze (2001) on Germany, Stanziani (1998) and Zweynert (2002) on Russia, and Daunton and Trentmann (2005) on comparative economics and politics are interesting examples of how the history of facts and the history of ideas can be combined, bringing about improved understanding of both spheres.

Because it can be applied to any intellectual product, even an apparently abstract one, the method goes far beyond more immediate aspects such as the study of economic nationalism, where a strong policy element makes the link between the two planes explicit (Finkelstein 2000; Hont 2005; Hoppit 2006). This happens, for example, in the powerful synthesis of Jean-Yves Grenier (1996). He has shown how the analytical framework and the conceptual elements developed by physiocracy help in understanding the operation of the French economy during the *ancien régime*. I myself have had occasion to experience the great utility of pursuing this itinerary backward, using economic history to throw light on economic thought (Boldizzoni 2008), but the course suggested by Grenier is equally valid. Until axiomatization started to prevail in the second half of the twentieth century, facts and theories of a given period were an indivisible whole, and they reflected each other. Wherever one starts from, there are good chances of reaching the intended goal, but with a word of warning. The economic ideas of the past were still the product of elites, and as such they could be biased, as the result of a particular social environment, or the sensibility of particular intellectuals. Because the economic historian is normally interested in the collective destinies of whole societies, this needs to be taken into account when using this invaluable tool.

## The Environment

Historians have been driven to question the past by the reawakening of environmental awareness in recent times and its preoccupations over health and the well-being of future generations. In any case, the impact of the environment on human history has been clear since the time of Braudel's *Mediterranean* and even before that—one has only to think of the influence of the geographer Paul Vidal de la Blache on Febvre (1911;

1922) and Bloch (1931). But at the same time humans act on the environment and transform it. Hence, the historian is interested in not only the natural environment with its associated problem of the exploitation of resources but especially the environment that has been modeled and remodeled by human culture. The close connection between the two planes is a powerful antidote against the temptation to transform human history into the natural history typified by environmental determinism (Crosby 1986; Diamond 1997). It is therefore positive that classics such as Emilio Sereni's (1961) history of the Italian landscape are being translated and rediscovered after many years, as well as more recent attempts in this direction (e.g., Ambrosoli 1997).

In 1983 Keith Thomas's book *Man and the Natural World* opened up new perspectives for a cultural and economic history of the environment. It showed how environmental attitudes changed radically with industrialization and the possibilities it offered. The idea that wild and uncontaminated nature predominated in preindustrial Europe is a myth. The landscape was constructed and the land often exploited to the last lump of earth. Paradoxically, therefore, the Arcadian conception of the environment made headway as a reaction to the agricultural revolution and then to industrialization.

Geographic factors such as soil quality and climate probably did have great bearing on the primacy of the Dutch and English in accomplishing the agricultural revolution. But the environmental perspective also helps to clarify the development of agriculture in relation to industry. First, there was the boost that agriculture gave to the first industrial revolution. Following that was the feedback from industry (in the first place, the chemical industry) to agriculture in the late nineteenth century, which definitively resolved the problem of decreasing returns that had so afflicted the classical economists. It is not only a question of the history of technology. Once again, behind the technology, there are human societies that bring about different solutions for the same problems. The controversy of the 1830s and 1840s comes to mind with the theories of Justus von Liebig conflicting with the experimental agriculture of the English (Warde 2009, pp. 82–83). On the one side there was the systematic approach based on plant and soil chemistry, while on the other there was the practical know-how proceeding by trial and error; on the one side innovation was planned and, in order to produce efficacious results, had to be applied on a large scale, while on the other it was left to the enterprising endeavor of individuals. In short, here was also a reflection of the cultural histories of German systematicity and British empiricism.

Nowadays, the more innovative directions of research are concerned with the study of the coexistence between ecology and the economy and the ever precarious balance between them. One particular current explores the relationship with energy sources, and emphasis has rightly been laid on the role played by the material constraints of the organic economy in shaping preindustrial Europe's specific character over the *longue durée* (Landers 2003). Studies have been made on land management and ways of coping with wood shortage in that period, including institutional responses (Warde 2006a). Strategies for the use of common land have been reexamined, and the traditional emphasis on the enclosures has been challenged (De Moor et al. 2002). In the modern period, on the other hand, the coexistence between ecology and economy relates to urbanization and the repercussions of the industrial process on the environment: a case in point is the evolution of the relationship between the towns and waste through industrialization (Sori 2001; Cooper 2009).

But the most important puzzle that environmental history could help to resolve concerns the original conditions that have led to the great imbalances in the world. The real problem for future historians will not be to explain the reasons for Britain's economic primacy in the nineteenth century, the United States' primacy in the twentieth, and China's "only" in the twenty-first. These dynamics are interesting, but in the final analysis they are transitory. The central question will be why several human groups have not spontaneously abandoned even the state of hunter-gatherer society and gone through the Neolithic revolution. Is it because they settled on land unsuited to agriculture and were placed at a disadvantage by nature? Or is it because they were favored by nature and found themselves in a state of relative abundance and low demographic pressure? This is another way to reformulate problems that Boserup and Sahlins raised a few decades ago.

## Final Thoughts

Is economic history really going through a crisis? Judging from the extensive panorama that has just been looked at, and which represents only a small selection of what seem the most interesting approaches, the discipline is apparently full of new life and vitality. The eclecticism that is its hallmark is not undisciplined, and its development is following easily recognizable lines of research. However, it will not have gone unnoticed that most of the cited works are from European historians or historians based at European institutions, or else from practitioners outside the field in the conventional sense. It is very likely that over the next few decades we will see rapidly growing contacts with the historiography of the emerging countries, especially in Asia and hopefully also in Africa in a not-too-distant future. Scholars in these countries have already begun to write their histories, and the success of global history will contribute to integrating the perspectives.

At the same time, the cliometric threat hangs over Europe, as the spread over the past fifteen years of this approach shows (Grantham 1997; R. Tilly 2001; Malanima 2001). The fact that the new economic history is gaining a foothold outside its natural context is probably due to the prestige that economics enjoys in Western society rather than to a process of Americanization. As Richard Wilk points out, "Western culture has elevated economics far above other social sciences. Economists are on TV every day. They speak an exclusive language, they predict the future, and they occupy positions of high authority—in other words, they are the high priests of our culture" (1996, p. 33). Thus it is hardly surprising if, on this side of the Pillars of Hercules, the siren lure has also attracted so many.

For European economic historians, the rediscovery of the roots of their social science history tradition means having the appropriate tools to hold back these drifts. They need to organize themselves with greater awareness and regain the courage to construct the type of historical models of past generations. Certainly, this is more difficult nowadays than it was a few decades ago. The models were sometimes represented by the collective achievements of a particular school, and today there are no compact armies of scholars like those working in the 1970s behind the windows of 54 Boulevard Raspail in Paris or within the thick walls of Cambridge colleges. The schools have disintegrated practically everywhere, a sign of liquid modernity, but this circumstance also offers extraordinary opportunities for individual creativity, and not having strong paradigms is not in itself an obstacle. It should not be forgotten that original and innovative constructions, like those of Kula and Finley, were the work of solitary scholars who were able to draw out the best from a transnational environment. There is no lack of brilliant minds, and it is hoped that what has been written here is an invitation for reflection.

However, this book is addressed primarily to American scholars, to historians of each specialty, as well as to those in the humanities and social sciences. The American historiographical tradition is an important one, and it is a pity that economic history, which was such a dynamic field in the mid-twentieth century, has declined in the way we have seen. The intellectual crisis that it is in is confirmed by the growing marginalization of the discipline in the universities. In the economics departments, it just about survives totally subordinated to economics and acting as its handmaid. But from the history departments, economic history has all but disappeared (see Whaples 2010).

Indeed, academic communities increasingly absorbed in the labyrinths of subjectivity have been discouraged from an earthly subject like economic history by the postmodern turn of the late twentieth century, as O'Brien (2008) has pointed out. Yet postmodernism is now in its twilight, crushed under the weight of its own exaggerations. It has become clear to the overwhelming majority of historians that not all reality is fiction; and, no matter how important it is to read between the lines of a text, the text is still the text (Appleby et al. 1994). If there is a consensus in the profession today, it focuses on more traditional forms of cultural history, alongside the revival of social history (Burke 2008, ch. 6).

The coexistence of a wide variety of orientations in the history departments of American research universities makes them training centers for methodological pluralism. The type of approach to economic history advocated in this book is compatible with the emerging sensibilities. The economy, in a substantive sense, is an important part of the human past, and investigating the production, distribution, and consumption of wealth in societies with regard to their value systems, their geography, scientific knowledge, and intellectual dimension would make a major contribution. It should be clear to humanistic historians that it is not a question of choosing between the economy and culture: in its concrete historical forms, the economy is a manifestation of culture.

Economic history has to also, and especially, lift itself out of the difficult situation it is now in by becoming involved with the genuinely "social" sciences and with all those scholars who are interested in an innovative interaction with historians without imposing any particular point of view. Mention has been made of economic sociology, which has remained faithful to its roots and developed into an influential group. This success story shows that the capacity to think independently and to innovate is ultimately rewarded. Economic historians, sociologists, anthropologists, geographers, and demographers should enter into a dialogue with each other more often. They should organize joint conferences, compare each others' methods, and learn from each other. Today, as in Durkheim's time, social theory can remind historians of the need for conceptualization and help them to formulate their hypotheses and theses more clearly—in short, to produce a more analytical and reasoned history. In their turn, historians can bring depth of vision to the theory, make it more sensitive to changes in circumstances, and warn it of the limits of generalization. In the first quarter of the twentieth century, this interaction gave rise to a historical revolution that started in Alsace. Today a new encounter could lead to a profound renewal of methods on all fronts.

What we need is not applied social science, let alone applied economics, but a science of men in time. History is not made for studying "well-walled gardens," or it would fail in its most important task, which is to understand the world. "It is the fear of history, the fear of its great ambitions, which has killed history," wrote Braudel (1949, p. 351), citing Edmond Faral. One can only conclude by taking up his wish: "May it live again!"

# References _____

Abel, Wilhelm. 1974. *Massenarmut und Hungerkrisen im vorindustriellen Europa: Versuch einer Synopsis.* Hamburg: Paul Parey.

Acemoglu, Daron, Simon Johnson, and James Robinson. 2005. "The Rise of Europe: Atlantic Trade, Institutional Change, and Economic Growth." *American Economic Review* 95.3, 546–79.

Acemoglu, Daron, and James A. Robinson. 2006. *Economic Origins of Dictatorship and Democracy.* New York: Cambridge University Press.

Acheson, James M. 1994. *Anthropology and Institutional Economics.* Lanham, MD: University Press of America.

———. 2002. "Transaction Cost Economics: Accomplishments, Problems, and Possibilities." In Ensminger (2002), 27–58.

Akerlof, George A. 1970. "The Market for 'Lemons': Quality Uncertainty and the Market Mechanism." *Quarterly Journal of Economics* 84.3, 488–500.

Alberti, Leon Battista. 1441. *I libri della famiglia.* Ed. Ruggiero Romano and Alberto Tenenti. Turin: Einaudi, 1994.

Alchian, Armen A. 1950. "Uncertainty, Evolution, and Economic Theory." *Journal of Political Economy* 58.3, 211–21.

Alexander, Jeffrey C. 1995. *Fin de Siècle Social Theory: Relativism, Reduction, and the Problem of Reason.* London: Verso.

Alexander, Jeffrey C., and Bernhard Giesen. 1987. "From Reduction to Linkage: The Long View of the Micro-Macro Link." In *The Micro-Macro Link,* ed. Jeffrey C. Alexander et al. Berkeley: University of California Press, 1–44.

Alford, B.W.E. 2004. "New Frame—Same Picture?" *Business History* 46.4, 640–44.

Alighieri, Dante. 1304–21. *La Commedia secondo l'antica vulgata.* Ed. Giorgio Petrocchi. Florence: Le Lettere, 1994.

Allen, Robert C. 2001. "The Great Divergence in European Wages and Prices from the Middle Ages to the First World War." *Explorations in Economic History* 38, 411–47.

———. 2005. "Real Wages in Europe and Asia: A First Look at the Long-Term Patterns." In *Living Standards in the Past: New Perspectives on Well-Being in Asia and Europe,* ed. Robert C. Allen, Tommy Bengtsson, and Martin Dribe. New York: Oxford University Press, 111–30.

———. 2009a. "How Prosperous Were the Romans? Evidence from Diocletian's Price Edict (AD 301)." In *Quantifying the Roman Economy: Methods and Problems,* ed. Alan Bowman and Andrew Wilson. Oxford: Oxford University Press, 327–45.

———. 2009b. *The British Industrial Revolution in Global Perspective.* Cambridge: Cambridge University Press.

Ambrosoli, Mauro. 1997. *The Wild and the Sown: Botany and Agriculture in Western Europe, 1350–1850.* Cambridge: Cambridge University Press.

Amemiya, Takeshi. 2007. *The Economy and Economics of Ancient Greece*. New York: Routledge.

Andreano, Ralph L., ed. 1970. *The New Economic History: Recent Papers on Methodology*. New York: Wiley.

Andreau, Jean. 1999. *Banking and Business in the Roman World*. Cambridge: Cambridge University Press.

———. 2002a. "Markets, Fairs and Monetary Loans: Cultural History and Economic History in Roman Italy and Hellenistic Greece." In Cartledge et al. (2002), 113–29.

———. 2002b. "Twenty Years after Moses I. Finley's *The Ancient Economy*." In Scheidel and von Reden (2002), 33–49.

Ankarloo, Daniel, and Giulio Palermo. 2004. "Anti-Williamson: A Marxian Critique of New Institutional Economics." *Cambridge Journal of Economics* 28.3, 413–29.

Annis, Sheldon. 1987. *God and Production in a Guatemalan Town*. Austin: University of Texas Press.

Appian. *The Civil Wars*. Loeb Classical Library edition of Appian, vols. 3–4. Cambridge, MA: Harvard University Press, 1913.

Appleby, Andrew B. 1978. *Famine in Tudor and Stuart England*. Stanford: Stanford University Press.

Appleby, Joyce. 2010. *The Relentless Revolution: A History of Capitalism*. New York: Norton.

Appleby, Joyce, Lynn Hunt, and Margaret Jacob. 1994. *Telling the Truth about History*. New York: Norton.

Archer, Margaret S. 2000. "Homo Oeconomicus, Homo Sociologicus *and* Homo Sentiens." In Archer and Tritter (2000), 36–56.

———. 2003. *Structure, Agency and the Internal Conversation*. Cambridge: Cambridge University Press.

Archer, Margaret S., and Jonathan Q. Tritter. 2000. Introduction. In Archer and Tritter (2000), 1–16.

———, eds. 2000. *Rational Choice Theory: Resisting Colonization*. London: Routledge.

Aristotle. *Nicomachean Ethics*. Loeb Classical Library edition of Aristotle, vol. 19. Cambridge, MA: Harvard University Press, 1926.

———. *Politics*. Loeb Classical Library edition of Aristotle, vol. 21. Cambridge, MA: Harvard University Press, 1944. (Trans. Stephen Everson. Cambridge Texts in the History of Political Thought. Cambridge: Cambridge University Press, 1996.)

Aston, Trevor, ed. 1965. *Crisis in Europe, 1560–1660: Essays from "Past and Present."* London: Routledge and Kegan Paul.

Austin, M. M., and P. Vidal-Naquet. 1972. *Economic and Social History of Ancient Greece: An Introduction*. Berkeley: University of California Press, 1977.

Aymard, Maurice. 1972. "The *Annales* and French Historiography, 1929–72." In S. Clark (1999), vol. 1, 3–23.

———. 1983. "Autoconsommation et marchés: Chayanov, Labrousse ou Le Roy Ladurie?" *Annales E.S.C.* 38.6, 1392–1410.

———. 2009. "La longue durée aujourd'hui: bilan d'un demi-siècle, 1958–2008." In *From Florence to the Mediterranean and Beyond: Essays in Honour of Anthony Molho*, ed. Diogo Ramada Curto, Eric R. Dursteler, Julius Kirshner, and Francesca Trivellato. Florence: Olschki, 559–79.

Baehrel, René. 1961. *Une croissance: la Basse-Provence rurale, fin XVIe siècle–1789. Essai d'économie historique statistique.* Paris: SEVPEN.

Baines, Edward. 1835. *History of the Cotton Manufacture in Great Britain.* London: Fisher and Jackson.

Bairoch, Paul. 1963. *Révolution industrielle et sous-développement.* Paris: SEDES.

———. 1971. *Le Tiers-Monde dans l'impasse. Le démarrage économique du XVIIIe au XXe siècle.* Paris: Gallimard.

———. 1973. "Agriculture and the Industrial Revolution, 1700–1914." In *The Fontana Economic History of Europe*, vol. 3: *The Industrial Revolution*, ed. Carlo M. Cipolla. Glasgow: Fontana/Collins, 452–506.

———. 1975. *The Economic Development of the Third World since 1900.* London: Methuen.

———. 1985. *Cities and Economic Development: From the Dawn of History to the Present.* Chicago: University of Chicago Press, 1988.

———. 1993. *Economics and World History: Myths and Paradoxes.* Chicago: University of Chicago Press.

———. 1997. *Victoires et déboires. Histoire économique et sociale du monde du XVIe siècle à nos jours.* Paris: Gallimard.

Baker, Wayne E. 1984. "The Social Structure of a National Securities Market." *American Journal of Sociology* 89.4, 775–811.

Bang, Peter F. 2008. *The Roman Bazaar: A Comparative Study of Trade and Markets in a Tributary Empire.* Cambridge: Cambridge University Press.

Barbagli, Marzio. 2000. *Sotto lo stesso tetto: mutamenti della famiglia in Italia dal XV al XX secolo.* Bologna: Il Mulino.

Barlett, Peggy F., ed. 1980. *Agricultural Decision Making: Anthropological Contributions to Rural Development.* New York: Academic Press.

Barnes, John A. 1947. "Postscript: Structural Amnesia." In *Models and Interpretations: Selected Esssays.* Cambridge: Cambridge University Press, 1990, 227–28.

Bates, Robert H., Avner Greif, Margaret Levi, Jean-Laurent Rosenthal, and Barry R. Weingast. 1998. *Analytic Narratives.* Princeton: Princeton University Press.

Becker, Gary S. 1965. "A Theory of the Allocation of Time." *Economic Journal* 75, 493–517.

———. 1976a. "Altruism, Egoism, and Genetic Fitness: Economics and Sociobiology." In *The Economic Approach to Human Behavior.* Chicago: University of Chicago Press, 282–94.

———. 1976b. *The Economic Approach to Human Behavior.* Chicago: University of Chicago Press.

———. 1991. *A Treatise on the Family.* Enlarged ed. Cambridge, MA: Harvard University Press.

———. 1996. *Accounting for Tastes.* Cambridge, MA: Harvard University Press.

Beckert, Jens. 2002. *Beyond the Market: The Social Foundations of Economic Efficiency*. Princeton: Princeton University Press.

———. 2009. "The Great Transformation of Embeddedness: Karl Polanyi and the New Economic Sociology." In Hann and Hart (2009), 38–55.

Bedford, Peter R. 2005. "The Economy of the Near East in the First Millennium BC." In Manning and Morris (2005), 58–83.

Ben-Amos, Ilana C. 2008. *The Culture of Giving: Informal Support and Gift-Exchange in Early Modern England*. Cambridge: Cambridge University Press.

Benedict, Ruth. 1934. *Patterns of Culture*. Boston: Houghton Mifflin.

Bentley, Michael. 2005. "The Evolution and Dissemination of Historical Knowledge." In *The Organisation of Knowledge in Victorian Britain*, ed. Martin Daunton. Oxford: Oxford University Press, 173–98.

Berg, Maxine. 1980. *The Machinery Question and the Making of Political Economy, 1815–1848*. Cambridge: Cambridge University Press.

———. 2005. *Luxury and Pleasure in Eighteenth-Century Britain*. Oxford: Oxford University Press.

Berg, Maxine, and Helen Clifford, eds. 1999. *Consumers and Luxury: Consumer Culture in Europe, 1650–1850*. Manchester: Manchester University Press.

Berg, Maxine, and Elizabeth Eger, eds. 2003. *Luxury in the Eighteenth Century: Debates, Desires and Delectable Goods*. Basingstoke: Palgrave Macmillan.

Bird-David, Nurit. 1992. "Beyond 'The Original Affluent Society': A Culturalist Reformulation." *Current Anthropology* 33.1, 25–47.

Bloch, Marc. 1924. *The Royal Touch: Sacred Monarchy and Scrofula in England and France*. London: Routledge and Kegan Paul, 1973.

———. 1928. "Pour une histoire comparée des sociétés européennes." *Revue de synthèse historique* 46, 15–50.

———. 1931. *French Rural History: An Essay on Its Basic Characteristics*. Berkeley: University of California Press, 1966.

———. 1949. *The Historian's Craft*. Manchester: Manchester University Press, 1992.

———. 1954. *Esquisse d'une histoire monétaire de l'Europe*. Paris: Colin.

Boas, Franz. 1897. "The Social Organization and the Secret Societies of the Kwakiutl Indians." *Report of the U.S. National Museum for 1895*. Washington, DC, 311–738.

———. 1911. *The Mind of Primitive Man*. New York: Free Press, 1963.

Boehm, Stephan, Christian Gehrke, Heinz D. Kurz, and Richard Sturn, eds. 2002. *Is There Progress in Economics? Knowledge, Truth and the History of Economic Thought*. Cheltenham: Elgar.

Bohannan, Paul, and George Dalton, eds. 1962. *Markets in Africa: Eight Subsistence Economies in Transition*. Evanston, IL: Northwestern University Press.

Boldizzoni, Francesco. 2003. "Il governo della moneta a Milano dal 1650 alla Guerra di successione spagnola." *Storia economica* 6.3, 387–433.

———. 2008. *Means and Ends: The Idea of Capital in the West, 1500–1970*. Basingstoke: Palgrave Macmillan.

Bonney, Richard, ed. 1995. *The Origins of the Modern State in Europe, 13th to 18th Centuries: Economic Systems and State Finance.* Oxford: Clarendon Press.

———, ed. 1999. *The Rise of the Fiscal State in Europe, c. 1200–1815.* Oxford: Oxford University Press.

Booth, W. James. 1993. *Households: On the Moral Architecture of the Economy.* Ithaca, NY: Cornell University Press.

Boserup, Ester. 1965. *The Conditions of Agricultural Growth: The Economics of Agrarian Change under Population Pressure.* London: Allen & Unwin.

Botticini, Maristella. 1999. "A Loveless Economy? Intergenerational Altruism and the Marriage Market in a Tuscan Town, 1415–1436." *Journal of Economic History* 59.1, 104–21.

Botticini, Maristella, and Aloysius Siow. 2003. "Why Dowries?" *American Economic Review* 93.4, 1385–98.

Bourdelais, Patrice. 1984. "French Quantitative History: Problems and Promises." *Social Science History* 8.2, 179–92.

Bourdieu, Pierre. 1963. "The Attitude of the Algerian Peasant towards Time." In *Mediterranean Countrymen: Essays on the Social Anthropology of the Mediterranean,* ed. Julian A. Pitt-Rivers. Paris: Mouton, 55–72.

———. 1972. *Outline of a Theory of Practice.* Cambridge: Cambridge University Press, 1977.

———. 1979. *Distinction: A Social Critique of the Judgement of Taste.* Cambridge, MA: Harvard University Press, 1984.

———. 1980. *The Logic of Practice.* Cambridge: Polity Press, 1990.

———. 2000. *The Social Structures of the Economy.* Cambridge: Polity Press, 2005.

Bouvier, Jean. 1961. *Le Crédit Lyonnais de 1863 à 1882: les années de formation d'une banque de dépôts.* Paris: SEVPEN.

Boyd, Robert, and Peter J. Richerson. 1985. *Culture and the Evolutionary Process.* Chicago: University of Chicago Press.

———. 2005. *Not by Genes Alone: How Culture Transformed Human Evolution.* Chicago: University of Chicago Press.

Boyer, Pascal. 2001. *Religion Explained: The Evolutionary Origins of Religious Thought.* New York: Basic Books.

Boyer, Robert. 2009. "Historiens et économistes face à l'émergence des institutions du marché." *Annales H.S.S.* 64.3, 665–93.

Braudel, Fernand. 1949. "Préface de *La Méditerranée.*" In Braudel (1997), 343–51.

———. 1955. "L'impérialisme de l'histoire." In Braudel (1997), 163–90.

———. 1958. "La longue durée" (original title: "Histoire et sciences sociales"). In Braudel (1997), 191–230.

———. 1959. "Histoire des civilisations: le passé explique le présent." In Braudel (1997), 254–313.

———. 1966. *The Mediterranean and the Mediterranean World in the Age of Philip II.* 2nd ed. Berkeley: University of California Press, 1995.

Braudel, Fernand, ed. 1974. *Conjoncture économique structures sociales. Hommage à Ernest Labrousse*. Paris: Mouton.

———. 1977. *Afterthoughts on Material Civilization and Capitalism*. Baltimore: Johns Hopkins University Press.

———. 1979. *Civilization and Capitalism, 15th–18th Century*. 3 vols. Berkeley: University of California Press, 1992.

———. 1987. *A History of Civilizations*. New York: Penguin, 1995.

———. 1997. *Les ambitions de l'histoire*. Ed. Maurice Aymard. Paris: Editions de Fallois.

Brewer, John, and Frank Trentmann, eds. 2006. *Consuming Cultures, Global Perspectives: Historical Trajectories, Transnational Exchanges*. Oxford: Berg.

Brunner, Otto. 1939. *Land und Herrschaft. Grundfragen der territorialen Verfassungsgeschichte Südostdeutschlands im Mittelalter*. Baden bei Wien: Rohrer.

———. 1958. "Das 'ganze Haus' und die alteuropäische Ökonomik." In *Neue Wege der Verfassungs- und Sozialgeschichte*. 2nd ed. Göttingen: Vandenhoek und Ruprecht, 1968, 103–27.

Bücher, Karl. 1901. *Die Entstehung der Volkswirtschaft: Vorträge und Versuche*. 3rd ed.Tübingen: Laupp.

Burford, Alison. 1993. *Land and Labor in the Greek World*. Baltimore: Johns Hopkins University Press.

Burguière, André. 2009. *The Annales School: An Intellectual History*. Ithaca, NY: Cornell University Press.

Burke, Edmund. 1790. *Reflections on the Revolution in France*. Ed. J.C.D. Clark. Stanford: Stanford University Press, 2001.

Burke, Peter. 1987. *The Historical Anthropology of Early Modern Italy: Essays on Perception and Communication*. Cambridge: Cambridge University Press.

———. 1990. *The French Historical Revolution: The Annales School, 1929–89*. Cambridge: Polity Press.

———. 2005. *History and Social Theory*. 2nd ed. Cambridge: Polity Press.

———. 2008. *What Is Cultural History?* 2nd ed. Cambridge: Polity Press.

———. 2009. *Cultural Hybridity*. Cambridge: Polity Press.

Campbell, Bruce M. S. 2005. "The Agrarian Problem in the Early Fourteenth Century." *Past and Present* 188, 3–70.

Cancian, Frank. 1966. "Maximization as Norm, Strategy, and Theory: A Comment on Programmatic Statements in Economic Anthropology." *American Anthropologist* 68.2, 465–70.

———. 1989. "Economic Behavior in Peasant Communities." In Plattner (1989), 127–70.

Caron, François. 1973. *Histoire de l'exploitation d'un grand réseau: la Compagnie du Chemin de Fer du Nord, 1846–1937*. Paris: Mouton.

———. 1997. *Histoire des chemins de fer en France*, vol. 1: *1740–1883*. Paris: Fayard.

———. 2005. *Histoire des chemins de fer en France*, vol. 2: *1883–1937*. Paris: Fayard.

Carrier, James G. 1995. *Gifts and Commodities: Exchange and Western Capitalism since 1700*. London: Routledge.

Carruthers, Bruce G. 1996. *City of Capital: Politics and Markets in the English Financial Revolution.* Princeton: Princeton University Press.

Cartledge, Paul. 2002a. "The Economy (Economies) of Ancient Greece." In Scheidel and von Reden (2002), 11–32.

———. 2002b. "The Political Economy of Greek Slavery." In Cartledge et al. (2002), 156–66.

Cartledge, Paul, Edward E. Cohen, and Lin Foxhall, eds. 2002. *Money, Labour and Land: Approaches to the Economies of Ancient Greece.* London: Routledge.

Cashdan, Elizabeth. 1989. "Hunters and Gatherers: Economic Behavior in Bands." In Plattner (1989), 21–48.

———, ed. 1990. *Risk and Uncertainty in Tribal and Peasant Economies.* Boulder, CO: Westview Press.

Cattini, Marco. 1973. "Produzione, auto-consumo e mercato dei grani a San Felice sul Panaro, 1590–1637." *Rivista Storica Italiana* 85.3, 698–755.

———. 1984. *I contadini di San Felice: metamorfosi di un mondo rurale nell'Emilia dell'età moderna.* Turin: Einaudi.

———. 2005. "Sui caratteri della civiltà ligure." In *La città e il mare: dalla Liguria al mondo*, ed. Giorgetta Revelli. Pisa: ETS, 381–87.

Cattini, Marco, and Marzio A. Romani. 2009. "Legami di sangue: relazioni politiche, matrimoni e circolazione della ricchezza nelle casate sovrane dell'Italia centro-settentrionale nei secoli XV–XVIII (ricerche in corso)." In *La famiglia nell'economia europea. Secc. XIII–XVIII*, ed. Simonetta Cavaciocchi. Florence: Firenze University Press, 47–68.

Chan, Selina C. 2006. "Love and Jewelry: Patriarchal Control, Conjugal Ties, and Changing Identities." In *Modern Loves: The Anthropology of Romantic Courtship and Companionate Marriage*, ed. Jennifer S. Hirsch and Holly Wardlow. Ann Arbor: University of Michigan Press, 35–50.

Chapman, Malcolm, and Peter J. Buckley. 1997. "Markets, Transaction Costs, Economists and Social Anthropologists." In *Meanings of the Market: The Free Market in Western Culture*, ed. James Carrier. Oxford: Berg, 225–50.

Chaudhuri, K. N. 1990. *Asia before Europe: Economy and Civilisation of the Indian Ocean from the Rise of Islam to 1750.* Cambridge: Cambridge University Press.

Chaunu, Pierre. 1964. "Histoire quantitative ou histoire sérielle." In Chaunu (1978), 20–27.

———. 1970. "L'histoire sérielle: bilan et perspectives." In Chaunu (1978), 121–38.

———. 1978. *Histoire quantitative histoire sérielle.* Paris: Colin.

Chaunu, Pierre, and Huguette Chaunu. 1955–60. *Séville et l'Atlantique, 1504–1650.* Paris: SEVPEN.

Chayanov, Alexander. 1924. "On the Theory of Non-capitalist Economic Systems." In Thorner et al. (1966), 1–28.

———. 1925. "Peasant Farm Organization." In Thorner et al. (1966), 29–269.

Cicero. *De officiis.* Loeb Classical Library edition of Cicero, vol. 21. Cambridge, MA: Harvard University Press, 1913.

Cicero. *De senectute*. Loeb Classical Library edition of Cicero, vol. 20. Cambridge, MA: Harvard University Press, 1923.

Cipolla, Carlo M. 1956. *Money, Prices, and Civilization in the Mediterranean World: Fifth to Seventeenth Century*. Princeton: Princeton University Press.

———. 1962. *The Economic History of World Population*. Harmondsworth: Penguin.

———. 1973. "Il ruolo delle spezie (e del pepe in particolare) nello sviluppo economico del Medioevo." In *Allegro ma non troppo*. Bologna: Il Mulino, 1988, 11–40.

———. 1991. *Between Two Cultures: An Introduction to Economic History*. New York: Norton.

———. 1993. *Before the Industrial Revolution: European Society and Economy, 1000–1700*. 3rd ed. London: Routledge.

Clapham, J. H. 1922. "Of Empty Economic Boxes." *Economic Journal* 32, 305–14.

Clark, Gregory. 1998. "A Precocious Infant? The Evolution of the English Grain Market, 1208–1770." In *Integration of Commodity Markets in History*, ed. Clara E. Núñez. Madrid: Proceedings of the Twelfth IEHA Congress, 17–29.

———. 2007. *A Farewell to Alms: A Brief Economic History of the World*. Princeton: Princeton University Press.

Clark, Peter, ed. 1985. *The European Crisis of the 1590s: Essays in Comparative History*. London: Allen & Unwin.

Clark, Stuart, ed. 1999. *The Annales School: Critical Assessments*. London: Routledge.

Coase, R. H. 1937. "The Nature of the Firm." *Economica* 4, 386–405.

Coats, A. W. 1980. "The Historical Context of the 'New' Economic History." *Journal of European Economic History* 9.1, 185–207.

———. 1990. "Disciplinary Self-Examination, Departments, and Research Traditions in Economic History: The Anglo-American Story." *Scandinavian Economic History Review* 38.1, 3–18.

Cochran, Thomas C. 1969. "Economic History, Old and New." *American Historical Review* 74.5, 1561–72.

*Codice diplomatico della Repubblica di Genova*. Rome: Tipografia del Senato, 1936–42.

Cohen, Edward E. 1992. *Athenian Economy and Society: A Banking Perspective*. Princeton: Princeton University Press.

———. 2008. "The Elasticity of the Money-Supply at Athens." In Harris (2008b), 66–83.

Cohen, Lizabeth. 2003. *A Consumer's Republic: The Politics of Mass Consumption in Twentieth-Century America*. New York: Knopf.

Cohen, Percy S. 1967. "Economic Analysis and Economic Man: Some Comments on a Controversy." In *Themes in Economic Anthropology*, ed. Raymond Firth. London: Tavistock, 91–118.

Conrad, Alfred H., and John R. Meyer. 1958. "The Economics of Slavery in the Ante Bellum South." *Journal of Political Economy* 66.2, 95–130.

Cook, Scott. 1966. "The Obsolete 'Anti-Market' Mentality: A Critique of the Substantive Approach to Economic Anthropology." *American Anthropologist* 68.2: 323–45.

Cooper, Tim. 2009. "Modernity and the Politics of Waste in Britain." In Sörlin and Warde (2009), 247–72.

Corritore, Renzo P. 2007. "La costituzione di scorte granarie pubbliche e la politica economica degli stati in età pre-industriale." In *Tra vecchi e nuovi equilibri: domanda e offerta di servizi in Italia in età moderna e contemporanea,* ed. Iginia Lopane and Ezio Ritrovato. Bari: Cacucci, 487–501.

Crafts, N.F.R. 1985. *British Economic Growth during the Industrial Revolution.* Oxford: Clarendon Press.

Crosby, Alfred W. 1986. *Ecological Imperialism: The Biological Expansion of Europe, 900–1900.* New York: Cambridge University Press.

Cullen, Louis. 2005. "Labrousse, the Annales School, and Histoire sans Frontières." *Journal of European Economic History* 34.1, 309–50.

Cunningham, William. 1892. "The Perversion of Economic History." *Economic Journal* 2.7, 491–506.

Daileader, Philip, and Philip Whalen, eds. 2010. *French Historians, 1900–2000.* Oxford: Wiley-Blackwell.

Dake, Karl. 1991. "Orienting Dispositions in the Perception of Risk: An Analysis of Contemporary Worldviews and Cultural Biases." *Journal of Cross-Cultural Psychology* 22.1, 61–82.

Dalton, George. 1971. *Economic Anthropology and Development: Essays on Tribal and Peasant Economies.* New York: Basic Books.

Danziger, Eve. 2005. "The Eye of the Beholder: How Linguistic Categorization Affects 'Natural' Experience." In McKinnon and Silverman (2005), 64–80.

Daunton, Martin. 2001. *Trusting Leviathan: The Politics of Taxation in Britain, 1799–1914.* Cambridge: Cambridge University Press.

———. 2002. *Just Taxes: The Politics of Taxation in Britain, 1914–1979.* Cambridge: Cambridge University Press.

———. 2010. "Rationality and Institutions: Reflections on Douglass North." *Structural Change and Economic Dynamics* 21.2, 147–56.

Daunton, Martin, and Matthew Hilton, eds. 2001. *The Politics of Consumption: Material Culture and Citizenship in Europe and America.* Oxford: Berg.

Daunton, Martin, and Frank Trentmann, eds. 2005. *Worlds of Political Economy: Knowledge and Power in the Nineteenth and Twentieth Centuries.* Basingstoke: Palgrave Macmillan.

David, Paul A. 1985. "Clio and the Economics of QWERTY." *American Economic Review* 75.2, 332–37.

David, Paul A., Herbert G. Gutman, Richard Sutch, Peter Temin, and Gavin Wright. 1976. *Reckoning with Slavery.* New York: Oxford University Press.

Davies, John K. 2005. "Linear and Nonlinear Flow Models for Ancient Economies." In Manning and Morris (2005), 127–56.

Davies, R. W., ed. 1990. *From Tsarism to the New Economic Policy: Continuity and Change in the Economy of the USSR.* Basingstoke: Macmillan.

Davies, Wendy, and Paul Fouracre, eds. 1995. *Property and Power in the Early Middle Ages*. Cambridge: Cambridge University Press.

Davis, John. 1992. *Exchange*. Buckingham: Open University Press.

Davis, Lance E. 1968. "'And It Will Never Be Literature': The New Economic History; A Critique." In Andreano (1970), 67–83.

Davis, Natalie Zemon. 2000. *The Gift in Sixteenth-Century France*. Madison: University of Wisconsin Press.

Davis, Robert C. 1991. *Shipbuilders of the Venetian Arsenal: Workers and Workplace in the Preindustrial City*. Baltimore: Johns Hopkins University Press.

Dawkins, Richard. 1976. *The Selfish Gene*. Oxford: Oxford University Press.

Day, John. 1999. *Money and Finance in the Age of Merchant Capitalism*. Oxford: Blackwell.

de Grazia, Victoria. 2005. *Irresistible Empire: America's Advance through Twentieth-Century Europe*. Cambridge, MA: Belknap Press.

De Maddalena, Aldo. 1980. "Il mercantilismo." In *Storia delle idee politiche economiche sociali*, vol. 4.1: *L'età moderna*, ed. Norberto Bobbio. Turin: UTET, 637–91.

———. 1982. "'Pecunia pecuniam parit': anche nella Milano del Seicento. Debiti monetari e tassi d'interesse, 1620–1720." In *Dalla città al borgo: avvio di una metamorfosi economica e sociale nella Lombardia spagnola*. Milan: Angeli, 199–250.

De Moor, Martina, Leigh Shaw-Taylor, and Paul Warde, eds. 2002. *The Management of Common Land in North West Europe, c. 1500–1850*. Turnhout: Brepols.

de Vries, Jan. 1994. "The Industrial Revolution and the Industrious Revolution." *Journal of Economic History* 54.2, 249–70.

———. 2008. *The Industrious Revolution: Consumer Behavior and the Household Economy, 1650 to the Present*. New York: Cambridge University Press.

de Vries, Jan, and Ad van der Woude. 1997. *The First Modern Economy: Success, Failure, and Perseverance of the Dutch Economy, 1500–1815*. Cambridge: Cambridge University Press.

de Waal, Frans. 2006. "Morally Evolved: Primate Social Instincts, Human Morality, and the Rise and Fall of 'Veneer Theory.'" In Macedo and Ober (2006), 1–80.

Deane, Phyllis. 1978. *The Evolution of Economic Ideas*. Cambridge: Cambridge University Press.

Delumeau, Jean. 1966. "Le commerce extérieur français au XVIIe siècle." *Dix-septième siècle* 70–71, 81–105.

Demélas, Marie-Danielle, and Nadine Vivier, eds. 2003. *Les propriétés collectives face aux attaques libérales, 1750–1914. Europe occidentale et Amérique latine*. Rennes: Presses Universitaires de Rennes.

Deyon, Pierre. 1967. *Amiens, capitale provinciale: étude sur la société urbaine au XVIIe siècle*. Paris: Mouton.

Diamond, Jared. 1997. *Guns, Germs, and Steel: The Fates of Human Societies*. New York: Norton.

Diamond, Jared, and James A. Robinson, eds. 2010. *Natural Experiments of History*. Cambridge, MA: Belknap Press.

Douglas, Mary. 1967. "Primitive Rationing: A Study in Controlled Exchange." In *Themes in Economic Anthropology*, ed. Raymond Firth. London: Tavistock, 119–47.

———. 1986. *How Institutions Think*. Syracuse, NY: Syracuse University Press.

Douglas, Mary, and Aaron Wildavsky. 1982. *Risk and Culture: An Essay on the Selection of Technological and Environmental Dangers*. Berkeley: University of California Press.

Drukker, J. W. 2003. *The Revolution That Bit Its Own Tail: How Economic History Changed Our Ideas on Economic Growth*. Amsterdam: Aksant, 2006.

Duby, Georges. 1973. *Guerriers et paysans, VIIe–XIIe siècle: premier essor de l'économie européenne*. Paris: Gallimard.

Duncan-Jones, Richard. 1990. *Structure and Scale in the Roman Economy*. Cambridge: Cambridge University Press.

———. 1994. *Money and Government in the Roman Empire*. Cambridge: Cambridge University Press.

Dupâquier, Jacques. 1968. "Sur la population française au XVIIe et au XVIIIe siècle." *Revue Historique* 239, 43–79.

Durkheim, Emile. 1895. *The Rules of Sociological Method*. Chicago: University of Chicago Press, 1938.

———. 1897. *Suicide: A Study in Sociology*. New York: Free Press, 1997.

Durrenberger E. Paul, and Nicola Tannenbaum. 1992. "Household Economy, Political Economy, and Ideology: Peasants and the State in Southeast Asia." *American Anthropologist* 94.1, 74–89.

———. 2002. "Chayanov and Theory in Economic Anthropology." In Ensminger (2002), 137–53.

Earle, Timothy. 2002. *Bronze Age Economics: The Beginnings of Political Economies*. Boulder, CO: Westview Press.

Ekelund, Robert B., Jr., Robert F. Hébert, and Robert D. Tollison. 2006. *The Marketplace of Christianity*. Cambridge, MA: MIT Press.

Elias, Norbert. 1939. *The Civilizing Process*. Oxford: Blackwell, 2000.

Ellickson, Robert C. 1993. "Property in Land." *Yale Law Journal* 102, 1315–1400.

Ellickson, Robert C., and Charles DiA. Thorland. 1995. "Ancient Land Law: Mesopotamia, Egypt, Israel." *Chicago-Kent Law Review* 71, 321–411.

Elster, Jon. 1984. *Ulysses and the Sirens: Studies in Rationality and Irrationality*. Rev. ed. Cambridge: Cambridge University Press.

———. 1989. *Nuts and Bolts for the Social Sciences*. New York: Cambridge University Press.

———. 2007. *Explaining Social Behavior: More Nuts and Bolts for the Social Sciences*. New York: Cambridge University Press.

Ensminger, Jean, ed. 2002. *Theory in Economic Anthropology*. Walnut Creek, CA: AltaMira Press.

Epstein, Stephan R. 1992. *An Island for Itself: Economic Development and Social Change in Late Medieval Sicily*. Cambridge: Cambridge University Press.

———. 1994. "Regional Fairs, Institutional Innovation, and Economic Growth in Late Medieval Europe." *Economic History Review* 47.3, 459–82.

———. 2000. *Freedom and Growth: The Rise of States and Markets in Europe, 1300–1750*. London: Routledge.

Epstein, Steven A. 1996. *Genoa and the Genoese, 958–1528*. Chapel Hill: University of North Carolina Press.

Erdkamp, Paul. 2005. *The Grain Market in the Roman Empire: A Social, Political and Economic Study*. Cambridge: Cambridge University Press.

Espeland, Wendy N., and Mitchell L. Stevens. 1998. "Commensuration as a Social Process." *Annual Review of Sociology* 24, 313–43.

Etemad, Bouda, and Jean Batou. 1999. "Paul Bairoch, 1930–1999." *Revue Suisse d'Histoire* 49.3, 391–94.

Etzioni, Amitai. 1988. *The Moral Dimension: Toward a New Economics*. New York: Free Press.

Eucken, Walter. 1940. *The Foundations of Economics: History and Theory in the Analysis of Economic Reality*. Chicago: University of Chicago Press, 1951.

Evans-Pritchard, E. E. 1940. *The Nuer: A Description of the Modes of Livelihood and Political Institutions of a Nilotic People*. Oxford: Oxford University Press.

Fassin, Didier. 2009. "Les économies morales revisitées." *Annales H.S.S.* 64.6, 1237–66.

Febvre, Lucien. 1911. *Philippe II et la Franche-Comté: étude d'histoire politique, religieuse et sociale*. Paris: Champion.

———. 1922. *A Geographical Introduction to History*. New York: Knopf, 1925.

———. 1942. *The Problem of Unbelief in the Sixteenth Century: The Religion of Rabelais*. Cambridge, MA: Harvard University Press, 1982.

Federico, Giovanni. 2005. *Feeding the World: An Economic History of Agriculture, 1800–2000*. Princeton: Princeton University Press.

Ferguson, Niall, ed. 1997. *Virtual History: Alternatives and Counterfactuals*. London: Picador.

Fine, Ben, and Dimitris Milonakis. 2003. "From Principle of Pricing to Pricing of Principle: Rationality and Irrationality in the Economic History of Douglass North." *Comparative Studies in Society and History* 45.3, 546–70.

———. 2009. *From Economics Imperialism to Freakonomics: The Shifting Boundaries between Economics and Other Social Sciences*. Abingdon: Routledge.

Finkelstein, Andrea. 2000. *Harmony and the Balance: An Intellectual History of Seventeenth-Century English Economic Thought*. Ann Arbor: University of Michigan Press.

Finley, M. I. 1970. "Aristotle and Economic Analysis." *Past and Present* 47, 3–25.

———. 1975. *The Use and Abuse of History*. London: Chatto & Windus.

———. 1976. Introduction. In *Studies in Roman Property*, ed. M. I. Finley. Cambridge: Cambridge University Press, 1–6.

———. 1977. *The World of Odysseus*. 2nd ed. London: Chatto & Windus.

———. 1980. *Ancient Slavery and Modern Ideology*. Princeton: Markus Wiener, 1998.

———. 1985. *The Ancient Economy*. 2nd ed. Berkeley: University of California Press.

Finn, Margot C. 2003. *The Character of Credit: Personal Debt in English Culture, 1740–1914*. Cambridge: Cambridge University Press.

Firth, Raymond. 1939. *Primitive Polynesian Economy*. London: Routledge.

Fishlow, Albert. 1965. *American Railroads and the Transformation of the Antebellum Economy*. Cambridge, MA: Harvard University Press.

Fleury, Michel, and Louis Henry. 1956. *Des registres paroissiaux à l'histoire de la population. Manuel de dépouillement et d'exploitation de l'état civil ancien*. Paris: INED.

Fligstein, Neil. 1996. "Markets as Politics: A Political-Cultural Approach to Market Institutions." *American Sociological Review* 61.4, 656–73.

———. 2001. *The Architecture of Markets: An Economic Sociology of Twenty-first-Century Capitalist Societies*. Princeton: Princeton University Press.

Florus. *Epitome of Roman History*. Loeb Classical Library. Cambridge, MA: Harvard University Press, 1929.

Floud, Roderick. 2001. "In at the Beginning of British Cliometrics." In P. Hudson (2001), 86–90.

Fogel, Robert W. 1964. *Railroads and American Economic Growth: Essays in Econometric History*. Baltimore: Johns Hopkins University Press.

Fogel, Robert W., and Stanley L. Engerman. 1974. *Time on the Cross: The Economics of American Negro Slavery*. New York: Norton.

Foley, William A. 2005. "Do Humans Have Innate Mental Structures? Some Arguments from Linguistics." In McKinnon and Silverman (2005), 43–63.

Fontaine, Laurence. 2008. *L'économie morale: pauvreté, crédit et confiance dans l'Europe préindustrielle*. Paris: Gallimard.

Foraboschi, Daniele. 1995. Review of E. Cohen (1992). *Rivista Storica Italiana* 107.1, 183–89.

Forster, Robert. 1978. "Achievements of the Annales School." *Journal of Economic History* 38.1, 58–76.

Foster, George M. 1965. "Peasant Society and the Image of Limited Good." *American Anthropologist* 67.2, 293–315.

Fowler, Catherine S., and Nancy J. Turner. 1999. "Ecological/Cosmological Knowledge and Land Management among Hunter-Gatherers." In *The Cambridge Encyclopedia of Hunters and Gatherers*, ed. Richard B. Lee and Richard Daly. Cambridge: Cambridge University Press, 419–25.

Foxhall, Lin. 2002. "Access to Resources in Classical Greece: The Egalitarianism of the Polis in Practice." In Cartledge et al. (2002), 209–20.

Freedman, Craig F. 2005. *Chicago Fundamentalism: Ideology and Methodology in Economics*. Singapore: World Scientific.

Freeman, Chris, and Francisco Louçã. 2001. *As Time Goes By: From the Industrial Revolution to the Information Revolution*. Oxford: Oxford University Press.

Freyre, Gilberto. 1933. *The Masters and the Slaves: A Study in the Development of Brazilian Civilization*. Berkeley: University of California Press, 1986.

Fukuyama, Francis. 1992. *The End of History and the Last Man*. New York: Free Press.

Furet, François. 1971. "Quantitative History." *Daedalus* 100.1, 151–67.

———. 1978. *Interpreting the French Revolution*. Cambridge: Cambridge University Press 1981.

Gabba, Emilio. 1988. *Del buon uso della ricchezza: saggi di storia economica e sociale del mondo antico*. Milan: Guerini.

Gallant, Thomas W. 1991. *Risk and Survival in Ancient Greece: Reconstructing the Rural Domestic Economy*. Cambridge: Polity Press.

Galor, Oded, and Omer Moav. 2002. "Natural Selection and the Origin of Economic Growth." *Quarterly Journal of Economics* 117.4, 1133–91.

Garnsey, Peter. 1988. *Famine and Food Supply in the Graeco-Roman World: Responses to Risk and Crisis*. Cambridge: Cambridge University Press.

———. 1999. *Food and Society in Classical Antiquity*. Cambridge: Cambridge University Press.

———. 2007. *Thinking about Property: From Antiquity to the Age of Revolution*. Cambridge: Cambridge University Press.

Geertz, Clifford. 1973. *The Interpretation of Cultures*. New York: Basic Books.

———. 1978. "The Bazaar Economy: Information and Search in Peasant Marketing." *American Economic Review* 68.2, 28–32.

Gerschenkron, Alexander. 1962. *Economic Backwardness in Historical Perspective: A Book of Essays*. Cambridge, MA: Belknap Press.

Gibbon, Edward. 1776–89. *The History of the Decline and Fall of the Roman Empire*. Ed. J. B. Bury. New York: Fred de Fau, 1906.

Gibson, Kathleen R. 2005. "Epigenesis, Brain Plasticity, and Behavioral Versatility: Alternatives to Standard Evolutionary Psychology Models." In McKinnon and Silverman (2005), 23–42.

Giddens, Anthony. 1979. *Central Problems in Social Theory*. London: Macmillan.

———. 1984. *The Constitution of Society: Outline of the Theory of Structuration*. Cambridge: Polity Press.

Ginzburg, Carlo. 1966. *The Night Battles: Witchcraft and Agrarian Cults in the Sixteenth and Seventeenth Centuries*. Baltimore: Johns Hopkins University Press, 1983.

Godelier, Maurice. 1966. *Rationality and Irrationality in Economics*. New York: Monthly Review Press, 1972.

Goldgar, Anne. 2007. *Tulipmania: Money, Honor, and Knowledge in the Dutch Golden Age*. Chicago: University of Chicago Press.

Goldin, Claudia, and Lawrence F. Katz. 2008. *The Race between Education and Technology*. Cambridge, MA: Belknap Press.

Goldstone, Jack A. 2002. "Efflorescences and Economic Growth in World History: Rethinking the 'Rise of the West' and the Industrial Revolution." *Journal of World History* 13.2, 323–89.

Goldthwaite, Richard A. 1993. *Wealth and the Demand for Art in Italy, 1300–1600*. Baltimore: Johns Hopkins University Press.

———. 2009. *The Economy of Renaissance Florence*. Baltimore: Johns Hopkins University Press.

Goodfriend, Marvin, and John McDermott. 1995. "Early Development." *American Economic Review* 85.1, 116–33.

Goody, Jack. 1977. *The Domestication of the Savage Mind*. Cambridge: Cambridge University Press.

———. 1983. *The Development of the Family and Marriage in Europe*. Cambridge: Cambridge University Press.

———. 1990. *The Oriental, the Ancient and the Primitive: Systems of Marriage and the Family in the Pre-industrial Societies of Eurasia*. Cambridge: Cambridge University Press.

———. 1996. *The East in the West*. Cambridge: Cambridge University Press.

———. 2004. *Capitalism and Modernity: The Great Debate*. Cambridge: Polity Press.

———. 2006. *The Theft of History*. Cambridge: Cambridge University Press.

Goody, Jack, and Stanley J. Tambiah. 1973. *Bridewealth and Dowry*. Cambridge: Cambridge University Press.

Goubert, Pierre. 1960. *Beauvais et le Beauvaisis de 1600 à 1730: contribution à l'histoire sociale de la France du XVIIe siècle*. Paris: SEVPEN.

Gould, S. J., and R. C. Lewontin. 1979. "The Spandrels of San Marco and the Panglossian Paradigm: A Critique of the Adaptationist Programme." *Proceedings of the Royal Society of London* B205, 581–98.

Granovetter, Mark S. 1973. "The Strength of Weak Ties." *American Journal of Sociology* 78.6, 1360–80.

———. 1974. *Getting a Job: A Study of Contacts and Careers*. Cambridge, MA: Harvard University Press.

———. 1985. "Economic Action and Social Structure: The Problem of Embeddedness." *American Journal of Sociology* 91.3, 481–510.

———. 1995. "The Economic Sociology of Firms and Entrepreneurs." In *The Economic Sociology of Immigration: Essays on Networks, Ethnicity, and Entrepreneurship*, ed. Alejandro Portes. New York: Russell Sage Foundation, 128–65.

———. 2002. "A Theoretical Agenda for Economic Sociology." In *The New Economic Sociology: Developments in an Emerging Field*, ed. Mauro F. Guillén, Randall Collins, Paula England, and Marshall Meyer. New York: Russell Sage Foundation, 35–60.

———. 2005a. "Comment on Liverani and Bedford." In Manning and Morris (2005), 84–88.

———. 2005b. "The Impact of Social Structure on Economic Outcomes." *Journal of Economic Perspectives* 19.1, 33–50.

Grantham, George. 1997. "The French Cliometric Revolution: A Survey of Cliometric Contributions to French Economic History." *European Review of Economic History* 1.3, 353–405.

Gregory, Paul R. 1994. *Before Command: An Economic History of Russia from Emancipation to the First Five-Year Plan*. Princeton: Princeton University Press.

Greif, Avner. 1998. "Self-Enforcing Political System and Economic Growth: Late Medieval Genoa." In Bates et al. (1998), 23–63.

———. 2005. "Comment on Hitchner and Saller." In Manning and Morris (2005), 239–42.

———. 2006. *Institutions and the Path to the Modern Economy: Lessons from Medieval Trade*. New York: Cambridge University Press.

Grenier, Jean-Yves. 1996. *L'économie d'Ancien régime: un monde de l'échange et de l'incertitude*. Paris: Albin Michel.

———. 2001. "Du bon usage du modèle en histoire." In *Le modèle et le récit*, ed. Jean-Yves Grenier, Claude Grignon, and Pierre-Michel Menger. Paris: Editions de la MSH.

Grossi, Paolo. 1981. *An Alternative to Private Property: Collective Property in the Juridical Consciousness of the Nineteenth Century*. Chicago: University of Chicago Press.

Gudeman, Stephen. 1986. *Economics as Culture: Models and Metaphors of Livelihood*. London: Routledge and Kegan Paul.

———. 2001. *The Anthropology of Economy: Community, Market, and Culture*. Oxford: Blackwell.

———. 2008. *Economy's Tension: The Dialectics of Community and Market*. New York: Berghahn Books.

Gudeman, Stephen, and Alberto Rivera. 1990. *Conversations in Colombia: The Domestic Economy in Life and Text*. Cambridge: Cambridge University Press.

Guerzoni, Guido. 1999. "*Liberalitas, Magnificentia, Splendor*: The Classic Origins of Italian Renaissance Lifestyles." In *Economic Engagements with Art*, ed. Neil De Marchi and Craufurd D. W. Goodwin. Durham, NC: Duke University Press, 332–78.

———. 2007. "The Social World of Price Formation: Prices and Consumption in Sixteenth-Century Ferrara." In O'Malley and Welch (2007), 85–105.

Guiso, Luigi, Paola Sapienza, and Luigi Zingales. 2006. "Does Culture Affect Economic Outcomes?" *Journal of Economic Perspectives* 20.2, 23–48.

Gutman, Herbert G. 1975. *Slavery and the Numbers Game: A Critique of "Time on the Cross."* Urbana: University of Illinois Press.

Guyer, Jane I. 2009. "Composites, Fictions, and Risk: Toward an Ethnography of Price." In Hann and Hart (2009), 203–20.

Gwako, Edwins L. M. 2002. "Property Rights and Incentives for Agricultural Growth: Women Farmers' Crop Control and Their Use of Agricultural Inputs." In Ensminger (2002), 3–25.

Halbwachs, Maurice. 1925. *Les cadres sociaux de la mémoire*. Paris: Alcan. (Abridged English trans., *On Collective Memory*. Chicago: University of Chicago Press, 1992.)

Halperin, Rhoda H. 1994. *Cultural Economies: Past and Present*. Austin: University of Texas Press.

Halperin, Rhoda H., and James Dow, eds. 1977. *Peasant Livelihood: Studies in Economic Anthropology and Cultural Ecology*. New York: St. Martin's Press.

Hann, Chris, and Keith Hart, eds. 2009. *Market and Society:"The Great Transformation" Today*. Cambridge: Cambridge University Press.

Hansen, Mogens H. 1998. *Polis and City-State: An Ancient Concept and Its Modern Equivalent*. Copenhagen: Royal Danish Academy of Sciences and Letters.

Hanson, Victor D. 1998. *Warfare and Agriculture in Classical Greece*. 2nd ed. Berkeley: University of California Press.

Harcourt, Geoffrey C. 1982. *The Social Science Imperialists*. London: Routledge and Kegan Paul.

Harris, W. V. 2006. "A Revisionist View of Roman Money." *Journal of Roman Studies* 96.1, 1–24.

———. 2008a. "The Nature of Roman Money." In Harris (2008b), 174–207.

———, ed. 2008b. *The Monetary Systems of the Greeks and Romans*. New York: Oxford University Press.

Harrison, A.R.W. 1968. *The Law of Athens*, vol. 1: *The Family and Property*. Oxford: Oxford University Press.

Harrison, Lawrence E., and Samuel P. Huntington, eds. 2000. *Culture Matters: How Values Shape Human Progress*. New York: Basic Books.

Haskell, Thomas L. 1975. "The True and Tragical History of *Time on the Cross*." *New York Review of Books* 22.15, 33–39.

Hayek, Friedrich A., ed. 1935. *Collectivist Economic Planning: Critical Studies on the Possibilities of Socialism*. London: Routledge.

Henrich, Joseph. 2002. "Decision Making, Cultural Transmission, and Adaptation in Economic Anthropology." In Ensminger (2002), 251–95.

Herlihy, David, and Christiane Klapisch-Zuber. 1985. *Tuscans and Their Families: A Study of the Florentine Catasto of 1427*. New Haven: Yale University Press.

Herskovitz, Melville J. 1940. *The Economic Life of Primitive Peoples*. New York: Knopf.

Hesiod. *Theogony*. Loeb Classical Library edition of Hesiod, vol. 1. Cambridge, MA: Harvard University Press, 2006.

Hicks, J. R. 1937. "Mr. Keynes and the 'Classics': A Suggested Interpretation." *Econometrica* 5.2, 147–59.

———. 1969. *A Theory of Economic History*. Oxford: Clarendon Press.

Hill, Polly. 1982. *Dry Grain Farming Families: Hausaland (Nigeria) and Karnataka (India) Compared*. Cambridge: Cambridge University Press.

———. 1986. *Development Economics on Trial: The Anthropological Case for a Prosecution*. Cambridge: Cambridge University Press.

Hilton, Matthew. 2003. *Consumerism in Twentieth-Century Britain: The Search for a Historical Movement*. Cambridge: Cambridge University Press.

Hirsch, Fred. 1976. *Social Limits to Growth*. London: Routledge and Kegan Paul.

Hirschman, Albert O. 1977. *The Passions and the Interests: Political Arguments for Capitalism before Its Triumph*. Princeton: Princeton University Press.

Hitchner, R. Bruce. 2002. "Olive Production and the Roman Economy: The Case for Intensive Growth in the Roman Empire." In Scheidel and von Reden (2002), 71–83.

Hobbes, Thomas. 1642. *De cive*. Molesworth edition of Hobbes's Latin works, vol. 2. Aalen: Scientia Verlag, 1961.

———. 1651. *Leviathan*. Ed. Richard Tuck. Cambridge: Cambridge University Press, 1991.

Hobsbawm, Eric J. 1959. *Primitive Rebels: Studies in Archaic Forms of Social Movement in the Nineteenth and Twentieth Centuries*. Manchester: Manchester University Press.

Hoch, Steven L. 1986. *Serfdom and Social Control in Russia: Petrovskoe, a Village in Tambov*. Chicago: University of Chicago Press.

Hodgson, Geoffrey M. 2000. "From Micro to Macro: The Concept of Emergence and the Role of Institutions." In *Institutions and the Role of the State*, ed. Leonardo Burlamaqui, Ana C. Castro, and Ha-Joon Chang. Cheltenham: Elgar, 103–26.

———. 2001. *How Economics Forgot History: The Problem of Historical Specificity in Social Science*. London: Routledge.

Hoffman, Philip T. 1996. *Growth in a Traditional Society: The French Countryside, 1450–1815*. Princeton: Princeton University Press.

Hont, Istvan. 2005. *Jealousy of Trade: International Competition and the Nation-State in Historical Perspective*. Cambridge, MA: Belknap Press.

Hopkins, Keith. 1980. "Taxes and Trade in the Roman Empire, 200 B.C.–A.D. 400." *Journal of Roman Studies* 70, 101–25.

———. 2002. "Rome, Taxes, Rents and Trade." In Scheidel and von Reden (2002), 101–25.

Hoppit, Julian. 2006. "The Contexts and Contours of British Economic Literature, 1660–1760." *Historical Journal* 49.1, 79–110.

Horn, Jeff. 2006. *The Path Not Taken: French Industrialization in the Age of Revolution, 1750–1830*. Cambridge, MA: MIT Press.

Howell, Martha C. 2010. *Commerce before Capitalism in Europe, 1300–1600*. New York: Cambridge University Press.

Hsia, R. Po-chia, ed. 2004. *A Companion to the Reformation World*. Oxford: Blackwell.

———. 2005. *The World of Catholic Renewal, 1540–1770*. 2nd ed. Cambridge: Cambridge University Press.

Hudson, Michael. 2010. "Entrepreneurs: From the Near Eastern Takeoff to the Roman Collapse." In Landes et al. (2010), 8–36.

Hudson, Pat, ed. 2001. *Living Economic and Social History*. Glasgow: Economic History Society.

———. 2006. "Choice and Habit in History." *Shakai-Keizaishigaku/Socio-Economic History* 72.3, 3–18.

———. 2010. "Closeness and Distance: A Response to Brewer." *Cultural and Social History* 7.3, 375–85.

Hughes, Jonathan R. T. 1991. "Interview." In Lyons et al. (2008), 232–47.

Huntington, Samuel P. 1996. *The Clash of Civilizations and the Remaking of World Order*. New York: Simon & Schuster.

Huxley, T. H. 1894. *Evolution and Ethics*. Princeton: Princeton University Press, 2009.

Imperiale, Cesare. 1936. Prefazione. In *Codice*, vol. 1, vii–xli.

Jacob, Margaret C. 1997. *Scientific Culture and the Making of the Industrial West*. New York: Oxford University Press.

Jacob, Margaret C., and Catherine Secretan, eds. 2008. *The Self-Perception of Early Modern Capitalists*. New York: Palgrave Macmillan.

Jacob, Margaret C., and Larry Stewart. 2004. *Practical Matter: Newton's Science in the Service of Industry and Empire, 1687–1851*. Cambridge, MA: Harvard University Press.

James, Harold. 2006a. *Family Capitalism: Wendels, Haniels, Falcks, and the Continental European Model*. Cambridge, MA: Belknap Press.

———. 2006b. *The Roman Predicament: How the Rules of International Order Create the Politics of Empire*. Princeton: Princeton University Press.

———. 2009. *The Creation and Destruction of Value: The Globalization Cycle*. Cambridge, MA: Harvard University Press.

Jones, A.H.M. 1974. *The Roman Economy: Studies in Ancient Economic and Administrative History*. Oxford: Oxford University Press.

Jones, E. L. 1988. *Growth Recurring: Economic Change in World History*. Oxford: Clarendon Press.

———. 2006. *Cultures Merging: A Historical and Economic Critique of Culture*. Princeton: Princeton University Press.

Jones, Richard. 1831. *An Essay on the Distribution of Wealth, and on the Sources of Taxation*. London: Murray.

Jongman, Willem M. 2007. "Gibbon Was Right: The Decline and Fall of the Roman Economy." In *Crises and the Roman Empire*, ed. Olivier Hekster, Gerda de Kleijn, and Daniëlle Slootjes. Leiden: Brill, 183–99.

Kahneman, Daniel, and Amos Tversky. 1974. "Judgement under Uncertainty: Heuristics and Biases." *Science* 185: 1124–31.

Kant, Immanuel. 1788. *Critique of Practical Reason*. Cambridge: Cambridge University Press, 1997.

Kaplan, Steven L. 1996. *The Bakers of Paris and the Bread Question, 1700–1775*. Durham, NC: Duke University Press.

Kaplan, Steven L., and Philippe Minard, eds. 2004. *La France, malade du corporatisme? XVIIIe–XXe.siècles*. Paris: Belin.

Kessler, David, and Peter Temin. 2007. "The Organization of the Grain Trade in the Early Roman Empire." *Economic History Review* 60.2, 313–32.

———. 2008. "Money and Prices in the Early Roman Empire." In Harris (2008b), 137–59.

Klapisch, Christiane. 1972. "Household and Family in Tuscany in 1427." In Laslett (1972), 267–81.

Knight, Frank H. 1941. "Anthropology and Economics." *Journal of Political Economy* 49.2, 247–68.

Kocka, Jürgen. 1984. "Theories and Quantification in History." *Social Science History* 8.2, 169–78.

Korsgaard, Christine M. 2006. "Morality and the Distinctiveness of Human Action." In Macedo and Ober (2006), 98–119.

Kriedte, Peter, Hans Medick, and Jürgen Schlumbohm. 1981. *Industrialization before Industrialization: Rural Industry in the Genesis of Capitalism.* Cambridge: Cambridge University Press.

Kron, Geoffrey. 2005. "Anthropometry, Physical Anthropology, and the Reconstruction of Ancient Health, Nutrition, and Living Standards." *Historia* 54.1, 68–83.

Kron, Geoffrey. Forthcoming. "Nutrition, Hygiene and Mortality: Setting Parameters for Roman Health and Life Expectancy Consistent with Our Comparative Evidence." In Lo Cascio (forthcoming).

Krugman, Paul. 2010. "Learning from Europe." *New York Times*, January 11, A17.

Kula, Witold. 1960. "Histoire et économie: la longue durée." *Annales E.S.C.* 15.2, 294–313.

———. 1962. *An Economic Theory of the Feudal System: Towards a Model of the Polish Economy, 1500–1800.* London: New Left Books, 1976.

———. 1963. *The Problems and Methods of Economic History.* Aldershot: Ashgate, 2001.

———. 1989. "Mon 'éducation sentimentale.'" *Annales E.S.C.* 44.1, 133–46.

Kurke, Leslie. 1991. *The Traffic in Praise: Pindar and the Poetics of Social Economy.* Ithaca, NY: Cornell University Press.

———. 1999. *Coins, Bodies, Games, and Gold: The Politics of Meaning in Archaic Greece.* Princeton: Princeton University Press.

Labrot, Gérard. 2004. "Eloge de la copie: le marché napolitain, 1614–1764." *Annales H.S.S.* 59.1, 7–35.

Labrousse, C.-E. 1933. *Esquisse du mouvement des prix et des revenus en France au XVIIIe siècle.* Paris: Dalloz.

———. 1944. *La crise de l'économie française à la fin de l'Ancien Régime et au début de la Révolution.* Preface by Jean-Claude Perrot. Paris: Presses Universitaires de France, 1990.

Lal, Deepak. 1998. *Unintended Consequences: The Impact of Factor Endowments, Culture, and Politics on Long-Run Economic Performance.* Cambridge, MA: MIT Press.

———. 2008. *Reviving the Invisible Hand: The Case for Classical Liberalism in the Twenty-first Century.* Princeton: Princeton University Press.

Lamoreaux, Naomi R. 1998. "Economic History and the Cliometric Revolution." In *Imagined Histories: American Historians Interpret the Past*, ed. Anthony Molho and Gordon S. Wood. Princeton: Princeton University Press, 59–84.

Landa, Janet T. 1994. *Trust, Ethnicity, and Identity: Beyond the New Institutional Economics of Ethnic Trading Networks, Contract Law, and Gift-Exchange.* Ann Arbor: University of Michigan Press.

Landers, John. 2003. *The Field and the Forge: Population, Production, and Power in the Pre-industrial West.* Oxford: Oxford University Press.

Landes, David S. 1969. *The Unbound Prometheus: Technological Change and Industrial Development in Western Europe from 1750 to the Present*. Cambridge: Cambridge University Press.

——. 1983. *Revolution in Time: Clocks and the Making of the Modern World*. Cambridge, MA: Belknap Press.

——. 1986. "What Do Bosses Really Do?" *Journal of Economic History* 46.3, 585–623.

——. 1998. *The Wealth and Poverty of Nations: Why Some Are So Rich and Some So Poor*. New York: Norton.

Landes, David S., Joel Mokyr, and William J. Baumol, eds. 2010. *The Invention of Enterprise: Entrepreneurship from Ancient Mesopotamia to Modern Times*. Princeton: Princeton University Press.

Laslett, Peter. 1965. *The World We Have Lost*. London: Methuen.

——, ed. 1972. *Household and Family in Past Time*. Cambridge: Cambridge University Press.

Lazear, Edward P. 2000. "Economic Imperialism." *Quarterly Journal of Economics* 115.1, 99–146.

Le Goff, Jacques. 1981. *The Birth of Purgatory*. Chicago: University of Chicago Press, 1984.

——. 1988. "L'histoire nouvelle." In *La nouvelle histoire*. Paris: Complexe, 35–75.

Le Roy Ladurie, Emmanuel. 1966. *Les paysans de Languedoc*. Paris: SEVPEN.

——. 1968. "L'historien et l'ordinateur." In *Le territoire de l'historien*. Paris: Gallimard, 1973, 11–14.

——. 1979. *Le Carnaval de Romans: de la Chandeleur au mercredi des Cendres, 1579–1580*. Paris: Gallimard.

——. 1983. *La sorcière de Jasmin*. Paris: Editions du Seuil.

——. 1995. "Un monarca che non capiva l'imprevedibile." *Corriere della sera*, October 28, 27.

Le Roy Ladurie, Emmanuel, and Joseph Goy. 1982. *Tithe and Agrarian History from the Fourteenth to the Nineteenth Century: An Essay in Comparative History*. Cambridge: Cambridge University Press.

LeClair, Edward. 1962. "Economic Theory and Economic Anthropology." *American Anthropologist* 64.6, 1179–1203.

Léon, Pierre. 1954. *La naissance de la grande industrie en Dauphiné, fin du XVIIe siècle–1869*. Paris: Presses Universitaires de France.

——. 1970. *Economies et sociétés préindustrielles, 1650–1780: les origines d'une accélération de l'histoire*. Paris: Colin.

Lévi-Strauss, Claude. 1962. *The Savage Mind*. Chicago: University of Chicago Press, 1966.

Lewis, W. Arthur. 1954. "Economic Development with Unlimited Supplies of Labour." *Manchester School* 22.2, 139–91.

Linton, Ralph. 1936. *The Study of Man: An Introduction*. New York: Appleton-Century.

Lippincott, Benjamin E., ed. 1938. *On the Economic Theory of Socialism*. Minneapolis: University of Minnesota Press.

List, Friedrich. 1841. *National System of Political Economy*. Philadelphia: Lippincott, 1856.

Lo Cascio, Elio, ed. Forthcoming. *L'impatto della "peste antonina."* Bari: Edipuglia.

Lopez, Robert S. 1971. *The Commercial Revolution of the Middle Ages, 950–1350*. Englewood Cliffs, NJ: Prentice-Hall.

Lucas, Robert E. 2002. *Lectures on Economic Growth*. Cambridge, MA: Harvard University Press.

Lucian. *How to Write History*. Loeb Classical Library edition of Lucian, vol. 6. Cambridge, MA: Harvard University Press, 1959.

Luebke, David M., ed. 1999. *The Counter-Reformation*. Oxford: Blackwell.

Lyons, John S., Louis P. Cain, and Samuel H. Williamson, eds. 2008. *Reflections on the Cliometric Revolution: Conversations with Economic Historians*. Abingdon: Routledge.

Macedo, Stephen, and Josiah Ober, eds. 2006. *Primates and Philosophers: How Morality Evolved*. Princeton: Princeton University Press.

Macfarlane, Alan. 1994. "The Origins of Capitalism in Japan, China and the West: The Work of Norman Jacobs." *Cambridge Anthropology* 17.3, 43–66.

———. 1998. "The Mystery of Property: Inheritance and Industrialization in England and Japan." In *Property Relations: Renewing the Anthropological Tradition*, ed. C. M. Hann. Cambridge: Cambridge University Press, 104–23.

Machiavelli, Niccolò. 1513. "To Francesco Vettori, His Benefactor (December 10)." In *The Letters of Machiavelli*. Ed. Allan Gilbert. Chicago: University of Chicago Press, 1988, 139–44.

———. 1531. *Discourses on Livy*. Ed. Julia Conaway Bondanella and Peter Bondanella. Oxford: Oxford University Press, 1997.

Maddison, Angus. 2006. *The World Economy*. Paris: OECD.

———. 2007. *Contours of the World Economy, 1–2030 AD: Essays in Macro-Economic History*. Oxford: Oxford University Press.

Malanima, Paolo. 2001. "From the Mediterranean: About Scylla and Charybdis." In P. Hudson (2001), 224–27.

———. 2003. "Measuring the Italian Economy, 1300–1861." *Rivista di storia economica* 19.3, 265–95.

Malinowski, Bronislaw. 1922. *Argonauts of the Western Pacific: An Account of Native Enterprise and Adventure in the Archipelagoes of Melanesian New Guinea*. London: George Routledge & Sons.

Malthus, T. R. 1820. *Principles of Political Economy*. Ed. John Pullen. Cambridge: Cambridge University Press, 1989.

Manning, Joseph G. 2004. "Property Rights and Contracting in Ptolemaic Egypt." *Journal of Institutional and Theoretical Economics* 160.4, 758–64.

Manning, Joseph G., and Ian Morris, eds. 2005. *The Ancient Economy: Evidence and Models*. Stanford: Stanford University Press.

Marczewski, Jean. 1964. "Buts et méthodes de l'histoire quantitative." *Cahiers Vilfredo Pareto* 3, 127–64.

Marin, Brigitte, and Catherine Virlouvet, eds. 2003. *Nourrir les cités de Méditerranée. Antiquité–Temps modernes*. Paris: Maisonneuve et Larose.

Maslow, A. H. 1943. "A Theory of Human Motivation." *Psychological Review* 50.4, 370–96.

Mauss, Marcel. 1914. "Les origines de la notion de monnaie." In *Œuvres*, vol. 2: *Représentations collectives et diversité des civilisations*. Paris: Editions de Minuit, 1969, 106–12.

———. 1923–24. "Essai sur le don. Forme et raison de l'échange dans les sociétés archaïques." *Année sociologique*, n.s., 1, 30–186.

McCants, Anne E. C. 2002. Review of Le Roy Ladurie (1966). EH.Net Economic History Services, http://eh.net/node/2737.

McClelland, David C. 1961. *The Achieving Society*. Princeton: Van Nostrand.

McCloskey, D. N. 1987. *Econometric History*. Basingstoke: Macmillan.

———. 1989. "The Open Fields of England: Rent, Risk, and the Rate of Interest, 1300–1815." In *Markets in History: Economic Studies of the Past*, ed. David W. Galenson. New York: Cambridge University Press, 5–51.

———. 2006. *The Bourgeois Virtues: Ethics for an Age of Commerce*. Chicago: University of Chicago Press.

———. 2010. *Bourgeois Dignity: Why Economics Can't Explain the Modern World*. Chicago: University of Chicago Press.

McKinnon, Susan. 2005. *Neo-liberal Genetics: The Myths and Moral Tales of Evolutionary Psychology*. Chicago: Prickly Paradigm Press.

McKinnon, Susan, and Sydel Silverman, eds. 2005. *Complexities: Beyond Nature and Nurture*. Chicago: University of Chicago Press.

McLean, Paul D., and John F. Padgett. 1997. "Was Florence a Perfectly Competitive Market? Transactional Evidence from the Renaissance." *Theory and Society* 26, 209–44.

———. 2004. "Obligation, Risk, and Opportunity in the Renaissance Economy: Beyond Social Embeddedness to Network Co-constitution." In *The Sociology of the Economy*, ed. Frank Dobbin. New York: Russell Sage Foundation, 193–227.

Meckler, Michael, ed. 2006. *Classical Antiquity and the Politics of America: From George Washington to George W. Bush*. Waco, TX: Baylor University Press.

Mendels, Franklin F. 1972. "Proto-industrialization: The First Phase of the Industrialization Process." *Journal of Economic History* 32.1, 241–61.

Menger, Carl. 1884. *Die Irrthümer des Historismus in der deutschen Nationalökonomie*. Vienna: Hölder.

Meuvret, Jean. 1977. *Le problème des subsistances à l'époque Louis XIV*, vol. 1: *La production des céréales dans la France du XVIIe et du XVIIIe siècle*. Paris: EHESS.

———. 1987. *Le problème des subsistances à l'époque Louis XIV*, vol. 2: *La production des céréales et la société rurale*. Paris: EHESS.

Milberg, William. 2009. "The New Social Science Imperialism and the Problem of Knowledge in Contemporary Economics." In *Economic Persuasions*, ed. Stephen Gudeman. New York: Berghahn, 43–61.

Miller, Judith A. 1999. *Mastering the Market: The State and the Grain Trade in Northern France, 1700–1860*. New York: Cambridge University Press.

Millett, Paul. 1991. *Lending and Borrowing in Ancient Athens*. Cambridge: Cambridge University Press.

——. 2001. "Productive to Some Purpose? The Problem of Ancient Economic Growth." In *Economies beyond Agriculture in the Classical World*, ed. David J. Mattingly and John Salmon. London: Routledge, 17–48.

Minard, Philippe. 1998. *La fortune du colbertisme. Etat et industrie dans la France des Lumières*. Paris: Fayard.

Mirowski, Philip. 1988. *Against Mechanism: Protecting Economics from Science*. Totowa, NJ: Rowman and Littlefield.

Mokyr, Joel. 1990. *The Lever of Riches: Technological Creativity and Economic Progress*. New York: Oxford University Press.

——. 1991. "Evolutionary Biology, Technological Change and Economic History." *Bulletin of Economic Research* 43.2, 127–49.

——. 2000. "Evolutionary Phenomena in Technological Change." In *Technological Innovation as an Evolutionary Process*, ed. John Ziman. Cambridge: Cambridge University Press, 52–65.

——. 2002. *The Gifts of Athena: Historical Origins of the Knowledge Economy*. Princeton: Princeton University Press.

——. 2003. Review of Drukker (2003). EH.Net Economic History Services, http://eh.net/book_reviews/de-revolutie-die-haar-eigen-staart-beet-hoe-de-econo mische-geschiedenis-onze-idee%C3%ABn-ove.

——. 2005. "Is There a Theory of Economic History?" In *The Evolutionary Foundations of Economics*, ed. Kurt Dopfer. Cambridge: Cambridge University Press, 195–218.

——. 2008. "The Institutional Origins of the Industrial Revolution." In *Institutions and Economic Performance*, ed. Elhanan Helpman. Cambridge, MA: Harvard University Press, 64–119.

——. 2009. *The Enlightened Economy: An Economic History of Britain, 1700–1850*. New Haven: Yale University Press.

Molho, Anthony. 1994. *Marriage Alliance in Late Medieval Florence*. Cambridge, MA: Harvard University Press.

More, Thomas. 1516. *Utopia*. Cambridge: Cambridge University Press, 2002.

Morineau, Michel. 1996. "Esquisse et Crise: une relecture nécessaire d'Ernest Labrousse." *Annales Historiques de la Révolution Française* 303, 77–107.

Morishima, Michio. 1982. *Why Has Japan "Succeeded"? Western Technology and the Japanese Ethos*. New York: Cambridge University Press.

Morley, Neville. 2007. *Trade in Classical Antiquity*. Cambridge: Cambridge University Press.

Morris, Ian. 2004. "Economic Growth in Ancient Greece." *Journal of Institutional and Theoretical Economics* 160.4, 709–42.

——. 2005. "Archaeology, Standards of Living, and Greek Economic History." In Manning and Morris (2005), 91–126.

Morris, Ian, and Barry R. Weingast. 2004. "Views and Comments on Institutions, Economics and the Ancient Mediterranean World: Introduction." *Journal of Institutional and Theoretical Economics* 160.4, 702–8.

Muldrew, Craig. 1998. *The Economy of Obligation: The Culture of Credit and Social Relations in Early Modern England*. Basingstoke: Macmillan.

Myrdal, Gunnar. 1968. *Asian Drama: An Inquiry into the Poverty of Nations*. London: Allen Lane.

Needham, Joseph. 1965. *Science and Civilisation in China*, vol. 4.2: *Mechanical Engineering*. Cambridge: Cambridge University Press.

Nef, John U. 1958. *Cultural Foundations of Industrial Civilization*. Cambridge: Cambridge University Press.

Nehring, Holger, and Florian Schui, eds. 2007. *Global Debates about Taxation*. Basingstoke: Palgrave Macmillan.

Nelson Jonathan K., and Richard J. Zeckhauser. 2008. *The Patron's Payoff: Conspicuous Commissions in Italian Renaissance Art*. Princeton: Princeton University Press.

Nelson, Richard, and Sidney Winter. 1982. *An Evolutionary Theory of Economic Change*. Cambridge, MA: Belknap Press.

Nelson, Robert H. 2001. *Economics as Religion: From Samuelson to Chicago and Beyond*. University Park: Pennsylvania State University Press.

Newman, Lucile F., ed. 1990. *Hunger in History: Food Shortage, Poverty, and Deprivation*. Oxford: Blackwell.

North, Douglass C. 1977a. "Markets and Other Allocation Systems in History: The Challenge of Karl Polanyi." *Journal of European Economic History* 6.3, 703–16.

———. 1977b. Review of Kula (1962). *Journal of European Economic History* 6.2, 508–10.

———. 1978. "Comment on McCloskey, Cohen, and Forster Papers." *Journal of Economic History* 38.1, 77–80.

———. 1981. *Structure and Change in Economic History*. New York: Norton.

———. 1990. *Institutions, Institutional Change and Economic Performance*. New York: Cambridge University Press.

———. 2005. *Understanding the Process of Economic Change*. Princeton: Princeton University Press.

———. 2008. "Further Reflections." In Lyons et al. (2008), 211–12.

North, Douglass C., John J. Wallis, and Barry R. Weingast. 2009. *Violence and Social Orders: A Conceptual Framework for Interpreting Recorded Human History*. Cambridge: Cambridge University Press.

North, Douglass C., and Barry R. Weingast. 1989. "Constitutions and Commitment: The Evolution of Institutions Governing Public Choice in Seventeenth-Century England." *Journal of Economic History* 49.4, 803–32.

Nozick, Robert. 1974. *Anarchy, State, and Utopia*. New York: Basic Books.

Nussbaum, Martha C. 2010. *Not for Profit: Why Democracy Needs the Humanities*. Princeton: Princeton University Press.

Ó Gráda, Cormac. 2009. *Famine: A Short History*. Princeton: Princeton University Press.

O'Brien, Patrick K. 2008. "The Shock, Achievements and Disappointments of the New." In Lyons et al. (2008), 437–43.

O'Brien, Patrick K. 2010. "Deconstructing the British Industrial Revolution." In *Reconceptualizing the Industrial Revolution*, ed. Jeff Horn, Leonard N. Rosenband, and Merritt Roe Smith. Cambridge, MA: MIT Press, 21–46.

Offer, Avner. 2006. *The Challenge of Affluence: Self-Control and Well-Being in the United States and Britain since 1950.* Oxford: Oxford University Press.

Ogilvie, Sheilagh. 2001. "The Economic World of the Bohemian Serf: Economic Concepts, Preferences, and Constraints on the Estate of Friedland, 1583–1692." *Economic History Review* 54.3, 430–53.

———. 2003. *A Bitter Living: Women, Markets, and Social Capital in Early Modern Germany.* Oxford: Oxford University Press.

O'Malley, Michelle, and Evelyn Welch, eds. 2007. *The Material Renaissance.* Manchester: Manchester University Press.

Orléan, André. 1990. "Le rôle des influences interpersonnelles dans la détermination des cours boursiers." *Revue économique* 41.5, 839–68.

———. 1992. "Contagion des opinions et fonctionnement des marchés financiers." *Revue économique* 43.4, 685–98.

Ormrod, W. Mark, Margaret Bonney, and Richard Bonney, eds. 1999. *Crises, Revolutions and Self-Sustained Growth: Essays in European Fiscal History, 1130–1830.* Stamford, England: Shaun Tyas.

Padgett, John. 2010. "Open Elite? Social Mobility, Marriage, and Family in Florence, 1282–1494." *Renaissance Quarterly* 63.2, 357–411.

Padgett, John F., and Paul D. McLean. 2006. "Organizational Invention and Elite Transformation: The Birth of Partnership Systems in Renaissance Florence." *American Journal of Sociology* 111.5, 1463–1568.

Pallot, Judith. 1999. *Land Reform in Russia, 1906–1917: Peasant Responses to Stolypin's Project of Rural Transformation.* Oxford: Clarendon Press.

Pareto, Vilfredo. 1906. *Manual of Political Economy.* New York: Kelley, 1971.

Parker, Geoffrey, and Lesley M. Smith, eds. 1997. *The General Crisis of the Seventeenth Century.* 2nd ed. London: Routledge.

Parsons, Stephen D. 2003. *Money, Time, and Rationality in Max Weber: Austrian Connections.* London: Routledge.

Parsons, Talcott, and Neil J. Smelser. 1956. *Economy and Society: A Study in the Integration of Economic and Social Theory.* Glencoe, IL: Free Press.

Pearson, Harry W. 1957. "Parsons and Smelser on the Economy." In Polanyi et al. (1957), 307–19.

Pearson, Heath. 2000. "*Homo Economicus* Goes Native, 1859–1945: The Rise and Fall of Primitive Economics." *History of Political Economy* 32.4, 933–89.

Perrot, Jean-Claude. 1992. *Une histoire intellectuelle de l'économie politique, XVIIe–XVIIIe siècle.* Paris: Editions de l'EHESS.

Perroux, François. 1973. *Pouvoir et économie.* Paris: Bordas.

———. 1983. *A New Concept of Development: Basic Tenets.* London and Paris: Croom Helm and Unesco.

Persson, Karl G. 1988. *Pre-industrial Economic Growth: Social Organization and Technological Progress in Europe.* Oxford: Blackwell.

———. 1999. *Grain Markets in Europe, 1500–1900: Integration and Deregulation.* Cambridge: Cambridge University Press.

Persson, Torsten, and Guido Tabellini. 2000. *Political Economics: Explaining Economic Policy*. Cambridge, MA: MIT Press.

Pinker, Steven. 1997. *How the Mind Works*. New York: Norton.

———. 2002. *The Blank Slate: The Modern Denial of Human Nature*. New York: Viking Press.

Plattner, Stuart, ed. 1975. *Formal Methods in Economic Anthropology*. Washington, DC: American Anthropological Association.

———, ed. 1989. *Economic Anthropology*. Stanford: Stanford University Press.

Plutarch. *Lives*, vol. 3: *Crassus*. Loeb Classical Library. Cambridge, MA: Harvard University Press, 1916.

Pocock, J.G.A. 1975. *The Machiavellian Moment: Florentine Political Thought and the Atlantic Republican Tradition*. Princeton: Princeton University Press.

Podolny, Joel M. 2005. *Status Signals: A Sociological Study of Market Competition*. Princeton: Princeton University Press.

Polanyi, Karl. 1944. *The Great Transformation: The Political and Economic Origins of Our Time*. Boston: Beacon Press, 2001.

———. 1957a. "Aristotle Discovers The Economy." In Polanyi et al. (1957), 64–94.

———. 1957b. "The Economy as Instituted Process." In Polanyi et al. (1957), 243–70.

Polanyi, Karl, and Conrad M. Arensberg. 1957. Preface. In Polanyi et al. (1957), v–xi.

Polanyi, Karl, Conrad M. Arensberg, and Harry W. Pearson, eds. 1957. *Trade and Market in the Early Empires: Economies in History and Theory*. Glencoe, IL: Free Press.

Pomeranz, Kenneth. 2000. *The Great Divergence: China, Europe, and the Making of the Modern World Economy*. Princeton: Princeton University Press.

Pomian, Krzysztof. 1978. "Impact of the Annales School in Eastern Europe." *Review* 1.3–4, 101–18.

Popkin, Samuel. 1979. *The Rational Peasant: The Political Economy of Rural Society in Vietnam*. Berkeley: University of California Press.

Posner, Richard A. 1980a. "A Theory of Primitive Society, with Special Reference to Law." *Journal of Law and Economics*. 23.1, 1–53.

———. 1980b. "Anthropology and Economics." *Journal of Political Economy* 88.3, 608–16.

Postan, M. M. 1966. "Medieval Agrarian Society in Its Prime: England." In *The Cambridge Economic History of Europe*, vol. 1: *The Agrarian Life of the Middle Ages*, ed. M. M. Postan. 2nd ed. Cambridge: Cambridge University Press, 548–632.

———. 1972. *The Medieval Economy and Society: An Economic History of Britain, 1100–1500*. Berkeley: University of California Press.

———. 1977. "The Feudal Economy." *New Left Review* 103, May–June, 72–77.

Procter, Ian. 2000. "'I Do': A Theoretical Critique of Becker's Rational Choice Approach to Marriage Decisions." In Archer and Tritter (2000), 147–66.

Putnam, Robert D. 1993. *Making Democracy Work: Civic Traditions in Modern Italy*. Princeton: Princeton University Press.

Radcliffe-Brown, A. R. 1952. *Structure and Function in Primitive Society: Essays and Addresses*. Glencoe, IL: Free Press.

Rathbone, Dominic. 1991. *Economic Rationalism and Rural Society in Third-Century AD Egypt: The Heroninos Archive and the Appianus Estate*. Cambridge: Cambridge University Press.

Rawski, Thomas G., et al. 1996. *Economics and the Historian*. Berkeley: University of California Press.

Redlich, Fritz. 1968. "Potentialities and Pitfalls in Economic History." In Andreano (1970), 85–99.

Reger, Gary. 1994. *Regionalism and Change in the Economy of Independent Delos, 314–167 BC*. Berkeley: University of California Press.

———. 2002. "The Price Histories of Some Imported Goods on Independent Delos." In Scheidel and von Reden (2002), 133–54.

Renger, Johannes. 1994. "On Economic Structures in Ancient Mesopotamia." *Orientalia* 63, 157–208.

———. 1995. "Institutional, Communal, and Individual Ownership or Possession of Arable Land in Ancient Mesopotamia from the End of the Fourth to the End of the First Millennium B.C." *Chicago-Kent Law Review* 71, 269–319.

Richet, Denis. 1968. "Croissance et blocage en France du XVe au XVIIIe siècle." *Annales E.S.C.* 23.4, 759–87.

Robbins, Lionel. 1932. *An Essay on the Nature and Significance of Economic Science*. London: Macmillan.

Robinson, Joan. 1970. *Freedom and Necessity: An Introduction to the Study of Society*. London: Allen & Unwin.

Roche, Daniel. 2000. *A History of Everyday Things: The Birth of Consumption in France, 1600–1800*. Cambridge: Cambridge University Press.

Romer, Paul M. 1990. "Endogenous Technological Change." *Journal of Political Economy* 98.5, part 2, S71–S102.

Rosenberg, Alexander. 1994. "Does Evolutionary Theory Give Comfort or Inspiration to Economics?" In *Natural Images in Economic Thought: "Markets Read in Tooth and Claw,"* ed. Philip Mirowski. New York: Cambridge University Press, 384–407.

Rosenbloom, Joshua L., ed. 2008. *Quantitative Economic History: The Good of Counting*. Abingdon: Routledge.

Rosental, Paul-André. 2003. "The Novelty of an Old Genre: Louis Henry and the Founding of Historical Demography." *Population* 58.1, 97–129.

Ross, Don. 2005. *Economic Theory and Cognitive Science: Microexplanation*. Cambridge, MA: MIT Press.

Rostow, Walt W. 1960. *The Stages of Economic Growth: A Non-Communist Manifesto*. New York: Cambridge University Press.

Rotberg, Robert I., and Theodore K. Rabb, eds. 1985. *Hunger and History: The Impact of Changing Food Production and Consumption Patterns on Society*. New York: Cambridge University Press.

Rublack, Ulinka. 2005. *Reformation Europe*. Cambridge: Cambridge University Press.

Rutherford, Malcolm. 1994. *Institutions in Economics: The Old and the New Institutionalism*. New York: Cambridge University Press.

Sahlins, Marshall. 1972. *Stone Age Economics*. Chicago: Aldine.

———. 1976a. *Culture and Practical Reason*. Chicago: University of Chicago Press.

———. 1976b. *The Use and Abuse of Biology: An Anthropological Critique of Sociobiology*. Ann Arbor: University of Michigan Press.

———. 2004. *Stone Age Economics*, 2nd ed. London: Routledge.

Said, Edward W. 2001. "The Clash of Ignorance." *Nation*, October 22, 1–4.

Saleh, Nabil A. 1986. *Unlawful Gain and Legitimate Profit in Islamic Law: Riba, Gharar and Islamic Banking*. Cambridge: Cambridge University Press.

Saller, Richard. 2005. "Framing the Debate over Growth in the Ancient Economy." In Manning and Morris (2005), 223–38.

Samuelson, Paul A., and William D. Nordhaus. 1998. *Economics*. 16th ed. New York: McGraw-Hill.

Sarti, Raffaella. 2004. *Europe at Home: Family and Material Culture, 1500–1800*. New Haven: Yale University Press.

Sauner-Leroy, Marie-H. 2001. "Les traditions culinaires de la Méditerranée: modèles, emprunts, permanences." In *L'anthropologie de la Méditerranée*, ed. Dionigi Albera, Anton Blok, and Christian Bromberger. Paris: Maisonneuve et Larose, 491–510.

Schabas, Margaret. 1995. "Parmenides and the Cliometricians." In *On the Reliability of Economic Models: Essays in the Philosophy of Economics*, ed. Daniel Little. Boston: Kluwer, 183–202.

Schama, Simon. 1987. *The Embarrassment of Riches: An Interpretation of Dutch Culture in the Golden Age*. New York: Knopf.

Scheidel, Walter. Forthcoming. "Roman Wellbeing and the Economic Consequences of the 'Antonine Plague.'" In Lo Cascio (forthcoming).

Scheidel, Walter, Ian Morris, and Richard Saller, eds. 2007. *The Cambridge Economic History of the Greco-Roman World*. Cambridge: Cambridge University Press.

Scheidel, Walter, and Sitta von Reden, eds. 2002. *The Ancient Economy*. Edinburgh: Edinburgh University Press.

Schlegel, Alice. 1991. "Status, Property, and the Value on Virginity." *American Ethnologist* 18.4, 719–34.

Schmoller, Gustav. 1883. "Zur Methodologie der Staats- und Sozialwissenschaften." *Jahrbuch für Gesetzgebung, Verwaltung und Volkswirtschaft im Deutschen Reich* 7, 975–94.

Schneider, Harold K. 1974. *Economic Man*. New York: Free Press.

Schumpeter, Joseph A. 1934. *The Theory of Economic Development*. 2nd ed. Cambridge, MA: Harvard University Press.

———. 1954. *History of Economic Analysis*. New York: Oxford University Press.

Scitovsky, Tibor. 1976. *The Joyless Economy: An Inquiry into Human Satisfaction and Consumer Dissatisfaction*. New York: Oxford University Press.

Scott, James. 1976. *The Moral Economy of the Peasant: Rebellion and Subsistence in Southeast Asia*. New Haven: Yale University Press.

Sella, Domenico. 2008. "Peasant Strategies for Survival in Northern Italy, 16th–17th Centuries." *Journal of European Economic History* 37.2–3, 455–69.

Sen, Amartya K. 1977. "Rational Fools: A Critique of the Behavioral Foundations of Economic Theory." *Philosophy and Public Affairs* 6.4, 317–44.

———. 1987. *On Ethics and Economics*. Oxford: Basil Blackwell.

Sereni, Emilio. 1961. *History of the Italian Agricultural Landscape*. Princeton: Princeton University Press, 1997.

Shepherd, Rupert. 2007. "Republican Anxiety and Courtly Confidence: The Politics of Magnificence and Fifteenth-Century Italian Architecture." In O'Malley and Welch (2007), 47–70.

Sherratt, Andrew. 1997. *Economy and Society in Prehistoric Europe: Changing Perspectives*. Edinburgh: Edinburgh University Press.

Shweder, Richard A. 2000. "Moral Maps, 'First World' Conceits, and the New Evangelists." In Harrison and Huntington (2000), 158–76.

Silver, Morris. 1992. *Taking Ancient Mythology Economically*. Leiden: Brill.

———. 1995. *Economic Structures of Antiquity*. Westport, CT: Greenwood Press.

———. 2004. "Modern Ancients." In *Commerce and Monetary Systems in the Ancient World: Means of Transmission and Cultural Interaction*, ed. Robert Rollinger and Christoph Ulf. Wiesbaden: Franz Steiner Verlag, 65–87.

Simiand, François. 1903. "Méthode historique et science sociale." In *Méthode historique et sciences sociales*. Ed. Marina Cedronio. Paris: Editions des Archives Contemporaines, 139–69.

———. 1912. *La méthode positive en science économique*. Paris: Alcan.

———. 1932a. *Le salaire, l'évolution sociale et la monnaie. Essai de théorie expérimentale du salaire*. Paris: Alcan.

———. 1932b. *Recherches anciennes et nouvelles sour le mouvement général des prix du XVIe au XIXe siècle*. Paris: Domat-Montchrestien.

———. 1934. "La monnaie réalité sociale." *Annales sociologiques*, série D, 1, 1–86.

Simon, Herbert A. 1955. "A Behavioral Model of Rational Choice." *Quarterly Journal of Economics* 69.1, 99–118.

Slicher van Bath, B. H. 1963a. *The Agrarian History of Western Europe, A.D. 500–1850*. London: Arnold.

———. 1963b. *Yield Ratios, 810–1820*. Wageningen: A.A.G. Bijdragen.

Smith, Adam. 1759. *The Theory of Moral Sentiments*. Ed. D. D. Raphael and A. L. Macfie. Oxford: Clarendon Press, 1976.

———. 1776. *An Inquiry into the Nature and Causes of the Wealth of Nations*. Ed. R. H. Campbell and A. S. Skinner. Oxford: Clarendon Press, 1976.

Smith, Mark M. 1998. *Debating Slavery: Economy and Society in the Antebellum American South*. Cambridge: Cambridge University Press.

Solow, Robert M. 1956. "A Contribution to the Theory of Economic Growth." *Quarterly Journal of Economics* 70.1, 65–94.

———. 1985. "Economic History and Economics." *American Economic Review* 75.2, 328–31.

Sombart, Werner. 1913. *Der Bourgeois. Zur Geistesgeschichte des modernen Wirtschaftsmenschen*. Munich: Duncker & Humblot, 1923.

Sori, Ercole. 2001. *La città e i rifiuti: ecologia urbana dal Medioevo al primo Novecento*. Bologna: Il Mulino.

Sörlin, Sverker, and Paul Warde, eds. 2009. *Nature's End: History and the Environment*. Basingstoke: Palgrave Macmillan.

Spence, A. Michael. 1974. *Market Signaling: Informational Transfer in Hiring and Related Screening Processes*. Cambridge, MA: Harvard University Press.

Spulber, Nicolas. 2003. *Russia's Economic Transitions: From Late Tsarism to the New Millennium*. Cambridge: Cambridge University Press.

Stanovich, Keith E. 2004. *The Robot's Rebellion: Finding Meaning in the Age of Darwin*. Chicago: University of Chicago Press.

Stanziani, Alessandro. 1998. *L'économie en révolution. Le cas russe, 1870–1930*. Paris: Albin Michel.

———. 2008a. "Free Labor–Forced Labor: An Uncertain Boundary? The Circulation of Economic Ideas between Russia and Europe from the 18th to the Mid-19th Century." *Kritika: Explorations in Russian and Eurasian History* 9.1, 27–52.

———. 2008b. "Serfs, Slaves, or Wage Earners? The Legal Status of Labour in Russia from a Comparative Perspective, from the Sixteenth to the Nineteenth Century." *Journal of Global History* 3.2, 183–202.

Steiner, Philippe. 2003. "Durkheim's Sociology, Simiand's Positive Political Economy and the German Historical School." *European Journal of the History of Economic Thought* 10.2, 249–78.

Stigler, George. 1984. "Economics—The Imperial Science?" *Scandinavian Journal of Economics* 86.3, 301–13.

Swedberg, Richard. 1998. *Max Weber and the Idea of Economic Sociology*. Princeton: Princeton University Press.

Tabellini, Guido. 2008. "Institutions and Culture." *Journal of the European Economic Association* 6.2–3, 255–94.

Tacitus. *Germania*. Loeb Classical Library edition of Tacitus, vol. 1. Cambridge, MA: Harvard University Press, 1970.

Tandy, David W. 1997. *Warriors into Traders: The Power of the Market in Early Greece*. Berkeley: University of California Press.

Tawney, Richard H. 1920. *The Acquisitive Society*. New York: Harcourt, Brace and Howe.

Temin, Peter, ed. 1973. *New Economic History: Selected Readings*. Harmondsworth: Penguin.

———. 2001. "A Market Economy in the Early Roman Empire." *Journal of Roman Studies* 91, 169–81.

———. 2002. "Price Behavior in Ancient Babylon." *Explorations in Economic History* 39, 46–60.

Temin, Peter, ed. 2004a. "Financial Intermediation in the Early Roman Empire." *Journal of Economic History* 64.3, 705–33.

———. 2004b. "The Labor Market of the Early Roman Empire." *Journal of Interdisciplinary History* 34.4, 513–38.

———. 2006a. "Estimating GDP in the Early Roman Empire." In *Innovazione tecnica e progresso economico nel mondo romano*, ed. Elio Lo Cascio. Bari: Edipuglia, 31–54.

———. 2006b. "Mediterranean Trade in Biblical Times." In *Eli Heckscher, International Trade, and Economic History*, ed. Ronald Findlay, Rolf G. H. Henriksson, Håkan Lindgren, and Mats Lundahl. Cambridge, MA: MIT Press, 141–56.

———. 2006c. "The Economy of the Early Roman Empire." *Journal of Economic Perspectives* 20.1, 133–51.

Tetlock, Philip E., Richard N. Lebow, and Geoffrey Parker, eds. 2006. *Unmaking the West: "What-If?" Scenarios That Rewrite World History*. Ann Arbor: University of Michigan Press.

Thomas, Keith. 1983. *Man and the Natural World: Changing Attitudes in England, 1500–1800*. London: Allen Lane.

Thomas, William I., and Florian Znaniecki. 1918. *The Polish Peasant in Europe and America*. New York: Dover, 1958.

Thompson, Edward P. 1967. "Time, Work-Discipline, and Industrial Capitalism." *Past and Present* 38, 56–97.

———. 1971. "The Moral Economy of the English Crowd in the Eighteenth Century." *Past and Present* 50, 76–136.

———. 1978. *The Poverty of Theory and Other Essays*. New York: Monthly Review Press.

Thorner, Daniel. 1964. "L'Economie paysanne concept pour l'histoire économique." *Annales E.S.C.* 19.3, 417–32.

Thorner, Daniel, Basile Kerblay, and R.E.F. Smith, eds. 1966. *The Theory of Peasant Economy*. Homewood, IL: Irwin.

Thurnwald, Richard. 1916. "Bánaro Society: Social Organization and Kinship System of a Tribe in the Interior of New Guinea." *Memoirs of the American Anthropological Association* 3.4, 251–391.

———. 1932. *Economics in Primitive Communities*. Oxford: Oxford University Press.

Thurow, Lester C. 1977. "Economics, 1977." *Daedalus* 106.4, 79–94.

———. 1983. *Dangerous Currents: The State of Economics*. New York: Random House.

Tilly, Louise A., and Joan W. Scott. 1987. *Women, Work, and Family*. 2nd ed. New York: Methuen.

Tilly, Richard. 2001. "German Economic History and Cliometrics: A Selective Survey of Recent Tendencies." *European Review of Economic History* 5.2, 151–87.

Tompkins, Daniel P. 2006. "The World of Moses Finkelstein: The Year 1939 in M. I. Finley's Development as a Historian." In Meckler (2006), 95–125.

———. 2008. "Weber, Polanyi, and Finley." *History and Theory* 47.1, 123–36.

Tooze, J. Adam. 2001. *Statistics and the German State, 1900–1945: The Making of Modern Economic Knowledge*. Cambridge: Cambridge University Press.

Toynbee, Arnold. 1884. *Lectures on the Industrial Revolution in England*. London: Rivingtons.

Trentmann, Frank, ed. 2006. *The Making of the Consumer: Knowledge, Power and Identity in the Modern World*. Oxford: Berg.

———. 2008a. *Free Trade Nation: Commerce, Consumption, and Civil Society in Modern Britain*. Oxford: Oxford University Press.

———. 2008b. Review of Offer (2006). *Journal of Modern History* 80.2, 416–19.

Trentmann, Frank, and Flemming Just, eds. 2006. *Food and Conflict in Europe in the Age of the Two World Wars*. Basingstoke: Palgrave Macmillan.

Tribe, Keith. 1995. *Strategies of Economic Order: German Economic Discourse, 1750–1950*. Cambridge: Cambridge University Press.

Trivers, Robert L. 1971. "The Evolution of Reciprocal Altruism." *Quarterly Review of Biology* 46.1, 35–57.

Turner, Victor. 1967. *The Forest of Symbols: Aspects of Ndembu Ritual*. Ithaca, NY: Cornell University Press.

Valenze, Deborah. 2006. *The Social Life of Money in the English Past*. New York: Cambridge University Press.

Van der Wee, Herman. 1977. "Monetary, Credit and Banking Systems." In *The Cambridge Economic History of Europe*, vol. 5: *The Economic Organization of Early Modern Europe*, ed. E. E. Rich and C. H. Wilson. Cambridge: Cambridge University Press, 290–392.

Van der Wee, Herman, and Paul M. M. Klep. 1977. "New Economic History of Europe since the Second World War." In *Frontiers of Quantitative Economics*, vol. 3B, ed. Michael D. Intriligator. Amsterdam: North-Holland, 417–28.

Van Doosselaere, Quentin. 2009. *Commercial Agreements and Social Dynamics in Medieval Genoa*. New York: Cambridge University Press.

van Zanden, Jan L. 1999. "Wages and the Standard of Living in Europe, 1500–1800." *European Review of Economic History* 3.2, 175–97.

———. 2001. "Early Modern Economic Growth: A Survey of the European Economy, 1500–1800." In *Early Modern Capitalism: Economic and Social Change in Europe, 1400–1800*, ed. Maarten Prak. London: Routledge, 69–87.

———. 2002. "The 'Revolt of the Early Modernists' and the 'First Modern Economy': An Assessment." *Economic History Review* 55.4, 619–41.

———. 2008. "The Road to the Industrial Revolution: Hypotheses and Conjectures about the Medieval Origins of the 'European Miracle.'" *Journal of Global History* 3.3, 337–59.

———. 2009. *The Long Road to the Industrial Revolution: The European Economy in a Global Perspective, 1000–1800*. Leiden: Brill.

Veblen, Thorstein. 1899. *The Theory of the Leisure Class*. Oxford: Oxford University Press, 2007.

Vilar, Pierre. 1962. *La Catalogne dans l'Espagne moderne. Recherches sur les fondements économiques des structures nationales*. Paris: SEVPEN.

Vilar, Pierre. 1964. *Crecimiento y desarrollo: economía e historia. Reflexiones sobre el caso español*. Barcelona: Ariel.

———. 1965. "Pour une meilleure compréhension entre économistes et historiens. 'Histoire quantitative' ou économétrie rétrospective?" *Revue Historique* 233, 293–312.

Volckart, Oliver. 2004. "The Economics of Feuding in Late Medieval Germany." *Explorations in Economic History* 41.3, 282–99.

von Reden, Sitta. 1995. *Exchange in Ancient Greece*. London: Duckworth.

———. 2002. "Money in the Ancient Economy: A Survey of Recent Research." *Klio: Beiträge zur Alten Geschichte* 84.1, 141–74.

———. 2007. *Money in Ptolemaic Egypt: From the Macedonian Conquest to the End of the Third Century BC*. Cambridge: Cambridge University Press.

Vovelle, Michel. 1972. *The Fall of the French Monarchy, 1787–1792*. Cambridge: Cambridge University Press, 1984.

Wagner, Peter. 2000. "The Bird in Hand: Rational Choice—The Default Mode of Social Theorizing." In Archer and Tritter (2000), 19–35.

Walker, Francis A. 1892. *Political Economy*. 3rd ed. London: Macmillan.

Walton, Gary M., ed. 1975. "A Symposium on *Time on the Cross*." *Explorations in Economic History* 12.4.

Ward, Keith. 1996. *God, Chance and Necessity*. Oxford: Oneworld.

Warde, Paul. 2006a. *Ecology, Economy and State Formation in Early Modern Germany*. Cambridge: Cambridge University Press.

———. 2006b. "Subsistence and Sales: The Peasant Economy of Württemberg in the Early Seventeenth Century." *Economic History Review* 59.2, 289–319.

———. 2009. "The Environmental History of Pre-industrial Agriculture in Europe." In Sörlin and Warde (2009), 70–92.

Weber, Max. 1920. *The Protestant Ethic and the Spirit of Capitalism*. Rev. ed. London: Routledge, 2001.

———. 1956–64. *Economy and Society*. 4th ed. Berkeley: University of California Press, 1978.

Weintraub, E. Roy. 2002. *How Economics Became a Mathematical Science*. Durham, NC: Duke University Press.

Welch, Evelyn. 2007. "Making Money: Pricing and Payments in Renaissance Italy." In O'Malley and Welch (2007), 71–84.

Whaples, Robert. 2010. "Is Economic History a Neglected Field of Study?" *Historically Speaking* 11.2, 17–20.

Whittaker, C. R. 1997. "Moses Finley, 1912–1986." *Proceedings of the British Academy* 94, 459–72.

Wickham, Chris. 2007. "Memories of Underdevelopment: What Has Marxism Done for Medieval History, and What Can It Still Do?" In *Marxist History-Writing for the Twenty-first Century*. Oxford: Oxford University Press, 32–48.

Wilk, Richard R. 1989. "Decision Making and Resource Flows within the Household: Beyond the Black Box." In *The Household Economy: Reconsidering the Domestic Mode of Production*. Boulder, CO: Westview Press: 23–52.

———. 1993. "Altruism and Self-Interest: Towards an Anthropological Theory of Decision Making." *Research in Economic Anthropology* 14, 191–212.

————. 1996. *Economies and Cultures: Foundations of Economic Anthropology*. Boulder, CO: Westview Press.

Williams, Simon J. 2000. "Is Rational Choice Theory 'Unreasonable'? The Neglected Emotions." In Archer and Tritter (2000), 57–72.

Williamson, Oliver E. 1975. *Markets and Hierarchies: Analysis and Antitrust Implications*. New York: Free Press.

Wilson, Edward O. 1975. *Sociobiology: The New Synthesis*. Cambridge, MA: Belknap Press.

Winch, Donald. 1978. *Adam Smith's Politics: An Essay in Historiographical Revision*. Cambridge: Cambridge University Press.

Winch, Donald, and Patrick K. O'Brien, eds. 2002. *The Political Economy of British Historical Experience, 1688–1914*. Oxford: Oxford University Press.

Wolf, Eric R. 1966. *Peasants*. Englewood Cliffs, NJ: Prentice-Hall.

Wright, Gavin. 1971. "Econometric Studies of History." In *Frontiers of Quantitative Economics*, ed. Michael D. Intriligator. Amsterdam: North-Holland, 412–59.

Wright, Robert. 1994. *The Moral Animal: The New Science of Evolutionary Psychology*. New York: Pantheon Books.

Wrightson, Keith. 2000. *Earthly Necessities: Economic Lives in Early Modern Britain*. London: Yale University Press.

Wrigley, E. A. 1988. *Continuity, Chance and Change: The Character of the Industrial Revolution in England*. Cambridge: Cambridge University Press.

Wrigley, E. A., and R. S. Schofield. 1981. *The Population History of England, 1541–1871: A Reconstruction*. London: Arnold.

Xenophon. *Oeconomicus*. Loeb Classical Library edition of Xenophon, vol. 4. Cambridge, MA: Harvard University Press, 1923.

Zelizer, Viviana A. 1979. *Morals and Markets: The Development of Life Insurance in the United States*. New York: Columbia University Press.

————. 1994. *The Social Meaning of Money*. New York: Basic Books.

————. 2005. *The Purchase of Intimacy*. Princeton: Princeton University Press.

————. 2010. *Economic Lives: How Culture Shapes the Economy*. Princeton: Princeton University Press.

Zuckerman, Phil. 2004. "Secularization: Europe—Yes, United States—No." *Skeptical Inquirer* 28.2, 49–52.

Zweynert, Joachim. 2002. *Eine Geschichte des ökonomischen Denkens in Rußland, 1805–1905*. Marburg: Metropolis.

# Index